Contents

THE NEWLY INDUSTRIALIZED COUNTRIES AND THE INFORMATION TECHNOLOGY REVOLUTION

To Alberto,

With whom I had the privilege of associating a rich academic experience for four years with a human adventure which I hope will last forever.

Un grande abrazo,

[signature]
12/I/96

For Aline, Augusto, André and Angelo
For Dalvinha

The Newly Industrialized Countries and the Information Technology Revolution

The Brazilian experience

ARLINDO VILLASCHI

Department of Economics
Federal University of Espírito Santo
Espírito Santo, Brazil

Avebury

Aldershot · Brookfield USA · Hong Kong · Singapore · Sydney

© A. Villaschi   1994

Published by
Avebury
Ashgate Publishing Company
Gower House
Croft Road
Aldershot
Hants GU11 3HR

Ashgate Publishing Company
Old Post Road
Brookfield
Vermont 05036
USA

British Library Cataloguing in Publication Data
Villaschi, Arlindo
 Newly Industrialized Countries and the
 Information Technology Revolution:
 Brazilian Experience
 I. Title
 338.0981
 ISBN 1 85628 699 1

Library of Congress Cataloging-in-Publication Data
Villaschi, Arlindo, 1947–
 The newly industrialized countries and the information technology
revolution : the Brazilian experience / Arlindo Villaschi
      p.   cm.
 Includes bibliographical references.
 ISBN 1-85628-699-1 : £34.00 ($59.95 U.S. : est) .
 1. Technological innovations--Economic aspects--Brazil.
2. Technological innovations--Government policy--Brazil. 3. Brazil-
-Industries. 4. Brazil--Economic conditions--1985– I. Title
HC190.T4V54 1994
338'.064'0981--dc20   94-18299
                                                                          CIP

Typeset by Lindinalva M. De Martin Silva
Rua Carlos Eduardo Monteiro de Lemos, 46/303
Ed. Icaro - Jardim da Penha
29.060-120 Vitoria, Esp. Sto., Brazil

Printed and Bound in Great Britain by
Athenaeum Press Ltd, Newcastle upon Tyne.

List of tables

Preface

This book seeks to present an alternative explanation for the economic performance of newly industrialized Brazil in the 1980s. Contrary to the more pessimistic tune of the 'lost decade' diagnosis, it is argued here that Brazil is well-positioned to take advantage of some 'windows of opportunities' which have been opened by the emergence of the IT techno-economic paradigm.

The analysis of the Brazilian national system of innovation (BNSI) provides evidence for the argument that the Brazilian socio-economic formation can take its associated-dependency beyond the spheres of exchange and production of goods and services. In other words, it can search for 'windows of opportunities' in the technological and production networks which are being built amongsts industrialized countries.

The degree of familiarity that the BNSI has gained with the funcionality of informatics and telecommunications technologies is one of its most important assets for the transformation of the country's dependence. Despite their small scale, capabilities exist today and are based on the country's manufacturing and product innovation capacities in these two dynamic industries.

These capabilities are spread throughout the system in state-owned, local and multinational enterprises; in R&D institutes; and in universities. As a result, these agents' negotiation position in the acquisition of foreign technology in the core areas of the new paradigm has been strengthened.

Despite the possible identification of these capabilities with the seeds of 'collective entrepreneurship' under the IT techno-economic paradigm, they are not, by any means, sufficient conditions for the transformation of dependency. The rigidity of the country's institutions has been a major obstacle to the emergence of a new hegemonic project aimed at building-up interdependencies under the new paradigm. This is not to say that there is lack of awareness of the need for a 'national project' which can take the country to a new development path. What is lacking is the ability to create a new regime of accumulation with appropriate institutional forms, social relations, and balance of social forces in the power bloc and amongst the population more generally.

Under these circumstances, the neo-liberal appeal for less state intervention as such is misplaced. In the past the state in Brazil has established policies which stimulated progress both along existing trajectories and in sectors which were to become 'core' areas of the new techo-economic paradigm. This books shows that the Brazilian State has played an important role in establishing some of the most positive features of the BNSI. That has been the case in (i) policies towards industrial and technological autonomy carried out by state-owned-enterprises and the externalities of these policies to the economy as a whole; (ii) the 'market reserve for informatics' which has strengthened industrial and technological capabilities amongst local enterprises in a 'core' area of the new techno-economic paradigm; and (iii) the attraction of foreign capital which has contributed to the diversification of the country's industrial production and its new role in the international division of labour.

Contrary to neo-liberal views that failures of the 1980s reflect inadequate liberalization, this book argues that the major loss of the 1980s has been in the opportunity of the Brazilian State to enhance the ability of internal agents to respond more adequately to the changes needed. An example of such a lost opportunity is the passive role played by the State in reshaping the country's education system.

Looking at the Brazilian socio-economic formation from a broader perspective than that privileged by the 'lost decade diagnosis' was made possible by the 'windows of opportunities' which were opened to me by Prof. Christopher Freeman of SPRU. I have also benefited from the academic environment at the Department of Economics / Birkbeck College, specially the patient advice of Prof. Ben Fine and Dr. Fiona Atkins.

This book is based upon the research work I did towards my Ph.D. in Economics between 1988 and 1992 whilst at the Department of Economics / Birkbeck College. Financial support by CNPq and UFES for that part of the work is acknowledged. BANDES (Espírito Santo state development bank) gave the means necessary in order to make this publication possible. I am specially grateful to Ms. Lindinalva Silva who was very patient in the preparation of the camera ready copy of the book.

My research work would still be under the format of a Ph.D. thesis if there had been not the incentive and encouragement of Prof. Chris Freeman, and Prof. Annibal Villela. They set examples, both as scholars and as human beings.

List of abbreviations

ABENGE - Brazilian association of engineering education
ABDIB - Brazilian association for the development of basis industry
ABICOMP - Brazilian association for computers and pefipheral equipment
      industries
ABIMAQ - Brazilian machinery producers trade association
ADTEN - programme for the support of national technology
AFCPqD - association of CPqD' employees
ANDES - association of university lecturers
ANPEC - association of posgraduate courses in economics
ANPEI - association for research and development in industrial enterprises
BACEN - central bank
BNDES - Brazilian national bank for economic and social development
BNSI - Brazilian national system of innovation
CA - computer aided
CACEX - Department of foreign trade
CAD - computer-aided-design
CAM - computer-aided-manufacturing
CAPES - Brazilian support programme for postgraduate education
CAPRE -   Brazilian commission for the co-ordination of electronic data
      processing activities
CATI - Co-operative Agreements and Technology Indicators
CEC - Commissions of the European Community
CEPAL - Economic commission for Latin America
CN - numerically controlled
CNC - computerized numerically controlled
CNI - national confederation of industries
CNPq - national council for scientific and technological development
CONFEA - federal council of engineers, architects and agronomists
CONIN - national council of informatics
COPPE - coordination of postgraduate programmes in engineering

CPqD - TELEBRAS' centre of research and development
CRUB - council of brazilian universities' rectors
CTA - centre of aerospatial technology
CTI - centre of informatics technology
CUT - confederation of labour unions
DIEESE - institute of statistics and socio-economic studies sponsored by labour unions
E.C.L.A. - Economic Commission for Latin America
FGV - Getulio Vargas foundation
FIESP - federation of industrial employers of São Paulo state
FINEP - Brazilian funding agency for studies and projects
FNDCT - Brazilian fund for scientific and technological development
FNT - national fund for telecommunications
GDP - gross domestic product
IA - industrial automation
IA-FEA - institute of management - school of economics and management
IAA - institute of sugar and alcohol
IBC - Brazilian institute of coffee
IBGE - Brazilian institute of geography and statistics
IBICT - Brazilian institute of information in science and technology
IDESP - Institute of socio-economic and political studies of São Paulo
IDS - Institute of Development Studies
IE - institute of economics
IEDI - institute of industrial development studies
IEI - institute of industrial economics
INPE - institute of spatial research
INPES - institute of economic research
INPI - institute of industrial property
IPEA - institute of social and economic planning
IPLAN - institute of planning
IPT - institute of technological research
IT - information technology
ITA - institute of aeronautics technology
LC - local capitals
MERIT - Maastricht Economic Research of Innovation and Technology
MNC - multinational corporations
MCT - ministry of science and technology
ME - ministry of education
NIC - newly-industrialized country
NOT - new organizational techniques
N.S.I. - national systems of innovation
OECD - Organization for Economic Cooperation and Development
PED - plan of strategic development

PUC - catholic university
PND - national development plan
R&D - research and development
SBPC - the Brazilian society for the progress of science
SEI - special secretariat for informatics
SENAI - national service of industrial training
SINDIMAQ - machinery and equipments producers trade union
SOE - state-owned enterprises
SPRU - Science Policy Research Unit
UFES - federal university of Espirito Santo
UFPb - federal university of Paraiba
UFRJ - federal university of Rio de Janeiro
UFSC - federal university of Santa Catarina
UFsC - federal university of São Carlos
UNICAMP - state university of Campinas
USP - university of São Paulo

1 Introduction

1.1 Establishing the object

The 1980s witnessed a turning point for mainstream economics just as the Brazilian economy ceased to be seen as a successful case of economic development in the periphery and became a key subject in discussions concerning international financial debt and macro-economic stabilization programmes. The centre of analysis of Brazil shifted from the highly-praised mechanisms that were used to promote high growth rates, to the need to comply with 'recipes' for short-run stabilization and long-run adjustments; from the achievements of authoritarian and interventionist governments to the need to transform the developmental-State into a liberal government which should rely mainly on the virtues of the market, as part of a programme for economic and political democracy.

Whilst recognizing the importance of Brazil's problems - such as inflation, external debt, and others privileged by mainstream economics - this book looks at the Brazilian socio-economic formation from an entirely different perspective. Its starting point is the changes which are taking place in the technological base of world economic development. It, then, refers to conditions in the Brazilian socio-economic formation and examines their possibilities and constraints relative to changes in the international division of labour due to shifts in the world technological base.

This alternative way of analyzing the Brazilian socio-economic formation embraces the central concerns of technology and dependency. The roots of such discussion can be found in two theoretical traditions. The first, and broader, one has its roots in classical economics which looks at technical progress through its roles in capitalist accumulation and distinguishes these under different historical and competitive conditions. In this vein, most recently, neo-Schumpeterians have emphasized the impact that different levels of technical progress have on specific industries/sectors/countries and on the

1

world economy as a whole. Thus, at the level of Schumpeter's 'creative gales of destruction' would be situated change in the techno-economic paradigm which has

> pervasive effects throughout the economy, ie it must not only lead to the emergence of a new range of products and services in its own right, it must also affect every other branch of the economy by changing the input cost structure and conditions of production and distribution throughout the system. It is the extension of the effects of a new technological system beyond the confines of a few branches to the economy as a whole. [Freeman (1984), p. 498, emphasis added].

Moreover, change of such techno-economic paradigm involves major changes in society. The pervasive characteristic of innovation at the centre of the techno-economic paradigm will have a widespread effect throughout the system but only after a period of changes and adaptations of many social institutions to the potential of the new technology.

> Inertia in the institutional and social framework, reinforced by the pressure of interest groups, conspires to frustrate a favourable course of development. The 'good match' between technology and social institutions ... [can] become a hindrance to further change and development (or in Marx's terminology becomes a 'fetter' on the forces of production). (ibid., p. 503) [1]

Under this theoretical perspective, with cheap microelectronics widely available, a new techno-economic paradigm is replacing the 'fordist/cheap energy' paradigm which prevailed until the 1970s. The new 'information--technology' techno-economic paradigm is changing the path of energy and materials intensity; it is bringing together management, production and marketing into one single integrated system. Under the IT techno-economic paradigm growth is being led by "the electronics and information sectors, propelling and being propelled by an all-encompassing telecommunications infrastructure, which would bring down to negligible levels the cost of access for producers and consumers alike." [Perez (1985, p. 445]. These accomplishments, however, are conditioned by institutional and social changes which are not expected to take place without social and international confrontation.

The roots for confrontation can be found in the differences in innovative capabilities, in the sources and uses of innovations, and in the technological strategies followed by firms, industries and nations. Confrontation can also occur because of technological gaps which are due to institutional conditions. According to Dosi et al. (1990), the latter are of fundamental importance in explaining the participation of each country in international trade flows, and international differences in income levels.

The second, and more specific, theoretical tradition followed by this thesis has its roots in the dependence argument developed by Cardoso and Falleto

(1979). There are two conceptualizations of the 'associated-dependent development' approach which are worth emphasizing in the context of this book. The first is the way they conceive the relationship between external and internal forces as forming a complex whole that is embedded in a world system. This world system is characterized by asymmetries such that some of its parts have more than their share of leadership and an almost exclusive possession of sectors crucial to production and capital accumulation. As a result, accumulation and expansion of capital cannot find its essential dynamic component within the periphery itself because of the absence of capital goods and financial sectors, the import of technology and penetration by foreign multinationals.

The second conceptualization to be emphasized is that Cardoso and Falleto (1979) take dependent development beyond the traditional dichotomy between the terms 'development' and 'dependence' in order to envisage the possibility of increasing development whilst maintaining and redefining the links of dependency. Hence, the use of the term 'associated-dependent' development. Moreover, they emphasize the need to analyze particular internal conditions of different socio-economic formations rather than to develop general theories [2].

1.2 Technological dependency in Brazil: some issues

Economic growth in Brazil has provided strong evidence for the associated--dependent argument. Industrialization changed radically the country's pattern of accumulation. Its links with the centre have been redefined by the role multinational corporations play in its socio-economic formation; by its increased reliance on international financing; and by the way it has transformed its dependence on foreign technology.

The analysis of Brazilian technological dependency became prominent in the literature after the pale results of the country's import-substitution-industrialization process based on capital-embodied foreign technology [3]. At first, the focus of analysis was the evolution of the factors which explained the incorporation of foreign technology into Brazilian industrialization. For Biato et al. (1971), for example, on the one hand, there are those factors which can be associated with the demand for technology. These would be mainly due to (i) pressures for the adoption of consumption patterns from the more developed countries which induce a demand for external technology; and (ii) the requirements of efficiency which drive local and multinational producers to search for 'proven' foreign technology. On the other hand, there are those factors that are associated with the specificities of the internal supply of technology which is limited due to the deficiencies in the local scientific and technological systems. These supply deficiencies coupled with the characte-

3

ristics of demand are perceived to lead to a "process of circular causation, in which the absence of response in the past inspires few requests in the present, which, in turn, impedes stimulation of ... any internal demand for know-how." [Biato et al. (1971), p. 139]

This view of technological dependency as both the cause and the consequence of the lack of articulation between the productive system and the scientific and technological systems is criticized because it takes what happens in Brazil as a 'functional anomaly' when compared with the model in the developed world. Thus, "this treatment reduces the importance of the specificity of the pattern of dependent development; it does not question the need for or the possibility of reproducing, within such pattern of development, a specific system of economic and social relationships developed under substantially different conditions." [Erber (1981), p. 10]

In a second 'stage', the technological problem of dependency in Brazil was investigated through analysis of its different technical levels. It has been done by, amongst others, Erber et al.(1974), Jorge (1978), Frenkel, coord. (1978), and Ferraz (1984) for, respectively, the capital goods, petrochemical, pharmaceutical, and shipbuilding industries. They analyze the different activities (research, design, production, etc.) that lead to technical progress in these industries and show the different technological capabilities that were actually acquired through technical transfers from abroad. Their findings show the limited scope of these transfers due mainly to the discountinuities that take place in technical knowledge [4].

This more critical interpretation of technological dependency has not remained unchallenged by mainstream analyses. For Figueiredo (1974), for instance, the introduction of technical progress in the economy should be interpreted as a major contribution to "a rational distribution of productive resources - investment resources especially - reflecting national, regional, and sectorial aptitudes for development, the economic requirements of scale of productions, etc." (ibid., p. 39). Thus, the objective should be to increase the incorporation of technical knowledge from abroad in order to improve the integration of the national economy with that of central countries [5].

The different interpretations given to technological dependency were clearly reflected in the policies which were prescribed. For the liberals, technological development is to be left to 'natural' forces (import of technology, for instance) until the country achieves the conditions that lead to the endogenous generation of technology [6]. Contrary to this position have stood those in the 'dependendista' camp who identify the need for state intervention if the country is to redefine its technology ties with the centre. The rationale for greater state intervention in matters of technological development in Brazil has been found in the example of countries in the centre. There, the argument goes, state support is usually behind scientific and technological initiatives.

4

One major obstacle to the policy recommendations of 'dependistas' has been the long time needed for the implementation of directives geared towards technological autonomy. Very often these directives have found unfavourable political conditions for the effective translation of a nationalist ideology into economic actions [7]. As Erber (1981, p. 12) points out "... the pattern of dependent development tends to build a powerful block of interests, strongly represented within the state, which does not favor a policy of greater technological autonomy or even opposes it altogether.".

A third 'stage' in the analysis of Brazil's technological dependency can be identified with the build-up of indigenous technological capabilities in the informatics and telecommunications-equipment industries. This has been interpreted as a break with past patterns of technological dependence. Despite the different approaches taken by the government in the two cases, its policies contributed for the emergence in the periphery of an entirely new industry (informatics), and a technologically transformed one (telecommunications--equipment). It has created locally controlled manufacturing capacity in two technologically complex industries; it has shifted their reliance on imports from final products to components. Moreover, fostering of informatics and telecommunications-equipment industries has generated capacity for product innovation in these technology-intensive industries.

Not surprisingly, the achievements in these two industries have been greeted [Evans (1986), Hobday (1985), Schmitz and Hewitt (1992)] as major transformations in the country's technological dependence. This is not to minimize criticisms that are made [Erber (1985), Pessini (1986), Baptista (1987), Rosenthal (1987), amongst others] of the policies' failure in pursuing synergies between the two industries. According to these critiques, synergies should have been sought by looking at informatics and telecommunications (along with electronic consumer goods, and microelectronics) from the perspective of the 'electronic complex'. This line of criticism highlights the industrial and technological linkages between these industries and the opportunities the country has forgone by not pursuing their synergies.

1.3 Aims and issues

The analysis carried out here takes the transformation of dependency beyond technological capabilities at the level of the industry or of industrial complex. Its objective is to address a question which is embedded in both the techno-economic paradigm and the associated-dependency approaches. That is, what are the conditions internal to the Brazilian socio-economic formation which enables its, or inhibits it from, transforming its technological dependency under the information technology (IT) techno-economic paradigm. Given the country's capabilities in the 'core' of the new techno-

-economic paradigm, the framework under which the book examines the possibilities of transformation of Brazilian associated-dependency is two-fold.

On the one hand, the external framework is given by the revolutionary character of changes that are taking place in world development under the IT techno-economic paradigm and which are fostering new patterns of division of labour throughout the world system. On the other hand, internal conditions are examined through the analysis of the Brazilian socio-economic formation and the possible 'matches' and 'mismatches' between its elements and the new patterns of division of labour.

The combination of the external and internal frameworks used here departs from traditional 'technology-dependence' analyses. The latter emphasizes the need for greater autonomy in order to avoid problems with balance of payments, employment, rate of growth and national sovereignty [Ratner (1974)]. The emphasis here is on the Brazilian socio-economic formation's need to engage in a qualitatively different form of dependency with the centre.

There are two reasons why the dependency linkages to be pursued by associate-dependent Brazil must be made to be qualitatively different. In the first place, under the new techno-economic paradigm the centre has enough scope to grow without the immediate 'need' for market expansion towards the periphery. Secondly, the major features of the last transformation of Brazil's dependence - natural resources and/or cheap, low skilled labour force - no longer guarantee the country a role of interdependence with the centre because these 'comparative advantages' do not remain essential to accumulation under the IT techno-economic paradigm.

By focusing on dynamic qualification for interdependence, the analysis brings to the forefront of the technological dependency discussion the need to pursue new forms of technological capabilities. In contrast to the more traditional approach, the major concern is not be with the ability to pursue 'marginally autonomist policies' [Cardoso and Faletto (1979), p. 185]. The analysis here concentrates on the possibilities of associate-dependent Brazil pursuing 'interdependent' technological capabilities with the centre. Under the present conditions of a changing world paradigm, more important than autonomy, the book argues, is the country's ability to participate in different information and production networks that are being built throughout the industrialized world.

Summing up, this book takes as its external framework of analysis the change of techno-economic paradigm of world development from 'cheap energy' into 'chips'. Moreover, it brings together features of the neo--Schumpeterian approach to world development and those put forward by the 'associated-dependent development' school in order to examine the implications of the 'IT techno-economic paradigm' for associate-dependent Brazil. That is done from a perspective that takes into account the country's system of innovation as a whole and its possibilities and constraints in

6

interacting within information and production networks that are being built amongst industrialized countries.

1.4 Structure of the book

This book is developed in two parts. Part I provides the historical background and the theoretical framework under which the analysis is performed. It comprises two chapters. Chapter 2 reviews the political economy of the Brazilian industrialization process from a perspective which privileges two peculiarities of its different moments. In the first place, the compromises that took place between mercantile and industrial capital with respect to the accumulation process. Secondly, the different institutional configurations given to the state in order to accommodate inter- (capital, bureaucracy, and labour) and intra- (industrialists, agro-exporters) group rivalries.

Chapter 3 examines three theoretical constructs of the neo-Schumpterian approach which provide the analytical framework for the book: Freeman and Perez' (1988) taxonomy of innovation; Lundvall's (1988) national systems of innovation; and Dosi's (1986) 'three self-regulating domains model'. Freeman and Perez' taxonomy emphasizes the permanent tension between technology, and social and economic agents in the process of world development. It moves towards a more comprehensive explanation of the so-called long wave question by making 'impressionistic approximations' between 'technological revolutions' and changes in paradigm in the natural sciences. Lundvall's n.s.i. gives theoretical relevance to the spatial (national) dimension of the innovation process and argues for the importance of 'learning-by-interacting' (formal/ informal) between agents at times of radical technological changes. Dosi's model provides the framework under which elements of a national system of innovations can be analyzed. The model places these elements into three self- -regulated domains: that of the system of technologies; the 'economic machine'; and the system of social relations and institutions.

Part II consists of three chapters and analyses the Brazilian national system of innovations in the 1980s [8]. Chapter Four examines those elements of the Brazilian economy which can contribute to 'matches' and 'mismatches' between the BNSI and the information and production networks which are being built in the industrialized world. On the one hand, attention is given to macro-economic conditionalities - inflation; debt and fiscal crises - which affect the response of agents to innovation and change. On the other hand, the Brazilian economy is examined from a perspective which privileges those elements that can play an important role in the IT techno-economic paradigm. These are taken to be the way state-owned, local and multinational enterprises structure the country's production system; the diversification of its exports; and the industrial and technological capabilities which have been accumulated in three 'strategic industries' - capital goods, informatics and telecommunications.

Chapter Five examines elements of the Brazilian socio-political framework. It privileges stability and flexibility as two basic characteristics of institutions if they are to favour innovation and change. The build-up of institutions under the Constituent Congress of 1987/1988 is analyzed in the light of the country's institutional path-dependence. The chapter also examines perceptions of agents with respect to the new techno-economic paradigm.

Chapter Six looks at three elements of the 'technological domain'. Its educational system, with special emphasis on the training of researchers and engineers; the R&D infrastructure and its interactions with the country's production sector; and the interplay of these three elements - the educational system, R&D laboratories and production sector - in the emergence of technological parks in the country.

The final chapter re-examines some of the ways by which dependency is being transformed at a world scale due to the characteristics of the new techno-economic paradigm. It then raises some policy issues that must be faced by Brazil if it is to transform its dependency under these new conditions. The last chapter also establishes some grounds for further studies of the implications of the new paradigm of world development for the Brazilian socio-economic formation.

1.5 Some methodogical considerations

Methodologically, this work approaches its main objective - that of examining the constraints upon, and the possibilities for, Brazil to transform its technological ties with the centre - in a different way from other studies. To begin with, the point of departure is the emergence of a new techno-economic paradigm that is taking place at a world scale and not - as is usually done - the impact of a 'radical innovation' on specific industries, sectors or complexes of the Brazilian economy [9].

In contrast to other examinations of the Brazilian national system of innovation which concentrate on organizational aspects involving technical progress [10], the present analysis privileges the linkages - formal and informal - between different agents - private/public; local/multinational; research related/non-academic - which comprise the BNSI. Moreover, given that some of the interactions which will be seen as crucial for the system under the new paradigm do not take place under the framework of the market, emphasis is given to new forms of interactions amongst agents and domains aside from the market.

The basic ground upon which this book develops its analysis of the BNSI was laid (i) on findings of sectoral analyses of innovations taking place in specific firm/industry (capital goods, informatics, telecommunications, etc.); and (ii) in analyses of performance of government agencies involved with scientific and technological development (universities, research institutes, etc.). The next step was to establish a theoretical framework under which these findings could be brought together under a perspective which emphasizes a 'system of innovation' comprising not just production units and research centres but also social capabilities which are built within the country's institutions.

Given the many interpretations that exist about what constitutes a 'system of innovation', I profited greatly from the debates that took place at the Maastricht's *Workshop on National Systems of Innovation* [11] where the findings of fifteen different 'national systems of innovation' were reported using various theoretical backgrounds. From then on, the framework that I used to analyze the BNSI was influenced by the 'learning-by-interacting--through the mail' opportunity I was given to establish with Prof. Lundvall, of Aasborg University, Denmark. From him I got a deeper understanding of the theoretical and policy issues that the concept allows one to explore. His studies of innovation and change from a non-Anglo/American perspective, have contributed to my better understanding of the 'learning-by-interacting' process [12]. This is particularly reflected in my work by the importance I have given to the interactions that have taken place amongst actors within a specific domain and between different domains [13].

These interactions are not 'measured' through regular data collecting activities [14]. They have also been changing quite fast as the new paradigm is established in different fields of technological, economic and institutional knowledge and action. These two facts made me think at first of a survey of the understanding that different agents in Brazil have of the new paradigm and their particular responses to these changes. The very low returns I got from more than 120 questionnaires I sent in late 1989 to individuals (academics, politicians, business and labour leaders), firms (mainly those in hi-tech activities and those active in manufacture exporting) and government agencies, made me put even greater effort in the interviews that were at first planned to be smaller in number and envisaged as a complement to the findings of the questionnaires. During a field trip to Brazil in August-October 1990, I interviewed forty-five people holding different positions and performing different activities in the Brazilian national system of innovation. In the intentional 'sampling' of people to be interviewed an effort was made to avoid repetition of those who had been interviewed by other research studies to which I had access [Rosenthal (1987), Castro (1990) and Castilhos (1992)]. Besides trying to avoid repetition, the reason for such 'precaution' was the fact that most of those interviewed in these studies were 'specialized' people/institutions and my aim was to get as much of 'outsiders' perspectives and understanding of the new techno-economic paradigm as possible.

The findings of most of these interviews - which were not meant to cover a 'statistical sample' - were enriched by the results of four different surveys that were conducted in Brazil in 1989/90 amongst leaders in different fields of activities in the country [15]. The importance of both levels of findings (those acquired through the interviews and those that were taken from the surveys) is established throughout the chapters concerning the BNSI.

The findings and analysis of this book, then, are not based on any long 'tested' theory of technical change. Nor are they the result of clearly established quantification of specific variables and parameters that 'explain' the behaviour of agents and the status of a specific socio-economic formation. Nevertheless, they have been geared towards a better understanding of the reasons why these tests and quantifications are to be avoided. This avoidance is important if one is interested in a better grasp of what is taking place in the world system as a whole and of the asymmetries that exist between the centre of the system and associate-dependent Brazil, in particular [17].

Notes

1. Paradigm is used in this thesis in two ways - in Kuhn's (1970) sense of a system of thought and as a functioning system. Chapter Three provides a discussion of this issue.

2. Cardoso (1980) and Palma (1981) provide analyses of the ways the different approaches to dependency in Latin America break with mainstream economic development and how they are rooted in the Marxist theory of imperialism and/or in the structuralist approach used by the United Nations' Economic Commission for Latin America to explain the major constraints to Latin American counties' late industrialization. Erber (1983) presents a good summary of the roots provided by E.C.L.A.'s structuralism and the Latin American dependence approach to the analysis of technological dependence in the continent.

3. In 1963 in its 'Problems and perspectives for Latin American industrial development', E.C.L.A. emphasized the need for Latin American industrialization to overcome one of its most important constraints which was seen to be its excessive dependence on foreign know-how. It is interesting to notice that there had been some 'progress' on E.C.L.A.'s diagnosis of the technological challenges to be faced by Latin American industrialization projects. In a previous report, a major constraint to be overcome by the periphery was the fact that "...technical progress only affected small sectors of the vast population as it usually only penetrated where it was needed to produce foodstuff and raw material at low cost for delivery to the great industrial centres." [E.C.L.A. (1951), p. 3]

4. This is so because of the discontinuities characteristic of technical knowledge; being skilled in operation procedures may allow the introduction of technical improvement that increase production and/or improve products. But it does not necessarily guarantee ability to design a new plant and/or foster a new product.

5. This perspective up-dates for technical progress the same liberal thinking which since the late 1930s stands against the 'artificial' (because not based on 'natural' comparative advantages) industrialization project for the Brazilian economy.

6. For a review of studies that reject the technological dependency postulates in different countries, see Fransman (1985a). Erber (1983) presents a discussion of both the technological dependency argument and that which is identified with the incremental indigenous learning school.

7. Cassiolato et al. (1981) describe the compensatory policies (and the organizations that were created in the government's apparatus to pursue them) that were designed in Brazil in the 1960s in order to cope with the need to supply local producers with instruments of innovation similar to those available to foreign producers. These policies - which have been implicitly and/or explicitly contemplated by all Brazilian development plans since the late 1960s - have centred their autonomy aims mainly on creating better competitive conditions for local producers.

8. The 1980s were chosen as time reference for the analysis because that was a decade when there was a break with economic trends which had prevailed since the 1930s in Brazil - that of high rates of industrial growth. Changes in the country's political regime were also significant. Moreover, in the 1980s the emergence of the IT techno-economic paradigm was shaped through concrete changes in the patterns of production, exchange and cooperation between firms and nations.

9. Sector-specific analyses are provided, for example, by Erber (1977), Tigre (1983), Hobday (1985), and Rosenthal (1987) for, respectively, the capital goods, the computer, the telecommunications-equipment, and the microelectronic industries. Coutinho and Suzigan (1990) appraises the technological gap of twelve Brazilian industrial complexes. Schmitz and Cassiolato (1992) analyzes the externalities of the informatics policy on four industrial sectors and on the learning process taking place in government. Drawing attention to the differences between the approach used in these studies and the one followed by this book, does not imply, however, any criticism of the former. Explicit recognition of their contribution to the understanding of the Brazilian system of innovation is made throughout this work. For an earlier approximation of the approach

used here, see Villaschi (1990).

10. Melo (1989) and Dahlman and Frischtak (1989) follow this organizational approach for the analysis of the Brazilian system of innovation.

11. The Maastricht workshop (2nd-4th November 1989) was followed by one in Stanford (June, 1990) with the purpose of putting together in a forthcoming book the experience of fifteen different national systems of innovation (Argentina, Australia, Brazil, Canada, China, France, Germany, Israel, Italy, Japan, Korea, Nordic countries, Taiwan, United Kingdom and United States of America).

12. See Freeman and Lundvall (1988), Lundvall (1988) and Johnson and Lundvall (1991). Prof. Lundvall and his colleagues of the IKE-group put together their last contribution on the theoretical relevance of national systems of innovation in a book which was published when I was about to finish the last draft of the thesis upon which the book is based.

13. A discussion concerning the 'autonomous' and 'interdependent' functioning of technological, economic and institutional domains as originally thought by Dosi (1986) is provided in the next chapter.

14. A first attempt to gather information on interactions amongst firms in the core countries in hi-tech industries is the CATI/MERIT Databank. See Hagerdoorn and Schakenraad (1990).

15. General descriptions of the surveys by C.N.I (the confederation of Brazilian industrial industries), IDESP (a non-governmental 'think-tank' based in São Paulo), *Gazeta Mercantil* (most influential Brazilian business newspaper) and Salm et al. (commissioned by business sponsored Institute of industrial training to the Institute of Industrial Economics / Federal University of Rio de Janeiro), are provided in Chapters 4/5/6.

16. For a discussion of the different asymmetries that arise in the economic and political interactions between countries from the centre and those in the periphery, see Cardoso (1980), especially 'Desenvolvimento na Berlinda'.

Part One
THE HISTORICAL AND ANALYTICAL FRAMEWORKS

2 The political economy of the Brazilian industrialization process: A review

2.1 Introduction

The main objective of this chapter is to establish the historical background under which the Brazilian national system of innovation will be examined in Part II of this book. The focus is on the associated-dependent industrialization of Brazil in the fifty years that followed the '1930 Revolution' [1]. Thus, attention is given to the different 'phases' of industrial development and to the institutional framework under which these phases took place between the early 1930s and the late 1970s.

Despite previous attempts [2] it was only in the post-1930 period that an industrialization process was established in Brazil. From the 1930s onwards internal forces were pulled together with the aim of substituting inward oriented industrial growth as the main source of capital accumulation for the outward model of agriculture export-led accumulation. The latter model had prevailed throughout the colonial period and the first fifty years of independent Brazil. Whilst recognizing the role played by external factors - such as balance of payments deficits and problems with foreign supplies due to war - the major focal point of this analysis is on the internal political forces associated with the industrialization process. It is due to them that direction was given towards new patterns of economic development.

In common with other late-comers Brazil has had the strong presence of the state in the process of economic development. Like Germany and Japan before and Asian NICs subsequently, the state in Brazil has led initiatives towards industrialization processes. Unlike those, though, in Brazil the process took place without breaking completely with the existing economic and political structures. The result of this conservative modernization process is that Brazil today is an extremely dualistic socio-economic formation where old/new; modern/traditional; rich/poor are all brought together. These dichotomies are why the Brazilian modernization process is called incomplete/ unfinished [inter alia Bacha et al. (1989), and Camargo (1990)].

In order to examine the different historical moments of the construction of this incomplete modernization process, two peculiarities of the Brazilian socio-economic formation are stressed. Firstly, the compromises that took place between mercantile and industrial capital as far as the accumulation process was concerned. Secondly, the different institutional configurations given to the State in order to accommodate inter- (capital, bureaucracy and labour) and intra- (industrialists, agro-exporters) group rivalries.

The analysis of the chapter covers the period from the early 1930s - when the deliberate industrialization process was begun [Suzigan (1975)] - to the late 1970s - when the undeveloped industrialized Brazilian model was consolidated. It is important to notice that during this period there was no substantial change in the technological paradigm of world development. This implies that the importance given to internal forces in pursuit of an industrialization process for the country does not necessarily minimize some favourable external conditions. The combination of a 'given' technological paradigm (fordism/cheap energy) with institutional innovations (Bretton Woods, emergence of multinational corporations), opened 'windows of opportunities' for countries like Brazil to push ahead some of their internal plans of industrial development. The point emphasized here, however, is that, without this internal political drive, favourable external conditions for 'catching-up' in industrial and technological capabilities could have become just another lost opportunity.

2.2   Structural changes in the Brazilian economy: some   figures for 1930/80

During the fifty years between 1930 and 1980 the Brazilian economy went through a substantial change in its dynamics of capital accumulation. Whilst in 1930, agriculture was responsible for over 40% of gross domestic product, by 1980 this had fallen to 13.2%. In 1980, 32.6% of GDP was generated in the industrial sector, with manufacture accounting for about 80% of that total.

More important than the composition of the Brazilian domestic product is the fact that, especially in the post-World War II period, manufacturing consolidated its role as the dynamic pole of capital accumulation in the Brazilian economy. Thus, data from national accounts (Fundação Getúlio Vargas) show that whilst the growth rate of GDP was about 7% per year between 1945 and 1980, manufacturing grew at 9% per year. Moreover, by 1980 over 35% of industrial production in Brazil was being generated by the production of metallurgical goods, machines and equipment. Such a qualitative performance was responsible for the fact that the Brazilian economy between 1930 and 1980 narrowed its productivity gap with the O.E.C.D. block, as I have shown elsewhere [Villaschi (1991)].

Table 2.1
Brazil: Sectors' contribution to GDP (% of total in c.v.)

Sectors	Years				
	1939	1949	1959	1970	1980
Agriculture	25.8	24.9	19.2	10.1	13.2
Industry	19.4	26.0	32.6	35.9	33.4
(Manufacturing)	-	(20.2)	(25.1)	(27.3)	(31.0)
Services	54.8	49.1	48.2	53.0	53.7

c.v. - current value
Sources: Serra (1982) and Baer (1989)

Table 2.2
Brazil - changes in industrial structure: gross value added (%)

	1949	1963	1975	1980
Non-metallic minerals	7.4	5.2	6.2	5.8
Metal products	9.4	12.0	12.6	11.5
Machines	2.2	3.2	10.3	10.1
Eletrical equipment	1.7	6.1	5.8	6.3
Transport equipment	2.3	10.5	6.3	7.6
Wood products	6.1	4.0	2.9	2.7
Furniture	-	2.0	1.8	-
Paper products	2.1	2.9	2.5	3.0
Rubber products	2.0	1.9	1.7	1.3
Leather products	1.3	0.7	0.5	0.6
Chemicals	-	12.0	14.7	-
Pharmaceuticals	9.4	15.5	2.5	1.6
Perfumes, soap, candles	-	12.0	0.9	-
Plastic products	-	2.2	2.4	-
Textiles	20.1	11.6	6.1	6.4
Clothing and shoes	4.3	3.6	3.8	4.8
Food products	19.7	14.1	11.3	10.0
Beverages	4.3	3.2	1.8	1.2
Tobbaco	1.6	1.6	1.0	0.7
Printing and publishing	4.2	2.5	3.6	2.6
Miscellaneous	1.9	1.4	3.7	4.0
TOTAL	100.0	100.0	100.0	100.0

Source: IBGE, Industrial Censuses, quoted in Baer (1989),
Table 15,5

Changes also took place with respect to the country's trade relations. Whilst GDP grew at a rate superior to 7% per year between 1947 and 1980,

17

the quantity of exports grew at a rate lower than 6% per year. During that period, the contribution of coffee in total exports decreased from over 50% in 1947 to less than 15% in 1978/79. Qualitative changes once again took place in the direction of manufacturing: between 1968 and 1980, manufacturing increased its share in total exports from just over 10% to 45%. As far as imports are concerned, whilst in 1947 13.7% of GDP was made out of imported goods, in 1980 import's share decreased to 7% [Serra (1982)].

Important changes also took place in the country's social structure. The percentage of the working force in the formal industrial sector grew from 10.1% in 1940 to about 25% in 1980; the illiteracy rate decreased from 56% in 1940 to less than 30% in 1980; enrolment in secondary and university education grew faster than population growth; a larger middle-class was formed. Nonetheless, the major characteristic of change in the country's social structure has been the growth in income inequality as will be seen later.

Table 2.3
Brazil: sectoral distribution (non-agricultural) - % of labour force

	1940	1950	1960	1970	1980
Total Ind.	10.1	13.7	12.9	18.0	24.4
Manufacturing	7.1	9.4	8.6	11.1	15.7
Construction	1.9	3.4	3.4	5.9	7.2
Others	1.1	0.9	0.9	1.1	1.5
Total services	25.9	26.4	33.1	37.3	45.7

Sources: Katzman (1989), Table 3.2

2.3 Mercantile and industrial capitalism in Brazil: some historical roots

The associated-dependent approach used here emphasizes the historical content of the transformations that the Brazilian socio-economic formation went through in the period from 1930 to 1980. Of particular concern are the shifts between mercantile and industrial capitalism and how compromises have always been found between these conflicting interests.

The analysis carried out here follows a historical theory of Brazilian underdevelopment which begins by denying a non-capitalist phase in the Brazilian socio-economic formation. In his *História Econômica do Brasil*, Prado Jr. (1945) shows that since the beginning of its colonization, Brazil was treated as a commercial enterprise. That is, despite the fact that slavery existed and economic growth was centred on self-sufficient, master-controlled, aristocratic ideologically dominated 'latifundios', the latter's main objective was profits raised through the selling of sugar in the international market and their profits were obtained through primitive accumulation [3].

What matters in the Brazilian associated-dependent socio-economic formation, then, is not the emergence of capitalism but the role played in it by mercantile 'vis-à-vis' industrial capital. Brazilian mercantile capital in its early version, was characterized by profits which were derived from the exploitation of slaves and from the distances that existed in international trade. It was not part of the mercantile capitalist's behaviour to pursue systematic increases in productivity and the incorporation of technical progress.

Such behaviour was not confined to growth led by sugar-cane production in the seventeenth century or by gold production in the eighteenth century. It was also present in the production of coffee for which there was no meaningful technical progress between 1830 and 1930. Given this dominant mercantile characteristic of capitalism in Brazil up to the first third of the twentieth century, growth was achieved by increase in production and not based on improvements in productivity.

Although there was room for improvements in the consumption pattern of the dominant elite, there was no development of the production forces. Thus, income per capita increased from the mid-1800s up to 1930 as the country specialized in the production of coffee, but the gap between Brazil's economic performance and that of the industrial world became larger. Population growth was not matched by growth in labour productivity. Thus, it seems appropriate the analysis of Bresser Pereira (1983) who identifies the roots of the country's underdevelopment in its late adherence to industrial capitalism, broadly seen as centred on any capital which extracts relative surplus value through the systematic introduction of technical progress in production.

The importance of identifying these roots is that when industrial capitalism emerges in the Brazilian socio-economic formation, it does so under the conditions of monopoly capitalism at a world level. As a result, the major surge of industrial development in Brazil (mid-1950s onwards) only took place under the strong presence of state-owned and multinational enterprises. Despite the fact that import-substitution in its first stage (1930/50) was mainly led by local small firms, the associated characteristic of the country's dependency took place when there was the convergence of interest between local forces led by the state and multinational corporations [4]. The framework for the analysis that follows is given, then, by the combination of deeply rooted rent-seeking behaviour on the part of mercantile capitalism, late-coming industrial capitalism which was never based on competition in the 'classical' English and American sense, and the emergence of the state and of multinational corporations as key actors in the industrialization process. Given this combination in the associated-dependent development of Brazil, the focus of the analysis is centred on the periodization of the country's industrialization process and the role played by internal forces in the way this process has been shaped.

2.4   Establishing the grounds for the import-substitution model (1930/55)

It is common amongst Brazilian economists [Furtado (1971), Castro (1971), Cano (1977), for example] to link the beginning of the country's industrialization process in 1930 with the crisis of accumulation that took place due to the problems faced by coffee in the international market. For these authors, a major impulse to industrialization was given by the combination of (i) increases in the prices of imported goods as the country's export earnings (mainly from coffee) dropped in the 1930s to less than half of what was achieved in the 1920s; and (ii) the government's policy which maintained aggregate demand through the acquisition (and burning) of existing coffee production.

According to the same line of reasoning, in the 1940s the main impulse to industrialization came from the impossibility of internal supply by imports due to the war. In these two decades, then, from an economic point of view the main motivation for industrialization came from 'exogenous shocks' which emerged either from a fall in the demand of the country's main tradable (coffee) or from a fall in the supply of imported goods.

The importance of these externally determined factors for the process of industrialization in Brazil is undeniable, but the emphasis here is placed on the internal conditions and political articulations that facilitated the shift in the existing mode of accumulation. That is, there were groups or fractions of the capitalist class in the country which aimed at a different pace of economic development which could only be obtained [Simonsen (1977)] through (i) the intensification of the industrialization process ["the nucleus part of a programme aimed at increasing production to the levels which are necessary to the needs of the nation, must be the industrial sector" (ibid., p. 33)]; and (ii) the establishment of a planning process which could assure the best utilization of existing resources.

The industrialization process which began in 1930 must be looked at from a perspective privileging the emergence of internal groups which saw industrial development as a necessary condition for the strengthening and the independence of the national economy. As Diniz (1981) points out, the struggle in favour of industrialization was identified as being the most important general interest of the nation [5].

Such vision and commitment of the industrial bourgeoisie did not imply, though, that they succeeded in carrying through a modernization process similar to that which took place in other late-comers such as Germany and Japan [6]. For they were never able to establish a hegemonic position in the state apparatus over the previously dominant agro-exporter interests which advocated anti-state and international liberal economic ideas. The state of compromise that was then established between these conflicting interests became characteristic of the Brazilian conservative modernization process [7].

20

During the first stage of the Brazilian import-substitution model (1930--1955), then, what seems important to emphasize is the struggle within the state apparatus in order to convey the specific interests of both the agro-exporter interests and those of the emerging industrialists and urban workers. Thus, whilst exchange rate policies favoured both groups, State investment in road construction and power generation were clearly aimed at creating market and production conditions for the emerging industries. Moreover, the increasing involvement of the State in production activities (steel and oil production, iron-ore export) and in institution building (BNDE - the Bank of National Development) was clearly driven by a task to foster industrialization [8].

The new directions taken by the State from 1930 onwards, but especially after the first half of the 1950s, were a direct response by segments of its bureaucracy (civil and military) committed to the industrialization project - along with the industrial bourgeoisie - to two internal conditions which were clear inhibitors of a new mode of accumulation in the country. The first was the fact that entrepreneurship in the Schumpeterian sense was very limited amongst Brazilian businessmen and that the private banking system would not be able to go beyond its traditional role of commercial financing. The second was that the strong arm of Brazilian capitalism - its mercantile side formed by agro-exporter activities - was not ready for voluntarily shifting its surpluses to a new mode of accumulation which would conflict with the interests of its foreign associates.

2.5 The second phase of the import-substitution model (1956-63)

The main results of the new role played by the state in the industrialization process came in the second phase of the import-substitution model (1956-62) [9]. Under the guidance of the explicit industrial policy of the Targets Plan (1956-60), and under the direct coordination by the State, an intense diversification of the country's industrial base took place. During that period were built the car industry, the ship industry, heavy electrical and other machines and equipments industry, followed by a significant increase in the capital goods sector. At the same time expansions took place in the production of steel, chemicals, petroleum and paper and pulp. Despite the role of innovation in these industries, the major concern at their implementation stage was with production capacities. This lack of concern with technological capabilities have had negative effects on the BNSI as will be seen later (especially Chapters 4 and 6).

In the rapid process of industrial diversification and consolidation of industrial capitalism in Brazil, the role of multinational corporations was significant, as can be seen in the jump in the average inflow of foreign capital.

That inflow increased from 17.6 million dollars per year in the 1947-55 period to more than 106 million dollars per year between 1956 and 1962.

Singer (1984) emphasizes, though, that more important than the amount of direct foreign investment brought in by multinationals, was the role they played in the compromise that was drawn in favour of the industrialization project. Given that the alternative to foreign capital was an even greater role for the State, because domestic private capital was not able to attain the necessary degree of monopolistic concentration, it is reasonable to conclude that "welcoming foreign capital was the compromise found by those within the power alliance in favour of industrialization and those against State capitalism in order to neutralize the opposition of other sectors within the alliance, especially those for whom priority should be given to agro-exporter activities, which strongly opposed both industrialization and a stronger role of the State." (ibid., p. 227, my translation).

Summing up, the qualitative changes that took place in the Brazilian socio-economic formation during the period of import-substitution (1930/62) were based on a strong role played by the populist State which was the result of an alliance of classes involving rural oligarchies, agriculture exporters, emerging industrial bourgeoisie, and parts of the civil and military bureaucracies, and of urban workers. Moreover, the change from mercantile accumulation to industrial accumulation took place within the framework of a triple alliance that was built between the State, and local/foreign capitals [10].

The implications of the power alliance on which the populist State was based, though, cannot be restricted to the period covered by the import--substitution model. When arrangements with urban workers within the alliance posed problems to the accumulation process in the 1960s, the populist State was replaced by the technocratic-authoritarian State which lasted until the mid-1980s. What is important to keep in mind is that compromises between mercantile and industrial capitalists and their counterparts in the civil and military bureaucracies are the common feature that remain throughout and beyond both periods. It will be shown in Part II that a new shift in the balance of power within 'the state of compromise' [11] built and consolidated around mercantile and industrial interests would considerably affect the way the State responds to the search for a new mode of accumulation in the 1980s.

As for the triple alliance that was build between State, and local/foreign capitals, it is important to emphasize that it consolidated both the internalization of the process of accumulation [12] and the ideological adherence of the Brazilian socio-economic formation to worldwide capitalism [13].

2.6 From import-substitution/populist State to export promotion/techno--bureaucratic State

The changes that took place in the Brazilian socio-economic formation in the period between 1930 and 1962 from rural, agro-exporter into urban-industrial, gave rise to two sorts of social expectations. The first one was that industrialization would bring development and economic independence to the country. The second was that the political role played by urban workers in the legitimation of the populist State could be expanded in such a way that they would have more to say about the sort of development path the country should follow.

Both expectations were increased by the fast economic growth that took place under Kubitschek (whose government's slogan was '50 years in 5') and by the favourable democratic environment that prevailed during those five years. The good performance of the economy - GDP grew at an average rate of 6.9% per year between 1957 and 1961 - was followed by a slower rate in 1962 (5.0%); by an increasing rate of inflation which went beyond 50% that year; and an increasing concern over balance of payments deficit and foreign debt which was over two billion American dollars in 1962.

Politically the country was going through a critical period in the sense that the mysterious resignation of the newly elected President Quadros in August 1961 led to a very unstable solution in the change of the regime to Parliamentarism. Elections for the Parliament in 1962 generated debate concerning the regime of government to be adopted and the need of the country to go through basic reforms in sectors such as education, banking and, always critical, land reform. Socially, the labour movement intensified its campaigns in favour of basic reforms and for wage increases which could at least cope with the inflationary process.

The economic policies followed by the Government under Goulart (1961-64) were contradictory. They sought both to control inflation in the interest of capital accumulation and simultaneously to appease the labour movement - its main political base. Under these circumstances, what emerged was not a crisis of realization. Despite problems in some sectors - mainly those producing wage-goods - the crucial aspect of the crisis which emerged was its institutional deadlock. In the words of Oliveira (1981)

> the struggle which was developed and that became the centre of the political debate took place at the heart of the relations of production. To think that under these circumstances it would be possible, to maintain (i) the horizons of economic calculations, and forecasts on investments; and (ii) the capacity of the State to mediate conflicts and to maintain a stable institutional environment, is to go back to economism. Investment fell not because it could not take place economically but because it could not be realized institutionally. (ibid., p. 63, my translation).

The major task of the authoritarian regime that came to power in 1964 was, then, to destroy the basis of the populist State and to replace it with the techno-bureaucratic-capitalist State. According to Bresser Pereira (1983), the main characteristic of the latter was to express the alliance of the dominant bourgeoisie class with the emerging techno-bureaucracy. The military group of this techno-bureaucracy took the role of leading the country politically whilst their civilian counterparts gave political tutelage to the bourgeoisie. Thus, "in economic matters the high techno-bureaucracy, despite satisfying its own interests, both in terms of high wages and power, responded mainly to the interests of the bourgeoisie for capital accumulation." (ibid., p. 55).

The economic policies and institutional rearrangements that emerged in the 1964-67 [14] period were consistent with the need to sustain accumulation based on the expansion of those industries that produced durable goods. Given that the authoritarian regime that emerged, by definition, did not require the popular legitimation that characterized the populist State, wage controls were high on the agenda of the stabilization program. The fall in the demand that followed was compensated for by an increase in the concentration process which resulted from the 'creative destruction' of less competitive firms through credit squeezing.

The State apparatus was reformed in order to respond more adequately (mainly through subsidized credit and fiscal incentives) to the needs of accumulation centred on manufactures both for the internal market and (since 1967 increasingly so) for exports. Moreover, although the authoritarian regime came to power in order to re-establish economic liberal ideas and ideals, in the 1964/67 period were established the principles under which State-owned enterprises came to play a crucial role in the circuit of productive capital, either on their own or in association with foreign and local capital.

With the new forms of associations between state-owned enterprises, and local/foreign capitals, the Brazilian economy was inserted differently into the international division of labour. From being mainly an exporter of agriculture products (coffee and sugar accounted for over 50% of exports in 1964), the country diversified its sales in the world market so that by 1973, manufactures already accounted for more than 20% of total exports (the same percentage as coffee).

More important than the diversification of exports and of marketing strategies (the American market accounted for over 33% of Brazil's total exports in 1967, but for less than 16% in 1975) was the switch in the ideological content of development that came about with the new regime of accumulation. Whilst under import substitution economic policy was mainly driven by nationalistic principles, under the new regime prevailed more internationalistic policies [15].

The changes that took place between 1964-67 were essential for the 'boom' in the economy from 1968 to 1973. The new approach to monetary policy used by policy-makers under the second and third authoritarian governments (1967/73), boosted the economy into the 'Brazilian miracle'. What followed was that GDP which had experienced yearly average growth of 3.7% between 1962 and 1967, boomed at an average rate of 11.3% per year between 1968 and 1974.

The priority that was given to industrial accumulation was reflected in the rates at which the industrial sector grew. According to the figures of *Conjuntura Econômica* from an annual average of 3.9% between 1962 and 1967, industrial growth was 13.3% in 1968, 12.2% in 1969, 10.4% in 1970, 14.3% in 1971, 13.4% in 1972, reaching 16% in 1973. As is to be expected from the wage squeeze (made politically viable through extreme controls over the unions) and the increasing inequality in income distribution that took place after 1964 (see Table 2.4), the highest growth rates observed within manufacturing were achieved by sectors such as transport equipment, machinery, and electrical equipment, whilst traditional sectors like textiles, clothing, and food products experienced much lower rates [16].

Table 2.4
Brazil: changes in income distribution - 1960-70

| | Share of income (%) | | Per capita income (US$) | |
	1960	1970	1960	1970
Lowest 40%	11.2	9.0	84	90
Next 40%	34.3	27.8	257	278
Next 15%	27.0	27.0	540	720
Top 5%	27.4	36.3	1,645	1,940
Total	100,0	100,0	300,0	400,0

Source: Baer (1989), Table 5.6

Despite the diversification of its industrial base, the Brazilian economy was still highly dependent on imports especially for the more sophisticated sectors upon which its growth was based during the years of the 'miracle'. Thus, whilst in the 1956-61 period the import/GDP ratio was 5.4% on average, in the 1967-73 period it was 8.6%. Furthermore, from a formal point of view, the contribution of import substitution to the growth of manufacturing was negative between 1968 and 1974 (about minus 5.4%), whilst between 1957 and 1961 it was positive (about 7.5%) [17].

This negative contribution of import-substitution to the growth of manufacturing was closely related to the strategy used during the industrialization process which privileged the diversification predominantly in the last stages of production. This meant that increases in demand - which was common either because there was rapid diffusion of the products now being produced internally or because their demand was restricted before import-substitution - had to be followed by additional imports. Under these circumstances, the increases in imports could end up being even greater than before import-substitution took place.

Consequently, as emphasized by Tavares (1972), import substitution has to be seen as a process which to a certain extent had to include a built-in feedback mechanism. That is, as it enlarged its horizontal base (through diversification into the production of final goods) it also became necessary to integrate the industrialization process vertically toward intermediate and capital goods. By the beginning of the 1970s the need to carry the process one stage further became more urgent because of the impact that increases in petroleum prices had on the country's trade balance [18] and on the patterns of international trade.

The identification of opportunities for both vertical integration of import-substitution and diversification of exports was the key tone of the last comprehensive development strategy put forward by the authoritarian regime. The political and economic implications of the new mode of accumulation are the subject of the next sub-section.

2.7 The political 'distensão' and the deepening of import-substitution and diversification of exports regime of accumulation (1974/79)

The economic strategy used by the Brazilian government in the 1974/79 period was, in the words of its Planning Minister, Reis Velloso (1977) that of a positive solution. The need to expand the internal production of basic inputs, which had been identified before the first oil shock in 1973, was seen by the second national development plan (II PND - 1975-79) as an imperative for the synchronization of the country's economy with the transformations that were taking place in the world economy.

The II PND's 'solution' was sought through the building-up of a modern industrial economy with the objective of developing new comparative advantages [19]. In order to achieve such a goal, the government had to respond to the 'natural' reactions of private (local and multinational) capital which was resistant to the idea of internalization of production of intermediate and capital goods. This was so on the supply side because these industries usually require long maturation periods, present higher risks and involve more sophisticated technologies. On the demand side, those industries (local and multinationals) using the goods to be produced internally argue that prices, quality and guarantee of supply are better achieved through purchases on the international market.

Given these different resistances amongst industrialists - which could not sound better to the 'always alert' agro-exporter groups - it should be of no surprise that a major role was played by state-owned enterprises in the process of the forced march [Castro (1985)] under which the Brazilian economy

26

searched for the development of capital-intensive and technology intensive industries. Thus, in order to keep the gross fixed capital formation/GDP ratio at the levels of the years of the 'miracle' (above 20%), the government had to increase the share of its state-owned enterprises in gross fixed capital formation from 20.3% in 1970 to 28.7% in 1979 (Table 2.5).

Table 2.5
Public and private share in gross capital formation (%)

	1965	1970	1975	1979
Private sector	61.9	61.2	58.0	56.3
Public sector	38.1	38.8	42.0	43.7
Government	24.8	18.5	16.9	15.0
State-enterprises	13.3	20.3	25.1	28.7

Source: Reichstul and Coutinho (1983), Table 2

Although there was no mention of it in any official document, the role of state-owned enterprises such as PETROBRAS (oil), ELETROBRAS (electricity power), SIDERBRAS (steel) and TELEBRAS (telecommunications) became central in the accumulation process that took place following the guidelines of the II PND [20]. The response from the liberals to the 'statization' of the Brazilian economy did not take long to emerge. The tone of the debate, however, was more grave than that which had been common throughout the industrialization process since the 1930s. Since industrialization in itself was no longer an issue (it had become a reality), the main target of well-known liberals such as Prof. Gudin and heralds of liberal ideals such as *O Estado de São Paulo* (a major daily newspaper from Sao Paulo), *O Globo* (a major newspaper from Rio de Janeiro) and Visao (a week business magazine) was the danger that the Brazilian economy would become socialist [21].

More important than the smoke-screen of the anti-statization campaign through the media was the realignment of forces within the dominant pact. The triple alliance of State techno-bureaucrats, and local/foreign capital was being questioned at two levels - the economic and the political - and from two perspectives - from within the alliance itself and from those who were left outside the dominant pact of 1964.

At the economic level, the major issues at the time were the refueling of inflation - which had more than doubled between 1973 and 1974 (from 16.2% to 33.8%) and was as high as 76.8% in 1979 - and the escalation of the foreign debt from 5.3 billion dollars in 1970, 12.6 billion in 1973, to 54 billion dollars in 1980. Thus, the managerial efficiency of the technocratic regime began to be questioned. At the political level, the 1974 election victory of the only opposition party was seen as a clear indication of lack of popularity of the regime. It became clear that the search for a new form of authoritarianism would have to go beyond the planned 'relative democracy' of 'distensão' (meaning the relaxation of certain authoritarian rules such as direct censorship of the press). Pressure was being build-up in favour of a 'distensão' which would contemplate direct elections for executive positions as well [22].

From the perspective of the local bourgeoisie, the growth of autonomy gained by the State techno-bureaucracy was unacceptable. Its ideology was in fact increasingly distancing itself from a position of subordination to the interests of the bourgeoisie. Moreover, the techno-bureaucracy was becoming too eager to present the State as the most efficient instrument for achieving high growth rates of income and productivity [23].

This internal fissure in the domination pact - clearly expressed in the open criticism by important associations of entrepreneurs such as FIESP (São Paulo state confederation of industrialists) and ABDIB (the national association of capital goods industries) - grew with the grievance of representative institutions, such as the Catholic Church and the Brazilian Bar Association, for human rights violations and poor social conditions in the country. They were certainly voicing the feelings of those who were left outside the domination pact that came to power in 1964. Despite the pledge of the II PND in favour of "a strategy of social development aimed at (i) guaranteeing to every class, and especially to the working and middle classes, substantial real income increases and (ii) eliminating, in as short a period as possible the sources of absolute poverty" (ibid., p. 27), the number of those marginalized by the domination pact was large (see Table 2.6).

Table 2.6
Brazil - Income distribution 1970 - 1980

Percent of Population		Percent of Total Income 1970	1980
Poorest	10 percent	.9	.8
	20	2.7	2.4
	30	5.5	5.0
	40	9.3	8.5
	50	14.1	13.1
	60	20.3	19.0
Richest	30	71.7	73.3
	20	61.0	62.7
	10	45.2	47.0
	5	32.9	34.6
	1	15.2	16.4

Source: Rossi, J (1986), 'Distribuição da Renda', RJ: IPEA/INPES

The political and economic results of these tensions within the dominant alliance and of those which grew between civil society and the State crystallized in the 1980s. By then the power struggle within the alliance - bourgeoisie versus techno-bureaucracy; productive capital versus finance capital; profit seekers versus rent-seekers, etc. - was quite widespread. Furthermore, the tensions between civil society and the State had mounted to such a point that a transition to democracy was seen as the only peaceful solution to the economic and political tensions that emerged as a result of the conservative modernization path followed since the 1930s.

These tensions, and the economic constraints that the country went through in the 1980s, are dealt with in Part II (mainly in chapters 4 and 5). Before that, the next section gives an overview of the way technology was seen at the different stages of industrial accumulation. The overview will focus on the struggle between forces which favoured the search for technological autonomy and those which were more concerned with production capabilities.

As the state apparatus was the privileged locus of that struggle, an appropriate source for identifying the different stages of the debate concerning technological development can be found in the development plans. They provide indications concerning the BNSI from a perspective which interest the analysis in this book. That is, possible dependency ties that were or were not major targets in the development process as perceived by forces within the Brazilian associated-dependent socio-economic formation.

2.8 Technology and development: tensions between production and technological capabilities

The analysis of the political economy of the Brazilian industrialization process provides a good illustration of Gerschenkron's (1966) 'advantages of backwardness'. Contrary to what took place in most cases of late-industrialization, however, the Brazilian development process can be pointed as singular in the sense of the marginal importance that has been given to scientific and technological capabilities [24].

Throughout most of the industrialization process which took place in Brazil since the 1930s, technological development has been the result of the incorporation of capital-embodied technical progress (25). Technology as a social process has become part of the public debate (even if circumscribed to mainly military circles) only in the post-World War II period. As is stressed in Part II, with the exception of ITA (an approximation to MIT's experience sponsored by the Air Force Ministry) and CENAP (training and research centre sponsored by state-owned PETROBRAS) which were established in the 1950s, the great majority of R&D initiatives in the country took place from the 1970s onwards.

Even when the debate was intensified under the ISI model implemented from 1955 onwards, most of it took place under the sponsorship of different government agencies. Thus, despite the limitations of analyses based on government plans only, the insertion of technology in the Brazilian political economy is better assessed through the indications of its relative importance in those plans.

The debate concerned with technology, in most cases, emerged because in the design and implementation of the planning process in Brazil, there has always been divergent objectives between agencies involved (or individuals concerned) with technological development and those in the implementation end of the policy-making process. Whilst the former have always perceived 'policies towards relative autonomy', at the implementation sectors of government, priority has always been given to 'response policies'. An example of government actions committed exclusively to a 'response policy' - broadly characterized as industrialization regardless of its technological content [Guimarães and Ford (1975)] - were those that took place in the industrialization period during the first stage of the import substitution model. Even though there was direct involvement of the government in basic sectors such as steel production, there was no genuine technological policy. As for 'policies towards relative autonomy' - characterized by the support given to national capacities in the creation/adaptation of technical knowledge - a good example is to be found in the definitions of the PED (Strategic Plan for Development 1968/70) when for the first time the need for a specific technological policy was made explicit.

Between the two, there is the Target Plan (1955/60) which, besides being an investment project, raised concern over technological matters. Thus, facing a technological demand from the production sector, the state responded with greater financial support for the import of equipment and as a mediator for the inflow of foreign embodied technology. This pragmatic approach went on until the late 1960s but these were times also of increasing concern over the need for a specific policy towards technological development [Jaguaribe (1987)].

The PED (Development Strategic Plan - 1968/70) can be taken as the starting point of active technological planning in Brazil. Its main characteristic was the intention of setting up a technological policy associated with an industrial strategy and an institutional framework. According to its formulation, "the import substitution of industrial products, as occurred in the post-war period, does not suffice for a self-sustained development process. It is necessary to complement it with technology substitution. That is to be taken as the adaptation of imported technology and the gradual creation of a process of autonomous technological development." (ibid., my translation).

The PED's strong wording in favour of greater technological autonomy can be identified with the beginning of systematic struggle between industrial, economic and technological planning in Brazil which was to take place in cycles [Erber et al. (1985a)]. It is interesting to notice, though, that under the PED technological development was seen like any other area of planning, not as a 'cement' to the development strategy as a whole.

A second cycle of struggles between industrial, economic and technological planning started with the first development plan (I PND - 1969/74). It established priority for nuclear energy, technology intensive industries, agriculture R&D, etc., and its strategy was based on local enterprises (private and state-owned). The intensification of technology imports, its adaptation to local needs, and investment in technological capability were once more seen as being able to result in innovation.

Again, contradiction occurred between the concerns with technological autonomy at the planning level, and the results of the implementation process. The 'national development' intentions were contradicted by the reality of strong roles being played by multinationals in key sectors. As put by Erber et al. (1985a), the strong ties between the Brazilian economy and the core of the capitalist world created the necessary conditions for the continuation of economic growth without depending on local technological capabilities.

A third impetus in the interplay between industrial, technological and economic policies took place with the second national development plan (II PND - 1975/79). The need for a systematic effort towards industrial and technological policies was made explicit and seen as basically necessary for the construction of a competitive economy and a modern industrial society. The argument was that "science and technology, at today's stage of the Brazilian society, represent a noble force, the outstanding conduit for the idea of progress and modernization." (ibid., p. 135, my translation).

More important than the wordings in the plan, however, were the actions taken in throughout the period of the II PND. As will seen in more details in Part II, the seeds of information technology in Brazil were planted during that period. The first systematic efforts towards informatics (the market reserve policy) [26] and towards strengthening R&D capabilities in telecommunications were taken during the II PND. Moreover, the institutional and financial support to R&D was made in such a way that substantial progress took place in the establishment of in-house and R&D institutes, and of research activities in Brazilian universities.

2.9 Summing up

The analyses provided in this chapter show that the industrialization process carried out in Brazil since the 1930s was based on a conservative modernization project. But, thanks to the alliance of the state with local and foreign capitals, it changed the form of dependency of Brazil in the

31

international division of labour. From a mainly agro-exporter position in the first half of the century, the country became one of the newly industrialized (and heavily indebted) countries of the post-World War II period. The compromises that were made between mercantile and industrial capitalists throughout the implementation of the industrialization process, however, left the country in a position where no hegemonic power prevails. Moreover, the 'state of compromise' resulted in a situation where growth has very seldom been driven by the 'creative destruction' of the inefficient.

The background provided in this chapter is used in Part II in order to emphasize the challenges the country must face if it is to maintain the relative economic gains it has achieved through the industrialization process described above. Given the institutional framework under which these gains were accomplished, emphasis is placed on the contradictions that exist between the diversification of the country's technological and economic base - even when changes in the techno-economic paradigm of the world economy are taken into consideration - and the conservative features of its institutional framework.

That is, the 'lost decade' of the 1980s is examined from a perspective which privileges, on the one hand, the results of past public policies and private decision-making which enabled the country to build technological capabilities in the core industry of the new paradigm. On the other hand, emphasis is given to both the adverse international conditions under which the Brazilian economy operated throughout the 1980s and the institutional boiling pot into which the country was immersed. Special attention is given to the forms taken by the 'state of compromise' between 'modern-industrial' Brazil and its 'traditional-rent seeking' counterpart which has been pointed to in this chapter.

Notes

1. The main objective of the '1930 Revolution' was to push political and administrative centralization in order to autonomise the state's ability to intervene in the different aspects of social and economic life. It is seen by many (Wanderley Guilherme dos Santos, for instance) as the necessary condition for the rapid expansion of capitalism in Brazil. For critical reviews of the different dimensions of the '1930 Revolution', see Fausto (1970) and Diniz (1981).

2. See Luz (1973) for an account of attempts of industrialization in Brazil before 1930.

3. Caio Prado's characterization of Brazil's agriculture development was in clear conflict with the existing interpretation given by the members of the Brazilian Communist Party (mainly Nelson Werneck Sodré) for the

country's stage of development. He was followed, though, by Frank (1964) and Marini (1969), amongst others. They agreed that labour relations in the country's primary sector were not the residue of feudal or semi-feudal practices. Much to the contrary, for those authors these labour relations were an indication that Brazil was already part of the world capitalist system since its colonial times. The indications of Brazil's early insertion in the world capitalist system are found by these authors mainly in the sphere of circulation. Nevertheless, even their critics agree that by the beginning of the century Brazil could also be considered capitalist if the sphere of production was taken into consideration. For a critique of the controversies and agreements amongst the left with respect to the origins and possible outcomes of Brazil's underdevelopment, see Mantega (1984).

4. This is not specific to the Brazilian socio-economic formation. According to the periodization of capitalism proposed by Fine and Harris (1979), in the third stage of capitalist development "the internationalization of productive capital divides capitals, not according to their ability to compete on the world market or gain access to world finance, but according to their ability to organize production across national boundaries. Associated with each stage, a section of national and foreign capital have a 'natural' alliance when interests come to dominate state intervention as the world economy develops." (ibid., p. 148).

5. In the words of Diniz (1981): "even though the [industrial] bourgeoisie could not define a specific project totally coherent with its interests, it participated (i) on the strengthening of ideological options more coherent with the industrialization process; (ii) on the state apparatus through its presence - side by side with civil and military bureaucrats and representatives of other economic groups - in committees specially designed for the formulation of economic policies. ... There was also the convergence between certain concepts of modernization that were advocated by those who supported the authoritarian regime and some aspects of the industrialization process that was supported by industry's leadership. Such convergence, amongst other consequences, created an appropriate political environment for the analogy between industrial growth and economic strengthening; between industrial growth and economic and political independence. All that made easier the identification of industry with nation, of industry with internal defense capability." (ibid., pages 97/98, my translation).

6. Significantly, it is easy to see strong similarities between the ideas of Brazilian industrialists like Roberto Simonsen, and those of Frederick Lizt, the German economist who in the eighteenth century questioned the

relevance of the theory of comparative advantage to late-comers because that theory was developed too closely connected to the interests of the 'centre' (mainly England).

7. Although the modernization of its economic structure through industrialization was not followed by a similar change in its political and social spheres, the Brazilian modernization process is said to be conservative because it has been based on subsidies and protection which have inhibited renewal and rationalization of the production process. For discussions of different aspects of the conservative/ incomplete modernization process in Brazil, see Velloso (1990b), Bacha and Klein, eds. (1989), and Fajnzylber (1983).

8. See Draibe (1985) for an analysis of the institution-building geared towards the industrialization of Brazil.

9. In the words of Fiori (1990, p. 50) "a strategic change of direction was needed. It meant the option in favour of an associated-development with international capital, the only way to finance an industrialization which was late and peripheral and which never became a truly national project in its Prussian sense ... An industrialization which lacked external ambitions and ambitions towards internal hegemonic powers." (my translation).

10. For an analysis of the triple alliance, see Evans (1979).

11. The 'state of compromise' is explained by Oliveira (1981) as a way found to make global accumulation feasible through: (i) the introduction of new relations in the archaic in such a way as to set free forces that could support urban-industrial accumulation; and (ii) the reproduction of old relations into the new in such a way as to preserve the potential for accumulation which was liberated exclusively for the expansion of the new.

12. Oliveira (1981) points out that "the affiliation of the Brazilian economy to the capitalist system, its structural transformation as occurred after 1930, is predominantly a possibility defined within itself; that is, the existing relations of production had in themselves the possibilities of restructuring the system. That was so even when the conditions given by the international division of labour were adverse." (ibid. p. 38, my translation).

13. This point is well established by Singer (1984) who points out that from the 1950s onwards "Brazil is no longer rebelling against its position in the international division of labour. On the contrary, it began to search for its opportunities of development within this division, in harmony with the tendency of international integration of national economies which was

dominant in the post-World War II up to at least 1974." (ibid., p. 236, my translation).

14. Besides the implementation of an orthodox stabilization programme based on the elimination of the fiscal deficit and tight credit and wage controls, the economic programme of the first authoritarian government (1964/67) also comprised a structural adjustment programme involving rapid growth of public revenues, the setting up of financial systems specialized in consumer credit and on housing financing, progressive liberalization of imports, less restrictions on foreign capital and the creation of incentives for the diversification of exports [Serra (1982)].

15. The shift in the ideological content of economic policies under the authoritarian regime is well captured by Singer (1984): "more important than the marginal profits that were acquired from international trade, were the effects of internationalization over the mentality of the dominant class, specially of its hegemonic fraction, which began to see the country from the same perspective that the multinationals' managers did. That is, as a 'segment of the world capitalist economy' each time more integrated internationally.   The new generation of economic policy-makers, recruited in its majority from the academia, not only made operational the new strategy of outward development but was also influenced by its logic. That is a reasonable explanation for the multinational strategies of important state-owned enterprises such as PETROBRAS and Bank of Brazil. From a practical point of view, within the circles of power nothing was left of the old nationalist ideology which saw in the progressive diversification of production for the internal market the most important base upon which could be built the strategy of development." (ibid., p. 241, my translation).

16. See Baer (1989).

17. Locatelli (1985) measured this negative contribution by disaggregating the sources of industrial growth through the use of input-output analysis. The three sources studied (expansion of internal demand, import substitution, and export expansion) contributed positively to industrial growth in the 1962/67 period (ibid., Table 3.4d, p. 74). In the 1968/74 period, however, whilst with regard to all 18 industrial sectors, expansion of internal demand and of exports contributed positively, import substitution contributed negatively in 16 of them (ibid., Table 3.4e, p. 75).

18. According to the Central Bank (*Boletim Mensal,* August 84), whilst imports had been just slightly ahead of exports in 1972 (4.2 billion dollars of imports and 3.9 billion dollars of exports) and in 1973 (6.1 billion of imports and 6.2 of exports), in 1974/75 imports jumped ahead

significantly to an average of over 12 billion dollars against an increase of exports which averaged about 8 billion dollars in those two years.

19. In this sense, the ideological content of the II PND can be seen as linked to the basic principles launched by the industrialization project of the 1930s. For Medeiros (1985) the political linkages between 1930 and 1974 were established through the fact that the generals who took power in 1974 (mainly President Geisel and his Home Secretary Golbery) were amongst the young officers who in 1930 backed the change of the political regime with the purpose of the country's modernization. As is shown in item 2.8 and in Chapters 4 and 6, the II PND played an important role in establishing the technological content of the modernization project.

20. See Lessa (1978), quoted in Castro (1985).

21. For an account of the anti-statization campaign which went through the implementation of the II PND, see Pessanha (1981).

22. Cardoso (1980) analyses the political crossroads of the authoritarian regime from 1974 onwards.

23. Bresser Pereira (1978) gives an account of the different reasons and different stages of the fissures that took place within the triple dominance alliance.

24. This is not to deny early achievements of the local scientific community. These achievements, however, were direct responses to specific problems of public health (malaria, Chagas disease, and yellow fever), of agriculture production ('rust' in coffee trees), and others. For a general assessment of the history of science in Brazil and the building-up of its scientific community, see Ferri and Motoyana (1979), and Schwartzman (1979).

25. The first systematic attempt of funding projects geared towards research and development was that of FUNTEC (the programme for technological development created by the National Bank for Economic Development). Its relevance for the BNSI should not be assessed by the limited amount of its financing (US$100 million between 1964 and 1974) but by the impact that it had in the emergence of many post-graduate courses in the country (COPPE in Rio de Janeiro, for example). BNDE (1974) and Romanini (1977) provide a general view of the institutional and financial support given to R&D activities in Brazil up to beginning of the 1970s. For the analysis of the cycles of systematic struggle between industrial, economic and technological planning, see Erber et al. (1985a).

26. See Langer (1989) for the identification of the roots of the Brazilian informatics programme with the physics research project being conducted by Schemberg in São Paulo since the 1950s.

3 Setting up the analytical framework

3.1 Introduction

In the first two chapters of this book attention was drawn to the dependent-
-associated characteristics of the Brazilian socio-economic formation and to
the important role played by technology in shaping different forms for this
dependency. The major objective of this chapter is to establish the theoretical
framework under which the performance of the Brazilian socio-economic
formation throughout the 1980s will be analyzed in Part II. Two concepts are
central to the presente discussion; that of techno-economic paradigm, and that
of national systems of innovation.

The concept of techno-economic paradigm emphasizes the revolutionary
content of certain clusters of innovations. Once identified, these clusters of
innovations can be examined from a perspective which focuses on their
pervasive impact on the technological, economic and institutional frameworks
of different socio-economic formations and of the world system as a whole.
The chapter's discussion of national systems of innovation is centred on its
theoretical relevance as a proper ground for understanding the learning process
which takes place amongst economic agents and which can foster and
facilitate innovation.

The chapter begins by drawing attention to the main characteristics of
innovation and by reviewing a taxonomy of innovations which emphasizes
their different impacts on economic development. At the highest 'level' of this
taxonomy are changes in techno-economic paradigms which have been
associated with shifts in the trajectories of economic development in the past
two hundred years. In this chapter changes in techno-economic paradigm are
taken as an alternative way of emphasizing the impact of information
technology on the prospects for world development. This proposition is
backed by a discussion of both the historical content and the status of techno-
-economic paradigm as a category for the analysis of long-term changes in the

pattern of economic development. Historical evidence is presented in order to stress the distinct impact that changes in techno-economic paradigms have had on different socio-cconomic formations

The chapter then discusses the learning process from a perspective which privileges interactions amongst agents. Emphasis is given to the 'learning-by--interacting' process because of the revolutionary content of innovations which take place at the 'level' of changes in techno-economic paradigm. The economic and technological uncertainties which permeate the innovative process under these revolutionary conditions can be minimized if the agents involved can draw on norms and procedures which are based on cooperation rather than on competition. Moreover, these norms and procedures run a better chance of facilitating and encouraging innovations if they are bounded by a common geographical and cultural terrain. For that reason the concept of national systems of innovation used here can be seen as having not only policy implications but also theoretical relevance.

Finally, the chapter draws on a 'self-regulating model' in order to make the concepts of techno-economic paradigm and of national systems of innovations more operational for the analysis of specific socio-economic formations. This model divides the socio-economic fabric under which innovations takes place in three domains: the system of technologies; the 'economic machine'; and the system of social relations and institutions.

3.2 Some basic characteristics of innovation

The importance of technology for economic change is not new to economists. Classical economists were already aware of it. Adam Smith's contribution to the questions of technical change and productivity improvement came in the first chapter of his *Wealth of the Nations*. Nevertheless, the work done afterwards was so limited that it led Marx to question why should not "the history of productive organs of man in society, of organs that are the material basis of every particular organization of society, deserve equal attention [to the one Darwin directed to the history of natural sciences]". (*Capital*, vol. I, p. 352)

Regardless of Marx's own contribution [1]; of the historical importance that has been given to technology as 'the unbound Prometheus' of economic development [Landes (1969)]; and of the efforts made by Schumpeter and his followers to emphasize the links that exist between firms' and nations' long-term competitiveness and their capacity to innovate, technology is still a 'black box'. In this 'black box' economists must be ready to dirty their hands if they are "to come to grips with [its] complexities, its interrelations with other components of the social system, and its social and economic consequences." [Rosenberg (1982)].

A first step towards coming to grips with technology's complexities is to draw attention to some characteristics of the innovative process [2]. The first one is that innovation is an ubiquitous phenomenon which combines aspects of gradual and cumulative changes (the Schumpeterian 'new combinations' content of innovations) with those of radical breaks with the past (the Marxian and Schumpeterian 'creative destruction' content of technological development) [3]. The revolutionary content of the latter is illustrated by Schumpeter (1934) when he stresses capitalist development as a process that does not simply consist in adding mailcoaches to the existing stock but in their elimination by railroads. Regardless of the form under which innovation takes place - that of gradual and cumulative change or that of radical breaks - a second characteristic of the innovation process is its element of uncertainty. Moreover, the uncertainties that come along with the innovative process go beyond a simple lack of information concerning both its technical and its commercial outcomes. This is so because in most innovative processes occurs also the lack of knowledge of both the precise cost and outcomes of different alternatives and of what the alternatives are. Dosi (1988) stresses that, in this respect, uncertainties associated with innovations are stronger than the imperfect information about the occurrence of known list of events which characterize uncertainty in economic analysis.

The plurality of sources involving the innovation process is a third element that must be emphasized. At the same time that innovation increasingly relies on the growth of scientific knowledge, it also involves elements of tacit and specific knowledge that are not and cannot be written down in a 'blue print' form. This plurality of sources that characterize innovation implies that an interactive process-perspective must be added if it is to be understood better [4]. Furthermore, given the above mentioned uncertainties under which this interactive process takes place, agents involved in such a process must be characterized by bounded rationality rather than by perfect rationality if they are to succeed in the process of learning and creation. This is so because only if technologies could be assumed stationary - which is by definition unrealistic - would it be reasonable to assume agents to concentrate on making successful transaction, and to regard them as calculating 'cartesians' [5].

A fourth characteristic of innovation which must be emphasized is that of cumulativeness. That is, despite significant variations with regard to specific innovations, the possibility of technological development of firms and/or countries increasingly rely on their mastering the 'state-of-the-art' of the technologies already in use. The cumulativeness element of technological capabilities and partial appropriability which accompany it creates permanent asymmetries between firms and countries in terms of their innovative capacity. Consequently, firms and countries can be ranked as 'better' or 'worse' according to their distance from different technological frontiers. Moreover, as they exploit these asymmetries as weapons for competition they can ultimately change the environment in which they operate [6].

3.3 Innovation and economic change: from piecemeal to paradigms

A second step in the direction of reaching a better understanding of innovations in the process of economic development is to come to grips with the different 'levels' under which innovation can take place. A way of doing this is to relate innovations to their impact on the economic structure and to take into consideration different combinations of demand pressures and socio--cultural factors which diversely affect the capability of firms, industries and countries to innovate.

An attempt to take these differences into consideration can be found in the taxonomy of innovation proposed by Freeman and Perez (1988) which emphasizes the distinctions between:

1   *incremental innovations* which are those innovations whose main economic impact refers to the extension of existing demand and an increase in the value added. They improve the efficiency in the use of all factors of production but are not necessarily related to deliberate research and development activity. They are mainly characterized by 'learning-by-doing' and 'learning-by-using' processes and are often the outcome of inventions and improvements suggested by those directly involved in the production process;

2   *radical innovations* comprise new production lines and a partial modification of existing demand. They are characterized by substantial change within existing industries and by the creation of new types of demands. Radical innovations result more and more from deliberate research and development activities in enterprises and/or university and government laboratories. Isolated radical innovations such as nylon or 'the pill' bring structural change but their aggregate economic and social impacts are relatively small and localized. This situation might change if "a whole cluster of radical innovations are linked together in the rise of new industries and services, such as the synthetic materials industry or the semiconductor industry." (ibid. p. 46)

3   *changes of 'technology system'* are characterized by major modifications on the demand system and the creation of new industries. They go beyond the combination of radical and incremental innovations to encompass organizational and managerial innovations as well. The example given by Freeman and Perez is the technically and economically interrelated 'constellation' of innovations that took place from the 1920s onwards in

41

synthetic materials, petro-chemicals, machinery innovations in injection molding and extrusion.

4   *changes in 'techno-economic paradigm' ('technological revolutions')* have a crucial impact throughout the economy with their new demand complexes, their substantial importance for the renewal of existing productive capital, their impact on the skill profile of the labour force, and the chain reaction they carry along which results in the creation of new growth complexes.

Even though the importance of all four 'levels' of innovations is recognized, here the main concern will be with the revolutionary ones. Three aspects of these revolutions are worth emphasizing [7]. The first one regards their widespread application and the drastic reduction in costs of many products and services. Beside their technical application in many areas of the economic system, these innovations must imply major and persistent changes in these areas' costs structure. They must be of an order of magnitude to affect both the behaviour of engineers, designers and researchers and the widespread perception of decision makers concerning opportunities for new profitable investments. The persistent reduction in the costs of integrated circuits throughout the 1970s and 1980s and its consequences for the diffusion of information technology is a good illustration of such changes.

A second important aspect concerning 'technological revolutions' is their social and political acceptability. This can take longer than the perception regarding the technical advantages of the innovation and its economicity because in many cases such acceptability must be expressed in legislative, educational and regulatory changes. Freeman (1992) provides an example of the importance of these changes with the cases of 'in-house' industrial R&D laboratory and the 'Technische Hochschule' which emerged in the U.S.A. and in Germany over a century ago. These two social innovations are taken as a positive reaction to "the increasing complexity and scale of the newer technologies emerging in the electrical and chemical industries in the second half of the 19th century and both greatly increased the scope and effectiveness of product and process innovation in those industries and in others." (ibid., p. 170).

Political acceptability cannot be taken for granted either because of the 'creative destruction' effects of revolutionary innovations and the vested interests behind the technology which is being replaced. An illustration of this point can be found in the reaction of English industrialists to the new organizational norms which emerged with fordism. According do Landes (1969, p. 315), "Many manufacturers would have plausibly argued that any effort to fix the form and structure of their products would rob them of that flexibility that is the strongest arm of the small or medium enterprise. It took initiative to break this conservative chain of logic, and it was rarely forthcoming. In most cases it took outside pressure, like the increasing inroads of Henry Ford on the British market, or extraordinarily favourable incentives, like the huge government orders of wartime, to induce a change.".

A third aspect concerning 'technological revolutions' which can be directly derived from the first two just mentioned is the time span they require to develop their impact fully on the socio-economic system. It is well recognized from past experiences of the introduction and diffusion of such revolutionary innovations that the changes that they bring about cannot possibly take place in a short period. They are a matter of decades rather than years or months.

This long-term characteristic of revolutionary innovations and their social-technical-economic consequences can be illustrated with the ex post analysis of Devine (1983) of technical-economic impact of the 'electric power revolution' and the ex ante precautions raised by Diebold (1952) regarding the full diffusion of the electronic computer. Thus, even though electric power was first introduced in the latter part of the nineteenth century, its diffusion process took half a century to mature and it was not until the 1920s that electricity overtook steam as the main source of industrial power in the United States. Moreover, it was not until the 1950s and 1960s that ownership of electrical consumer durables was widespread enough to become the norm in Western European and Japanese households [8].

As for the computer, Diebold - despite recognizing forty years ago the enormous potential of the electronic computer for the transformation of all industrial and office processes - was emphatic in predicting a long time span before these transformations would actually take place. Indeed, "most of the 'factory automation', which is today described as 'FMS' (flexible manufacturing systems) or 'CIM' (computer integrated manufacturing) did not show a really rapid take-off until the 1980s, even though most of the technical innovations which come under this heading were clearly foreseen by Diebold in 1952." [Freeman (1989), p. 45] [9].

The role of institutions in the time span required by techno-economic paradigms to develop their impact fully on the socio-economic system can be illustrated with the case of fordism. Despite being 'technologically available' since the beginning of the century, the fordist techno-economic paradigm had its pervasive effects on the world system delayed until the emergence of three institutional innovations in the Post-World War II period.

According to Maddison (1989) the unparalled prosperity of the world economy in the years 1950 to 1973 can be explained in three dimensions. Firstly, "a functioning international order with explicit and rational codes of behaviour, and a strong and flexible institutional underpinning which had not existed before. (...) The second element of strength was the changed character of domestic policies, which were self-consciously devoted to promoting high levels of demand and employment in the advanced countries, and usually oriented to development objectives elsewhere. Finally, one can explain improved performance more directly by the general and large increase in investment ratios, the accelerated growth of capital stock, the rise in foreign aid and technology transfers, the accelerated educational effort of developing countries, improvements in international trade and specialization and in domestic economic structure." (ibid., p. 65).

3.4 Techno-economic paradigm as a category of analysis

From the way technological revolutions have been characterized, two questions arise with respect to this higher 'level' of innovation in Freeman and Perez's proposed taxonomy. The first concerns a feature which is common to the term 'revolution' as seen in any context, such as politics, even if here it is applied specifically to an upward transition in the 'hierarchy' of technological change. It is implied that the existing institutions (and the social relations they embody) are unable to cope with the radical changes which are taking place, and their structural transformation comes about only through a more radical process of change.

The second question refers to possible reasons why technological revolutions come to a halt. In other words, what is that makes a specific technology lose its revolutionary content? From a Schumpeterian perspective, that can be explained by the life cycle of technologies. That is, despite the fact that revolutionary innovations have a longer life cycle, they also reach a point when their constellation of technologies give strong signals of diminishing returns and of approaching limits to their potential for further increasing productivity and/or for new profitable investment.

The institutional content of technological revolutions and the diminishing characteristics of their long term impact on the dynamics of technical and economic accumulation make it reasonable to draw 'impressionistic approximations' between the impact of technological revolutions in economic development and the changes that take place in the natural sciences as a result of switches in scientific paradigm [10]. Broadly defined as "universally recognized scientific achievements that for a time provide model problems and solutions to a community of practitioners" [Kuhn (1970)], scientific paradigms must share two essential characteristics. First of all, the novelties they achieve must be of such a magnitude that they attract a large and enduring number of adherents. In the second place, they must be sufficiently open-ended to leave different sorts of problems to be resolved by their group of practitioners.

Out of the different ways Kuhn describes paradigm [11], it seems important for the purpose of the present work to emphasize: (i) the way he equates paradigm with a standard, a new way of seeing, with an organizing principle governing perception itself, with a map, and with something which determines a large area of reality; (ii) the way he defines paradigm as a universally

44

recognized scientific achievement, as if it were a set of political institutions or an accepted judicial decision; (iii) the way he breaks with the tradition of seeing science as an enterprise which draws constantly to some goal set in advance. "If we can learn to substitute evolution-from-what-we- do-know for evolution-toward-what-we-wish-to-know, a number of vexing problems may vanish in the process." (ibid., p. 171).

The approximation with Kuhn's paradigm in natural sciences can be seen as permeating concepts such as Nelson and Winter's (1977) 'technological trajectories' (the 'normal' problem-solving activity determined by a paradigm) and Dosi's (1983) 'technological paradigms' ["a model and a pattern of solution of selected technological problems, based on selected principles derived from natural sciences and on selected material technologies." (ibid. p 83)].

Dosi draws on an approximation to Kuhn's notion of scientific paradigms in order to explain the 'zenith' and 'nadir' of those innovations that, given their powerful and influential effects, could be regarded as 'generalized natural trajectories'.

But it was under Freeman and Perez (1988) that the approximation to Kuhn was taken further in order to relate technological paradigms not just to a particular branch of industry but to the broad tendencies in the economy as a whole. Moreover, they put together the inadequacy of existing institutions to the full development of a technological revolution, and the state of crisis that sooner or later emerges from its diminishing revolutionary character. That is, they give some real content to the notion of 'successive industrial revolutions' by interpreting the long waves as increasing degrees of 'matches' between the techno-economic subsystem and the socio-institutional framework in the upswing followed by increasing degrees of 'mismatches' between these subsystems in the downswing.

Moreover, the approach proposed by Freeman and Perez is centred on a broader interpretation of Marxian and Schumpeterian 'creative destruction'. In their account of techno-economic paradigms attention is directed at the capacity of capitalism for fundamental reorganization during periods of crisis. This reorganization takes place in a sequence of historical constructs formed through the economic, technological and institutional dynamics of the crises. Between these major crises the framework established by the prevailing techno-economic paradigm allows for a range of technological trajectories and institutional arrangements which can take different forms in time and in space.

From an economic perspective, a change in techno-economic paradigm brings not only a whole range of new products but the new processes they bring about open new ways of doing old things. The latter is due to the fact that one underlying feature of a change in paradigm is the dynamics of the relative cost structure of all possible inputs into production.

From an institutional perspective changes of techno-economic paradigms involve major changes in society. The importance that is given by Freeman and Perez to the socio-institutional framework is reflected in their account of the spatial dimension of technological revolutions. They argue that the diffusion of innovations is highly dependent on attitudes, institutions, policy, etc. which are shaped differently on the different spaces where they take place. Moreover, the pervasive characteristic of innovations at the centre of the techno-economic paradigm will only have their widespread effect on profits throughout the system after a period of changes and adaptations of many social institutions to the potentialities of the new technology. "Inertia in the institutional and social framework, reinforced by the pressure of interest groups, conspires to frustrate a favourable course of development. The 'good match' between technology and social institutions ... [can] become a hindrance to further change and development (or in Marx's terminology becomes a 'fetter' on the forces of production)." [Freeman (1984), p. 503].

3.5 Changes in techno-economic paradigms - some illustrations

If a paradigm is taken to be its meta-content of the organizing principle governing perception itself, it is not hard to accept Freeman and Perez's (1988) 'impressionistic' approximation between Kuhn's concept and different modes of growth that have taken place in economic development in the last two hundred years. In order to illustrate such an approximation, they have identified the five Kondratieff waves (without any specific concern with rigorous time boundaries), with specific structural changes where "the new key factor does not appear as an isolated input, but rather at the core of a rapidly growing system of technical, social and managerial innovations, some related to the production of the key factor itself and others to its utilization." (ibid., p. 49).

These five long waves are 'early mechanization Kondratieff' (1770/80 - 1830/40); 'steam power and railway Kondratieff' (1830/40 - 1880-90); 'electrical and heavy engineering Kondratieff' (1880/90 - 1930/40); 'Fordist mass production Kondratieff' (1930/40 - 1980/90); and 'information and communication Kondratieff' (1980/90 - ?). The question addressed by the techno-economic paradigm approach, though, goes beyond a simple association of specific periods of economic history (1770/80 - 1830/40, or 1930/40 - 1980/90, for example) with certain key technological factors (early mechanization or fordist mass production, respectively). Thus, the so-called 'electrical and heavy engineering techno-economic paradigm' did not restrict itself to main 'carrier branches' such as electrical machinery, heavy armaments or steel ships, but can also be characterized by other economic sectors that grew rapidly from small bases such as aircraft, automobiles and telecommunications [12]. Each techno-economic paradigms can also be characterized by the emergence of a different labour process [13]. Thus, whilst the 'early mechanization techno-economic paradigm' (1770/80 - 1830/40) was marked by Adam Smith's idea that productivity would increase as a consequence of a labour process characterized by repetition of tasks, the 'steam power and railway techno-economic paradigm' (1830/40 - 1880/90) was marked by Babbage's principle that tasks in manufacturing can be separated in such a way that it is possible to employ lower-wage labour and to exercise such control over the labour process that recalcitrant workers would be sacked.

The 'electrical and heavy engineering techno-economic paradigm' (1880/90 - 1930/40) saw the emergence of taylorism, developed by the systematization of procedures for the detailed control over work, in such a way that "all possible brain work should be removed from the shop and centered in the planning and laying out department." [Taylor (1903)]. The fourth techno--economic paradigm (1930/40 - 1980/90), as its name shows, is characterized by the fordist mass production labour process. Ford's contribution was to add to the then existing process the mass production system based on moving production lines, specialized machinery and standardized products. The organization of firms and forms of cooperation and competition between them are another element used by Freeman and Perez to characterize the different techno-economic paradigms. Whilst under the first Kondratieff, for example, competition was restricted to individual entrepreneurs and small firms (less than 100 employees); in the second, the larger firms were employing thousands rather than hundreds; and during the third, monopoly and oligopoly became typical and there was the emergence of regulation or state ownership of 'natural monopolies' and 'public utilities'.

3.6   From 'cheap energy/Fordist' techno-economic paradigm to 'chips/IT techno-economic paradigm'

These sketches of some characteristics of successive long waves [14] are meant to highlight that moving from one paradigm into another is not solely 'determined' by economic and/or technological factors. Much to the contrary, a change of techno-economic paradigm comprises a wider combination of economic, technological and institutional responses to a crisis process that emerges out of mismatches between these different aspects of economic development.

Taking into consideration this permanent tension between technological, economic and social aspects of a techno-economic paradigm, and recognizing the possibility of a cyclical process emerging out of mismatches between them, is an important move towards a more comprehensive explanation of the so-called long wave question [15]. Furthermore, besides breaking with different degrees of monocausal economic determinism, the techno-economic paradigm approach can be seen as an important move towards a more unified theory of growth, crisis, and change. This heterodox approach seems more adequate than the vicious circle of mainstream social sciences where, on the one hand sociologists and political scientists try to explain weak social motivations, political apathy and political crisis in terms of economic trends. And, on the other hand, economists try to explain economic crisis tendencies as the result of the politicization of the economy on motivations and incentives.

As is pointed out by O'Connor (1987, p. 54), " 'crisis' comes from the Greek word meaning 'to separate or divide' and 'to sift, to decide', signifying the idea of 'discrimination or decision'. " In this sense, the crisis that emerges in the process of the changing techno-economic paradigms is not just a mark that separates or divides two historical periods but is also a process in which discriminations are made and decisions must be taken.

One way of seeing this in the context of moving from 'cheap energy' into 'chips' as the dominant techno-economic paradigm is to look at the solutions that were sought for the limitations of the 'Fordist' paradigm which were aggravated when the 'oil crisis' took place in the 1970s. Besides this disequilibrating phenomenon, the old model was being eroded, amongst other factors, by diminishing returns to further technical advance along existing trajectories, and the decline of the Keynesian welfare state.

Some of the responses given by the new paradigm based on information technology can be seen as solutions to technical and economic limitations of the previous 'norm'. To the challenges of diseconomies of scale and inflexibility of dedicated assembly-lines, IT offers the possibility of flexible manufacturing systems, networking and economies of scope. Electronic control systems open opportunities for 'dematerialization' of production by decreasing the need for energy and other material inputs. Furthermore, the uses of information and communication technologies to integrate the production plant with the design, marketing and administration, have expanded the notion of 'automation of production' into one of 'systemation' of design, production, control and marketing within the firm.

Parallel to these changes in intra-firm organization has been taking place the emergence of new forms of inter-firm relationship which enables them to operate in a more organic and system-like way. Networks of large and small firms are being built under the form of close cooperation in R&D, training, investment and production planning in such a way that a new pattern of systemofacture can be seen to be emerging [16].

'Networking' and 'economies of scope' have also had responses from the shop-floor through the emergence of a new labour-process. Thus, whilst under fordist mass production individual job tasks are segmented, work becomes increasingly specialized and monotonous, and the control of the production line is the responsibility of line foremen and middle management, in the new techno-economic paradigm, workers can be expected to undertake different tasks, machinery and plant layout are altered to facilitate rapid changes, and control over the movement of production lines shifts from line management to the responsibility of each worker [17].

Governments have also been involved in the search for new social and political solutions in areas such as industrial relations, education and training, regional policies, industrial policies, new financial systems, and access to data banks and networks at all levels and new telecommunication systems.

It is important, though, to emphasize that the scope for institutional changes is far greater than those related to intra- and inter-firms organization and cooperative schemes, capital/labour relations and specific policies in areas such as those just mentioned. Contrary to what might be implied in the neo--liberal discourse, the role of governments has to become increasingly more important in the provision of oversight and strategic direction for the network of technology alliances and strategic partnering which must take place between public/private R&D institutes/universities, public/private enterprises, local/international institutions. Moreover, in order to cope with the possibilities that are opened by the techno-economic system, governments need to perform major socio-institutional innovations both at the national and international levels of a scope similar to the Keynesian welfare state and Bretton Woods system, respectively, which were so important for the full development of the techno-economic paradigm which came to crisis in the 1970s [18].

3.7 An alternative (complement) to the techno-economic paradigm approach

Within the classical political economy tradition of giving historical context to short-term phenomena, two alternative (complementary) approaches have been drawn to explain the 'separate or divide' and the 'discrimination or decision' implied in the Greek origins of 'crisis' and which are needed as a response to the crisis of the 1970s/1980s [19]. Besides the neo-Schumpeterian [20] techno-economic paradigm approach just described, stand the neo--Marxist regulation theory [21].

The 'regulation approach' [22] explains the structural crisis of the 1970s as the result of four tendencies', viz.: (i) a decrease in productivity gains due to social and technical limits of fordism; (ii) the increasing difficulties found by national economic managers due to ever greater globalization of economic flows; (iii) the inflationary pressures and distributional conflicts that were embedded on growing social expenditure; and (iv) the changes in consumption pattern that were led by greater variety of use values and which were at odds with the standardization that could make mass production feasible.

49

The importance that the regulation approach gives to the specificities of national contexts is stressed in the way it considers the autonomy of the socio-institutional framework. Thus, Lipietz (1985) emphasizes the importance of the struggle over control of the process of production and reproduction and even the development of habits and conventions as important ingredients - along with the development of the productive forces - in the explanation of the different forms under which development takes place in different countries.

The analyses performed of different national economies by followers of the regulation approach are centred on concepts such as accumulation regime (regularities at the economy as a whole which enables a more or less coherent process of capital accumulation); mode of regulation (set of formal or informal norms that codify the main social relations); industrial paradigm (pattern of productive organization within firms which determines the way workers relate to the means of production); and mode of growth (regularities at the level of a national economy which explain its role in the international division of labour). They present a set of possible non-fordist developments for capital/labour relations in response to the challenges of flexibility and show different prospects for the national economies studied.

Thus, for Boyer (1990), firms, governments and unions are facing two major issues, to which contradictory responses can finally emerge according to the basic specificities of each national political process. The first issue regards how to use the advances in information technologies in the process of restructuring the process of work organization. The second is how should the dividends of this new configuration be distributed.

Boyer sees the emergence of three major strategies regarding these issues. Firstly there is the 'laissez-faire' strategy under which past fordist collective agreements should vanish and be replaced by purely individual strategies. A second strategy would be provided by meso-corporatism which comprises a compromise of workers, managers and firms holders regarding long- run rent-sharing, at least for large conglomerates. Labour mobility would provide a diffusion of this capital/labour relations to the rest of the economy. Under both strategies, state interventions would be as moderate as possible. Finally, under the social democratic compromise the diffusion process under the meso-corporatism strategy would be attained through state interventions via centralization of wage bargaining. Industrial restructuring and retraining of the labour force would be accomplished with subsidies via macroeconomic policy. The large social transfers implied in this strategies would require the construction of genuinely new institutions.

The background shared by techno-economic paradigm and the regulation approaches is the attempt to find an explanation for the structural crisis that emerged in the 1970s [23]. Despite their different starting point (change in the technological base of world development for the neo-Schumpeterians and the dialectics of techno-economic and political-institutional forces for the neo-

-Marxists), these two approaches leave room for reasonable syntheses [24]. For the purpose of this book, it is worth mentioning their common stress on the importance of analyzing the impact of new technologies at the national level. That is, despite the fact that there is no clear indication of which elements of each socio-economic formation are to be taken into account, a general strength is given to the choice of path at the national level similar to that of the associate-dependent approach discussed in Chapter 1.

They also bear in common the importance of information technology in the 'definition' of a new techno-economic paradigm and a new accumulation regime. But it is the neo-Schumpeterian approach that places greatest emphasis on the possibility of different over-all outcomes at countries' level as a result of the constraints and 'windows of opportunities' that emerge from the pervasive effects of the new technology. In this respect, the approach proposed by Freeman and Perez establishes a more appropriate framework for the analysis of associated-dependent countries. For these countries, a basic proposition of the present analysis is that regulation is strongly based on technological conditions. That is, a key issue for associated-dependent countries is their capacity to interact with the centre at a time when there is a radical change in the technological basis of capitalist development.

For this reason, the framework under which the Brazilian socio-economic formation will be analyzed in Part II will be the one that is being developed by the neo-Schumpeterian approach. This includes propositions regarding the singularities of the national system of innovation whose concept and impor-tance as a category of analysis will be the subject of the next section.

3.8 Nations in the context of changing techno-economic paradigm

It has long been recognized that whenever there is a radical change in the technological basis of the economy, questions must be posed regarding the structure of production and the institutional set-up of the specific country where that change is taking place. Even those who concentrate their analysis on technological capabilities [see review in Fransman (1985a)] recognize that, for those countries lagging behind the world technological frontiers, it is not sufficient to look at technology in isolation from structural economic and institutional questions.

A major proposition of the techno-economic paradigm approach to technological revolutions is that when the technological base of the economy goes through qualitatively radical changes, each single national system, regardless of their relative position in the previous paradigm, have to face questions regarding not only the organizational principles of its scientific/technological set-up but its structure of production and its institutional framework at large as well. Illustrations for this proposition can be found both in history [see Landes (1969) and Kennedy (1988)] and for the present situation of developed countries [Detouzos et al. (1988) provide a good example for the case of the U.S.A.].

In their analysis of the impact of technological revolutions on the specific position of countries, Freeman and Perez (1988) have shown that, whilst England held the technological hegemony in the first one hundred or so years after the 'industrial revolution', Germany and the United States took the leadership during the third and fourth paradigms, and it is clear that for the on-going 'information and communication' techno-economic paradigm, Japan has become the third 'partner' to share the hegemonic position.

But not only the leadership position has to be seen in a dynamic perspective. In each techno-economic paradigm, there are ascents and descents of countries that occupy a position in the so-called industrialized world. In the first paradigm, France and Belgium were second to England, whilst German states and the Netherlands were the newly industrialized countries. In the third techno-economic paradigm, England dropped to second position along with France, Belgium, Switzerland and the Netherlands, whilst Italy, Austria-Hungary, Canada were considered industrial countries, together with the newly industrialized Sweden, Denmark, Japan and Russia.

Moreover, as I show elsewhere [Villaschi (1991)], whilst countries that under a certain paradigm seemed to have the necessary conditions to converge with the technological leader(s), failed to do so in the paradigm that followed, others have 'leapfrogged' during the 'fordist mass production techno-economic paradigm' in ways which have been described as 'miracles' of economic development [25].

Thus, the claim made by List (1856) regarding the importance that must given to the nation as a category for political economy analysis due to

> its particular language, its literature, its history, its habits, its laws, its institutions, its right to existence, to independence, to progress, to a distinct territory; in a word, its personality and all the rights and duties involved. (ibid., p. X)

seems an up-to-date proposition. That is, despite the relevance of the rapid diffusion of an international business culture due to the telecommunications revolution and regardless of the prominent position that multinational corporations have acquired in establishing patterns for this international business culture, the institutional linkages that are established within the boundaries of a nation are still very relevant for political economy analysis.

3.9   Market forms and innovation: some theoretical issues

In order to cope with the theoretical relevance of the nation as a category of analysis of technological revolutions it is important to start by examining how innovation (especially product innovation) takes place in the real world. In general one can say that technological development takes place in situations characterized by mutual exchange of qualitative information and in many cases through direct cooperation between users and producers of the innovation [26].

That implies, then, as Arrow (1973) has long recognized, that the learning process under which innovation takes place goes beyond the limits of the firm and raises the possibility for externalities taking place. Since by definition externalities "occur where market priced transactions do not fully incorporate all the benefits and costs associated with transactions between economic agents" [Stewart and Ghani (1989), p. 1], their existence is a sign that there is a failure in the functioning of the market. Pure markets, then, a norm highly praised in the neoclassical analysis of allocation can be seen as an institutional form which is in part hostile to innovation. As is pointed out by Elster (1983), the neoclassical theoretical schemes can only cope, at most, with situations where innovation is marginal and accidental. If the process of technical change is taken beyond process innovations in order to consider product innovation, the pure market scheme would actually block innovation.

An alternative approach to the pure market scheme, that which focuses on increasing transaction costs [Williamson (1975/1985)] due to the search for optimal allocation of resources, is also hostile to product innovation. In order to minimize transaction costs, firms tend to verticalize their production process. Under these circumstances, innovation's uncertainties would be built into the commodity itself and information asymmetries, reflecting that the producer knows more about the characteristics of the new product than the user, whilst lacking knowledge about user needs, would be a typical phenomenon. The verticalization process, then, would transform product innovations into process innovation. That is, the institutional set-up designed to favour allocation in situations of increasing transaction costs would also be hostile to radical and frequent product innovations.

Lundvall (1985/88/89/90/92b) argues that in order to cope with the way innovation takes place in the real world, the theoretical framework must move away from hostile pure or verticalized markets, and focus its attention on the norms that prevail in organized markets. The micro-foundations for Lundvall's proposition can be found in modern microeconomic theories which emphasize the linkages associated with network information technology [Arthur (1988)] and externalities from one innovation to another [Romer (1986)]. As for the costs of rigidity, Arrow (1974) points out that the formation of an organization might be regarded as a process involving both growing efficiency and growing inflexibility. The negative aspect of bringing more and more activities into organizations - a direct implication of verticalization - is that they get locked into a network of communication codes and channels, very difficult to adjust when faced with radical change in the environment.

In his construct, Lundvall regards organized markets as a compromise which takes into account both the advantages of collective action towards the exploitation of the fruits of learning-by-interacting, and the costs of rigidity. The organized market represents, then, a degree of rigidity, necessary to produce the innovations that do not take place in pure markets for the reasons already discussed, but a rigidity of lesser degree than the one represented by the pure (verticalized) organization.

3.10 Organized markets, innovations and nations: some political implications

The selection process that takes place in the search for durable user-producer relationships (including those of dominance and trust) which characterize organized markets, takes time and involves the development of efficient codes of conduct and channels of information. This is more significant at times of radical changes in the technological foundations of economic development. At such times, the search and selection processes are intensified as can be seen from the data gathered by CATI [27]. In their analysis of new co-operation agreements in that data-bank, Hagedoorn and Schankenraad (1990) show that the number of new co-operative agreements has increased throughout the eighties in the core technologies (information, biotechnology and new materials). Two aspects of their analysis seem relevant for the 'nation as a category of analysis of innovation' argument. Firstly, from a strategic point of view, they found that four motives play a major role in forging cooperation between companies: the possibility to find and enter new markets; the reduction of the period of innovation; the technological competence of partners; and the prospect of monitoring technological opportunities. Financial constraints, very often mentioned in the literature, appear to be of relatively minor importance.

Secondly, from an international perspective, their findings point out that technology-related partnerships are to a very large extent restricted to companies from/within the triad United States-Japan-Western Europe: over 90% of the cooperation agreements on the core technologies analyzed by Hagegoorn and Schakenraad are related to companies from these economic blocks. This evidence seems to strengthen Lundvall's arguments regarding the importance of the nation as a theoretical category for the analysis of innovation at times of fast changes in the technological base of economic development. In the first case, that of the motives for cooperation, the framework under which the strategic partnerships take place is still that provided by nation(s), despite the increasing importance of supra-national institutions in the context of Europe.

As for the concentration of agreements of firms within the triad, it increases the relevance of the argument in favour of government intervention. It is relevant in small-developed countries because their governments should try to counterbalance the 'natural' tendency for the bulk of cooperation to be concentrated between the three leaders of the triad - U.S.A., Japan and Germany. In the case of newly industrialized countries, especially those not in the geographical proximity of these leaders - as is the case of Brazil - the rationale for national policies regarding technological development increases if the firms within their territories are to benefit from the cooperation networks that are being built.

3.11 National systems of innovation: stressing the territorial base of learning-by- interacting

A crucial point in the framework of organized markets is that the focus of the analysis moves one step beyond the original contributions of Arrow (1962) and Rosenberg (1976) regarding the economics of learning. Whilst in the former the emphasis was on the economics of 'learning-by-doing' [28], in the latter attention was called to the innovations that spring out of the experience process that is accumulated through the actual use of innovations, that is to the economics of 'learning-by-using'. Under both contributions the emphasis is given to the intra-firm learning process.

The learning processes that take place between users and producers of innovations and which are emphasized under Lundvall's framework of organized markets, adds the space dimension to the innovation process which is very often neglected or underestimated. Moreover, besides the economic, organizational and geographical spaces which are more commonly considered in economic analysis [29], it emphasizes the cultural dimension of space - "a loose and multidimensional concept, but it relates to important characteristics in the real world. (...) When cultural differences are present, certain types of messages will be difficult to transmit and decode. Complex, and ever--changing messages, combining explicit information with tacit assumptions regarding mutual obligations, will often be required in interactions involving innovative activities. Here, cultural differences between user and producer may block the interaction." [Lundvall (1992b), p. 56].

The framework proposed by Lundvall, then, responds to an aim of this book, i.e. that of building approximations between abstract technological, economic and institutional aspects of the new paradigm and the specificity of concrete socio-economic formations represented by the concept of nation as expressed by List in the above quotation. The approach proposed by Lundvall and followed here puts national systems of innovation at the centre of the analysis. It emphasizes the importance of the different dimensions of space and their relevance to the possibilities of, and constraints upon, the development of the highest level of technological development represented by a change in techno-economic paradigm [30].

The centre of the analysis becomes, then, how national institutional systems differ in the way they influence innovations, and how different countries' technological capabilities and economic structure define technological opportunities and bottlenecks [31]. Johnson (1991, p. 23) defines a national system of innovations as "all interrelated factors in a nation forming an environment, which selects, promotes, and diffuses innovation. (...) The terms select, promote and diffuse in this definition don't suggest that the national system of innovation necessarily stimulates innovation. In fact, it may also ignore, retard and isolate innovations.".

To this definition, this book adds the specificities of associated-dependent NICs in order to examine the possibilities of, and constraints upon, the 'learning-by-interacting' between the n.s.is. in associate-dependent countries and those in core countries. Qualifications are also added to the terms of the definition. Thus, national is to be understood as a spatial-institutional reference for interactions between agents within and beyond a country's geographical boundaries [32]. System is meant to capture the interactive processes and relations (not necessarily under legally binding forms) that occur between private and public, local and international actors along the innovation process. Innovations are to be taken in a broader sense than extension of markets or the diminution of the prices of material products. They are also to be taken for their influences upon the social connections, the productive forces, and the nation's economic strength as a whole [33].

3.12 A three domains approximation to national systems of innovations

From the elements used to describe n.s.i. it becomes clear that national systems are not restricted to organizations designed to pursue activities aimed at technological development, such as research institutes and R&D laboratories. These systems are conceived in a broader way in order to include aspects of the economic structure and the socio-political set up which affect the process of innovation of a nation. Moreover, the rate at which a country exploits the possibilities offered by the technological gap which is opened especially at times of revolutionary innovations, is seen as dependent on its ability to mobilize political and financial resources for transforming the social, institutional and economic structures which comprise its n.s.i.. The trajectories emerging from a techno-economic paradigm are seldom 'naturally' driven by endogenous scientific and technological factors. Economic and socio-political factors are very important in shaping trajectories and determining the way a techno-economic paradigm of world development is unfolded in different countries. A selection process, then, takes place through the interplay of economic, political and social forces, and the indigenous scientific, technological and industrial capabilities. The degree to which a country participates in the selection process that takes place at the international scale is - to a certain extent - the result of this interplay at the national level.

In order to capture the main characteristics of the interplays that take place at the country level, a national system of innovation must be seen from two interconnected and, at the same time, opposite angles. The first is that of the 'disequilibrating' content of the forces which interact within an n.s.i.. This is because changes and transformations are by nature non-equilibrating forces. The second angle through which an n.s.i. must be seen is that of the forces that maintain relatively ordered the configurations of the system and allow a broad consistency between the conditions of material reproduction.

In order to address these questions, a model proposed by Dosi (1984) will be followed. It divides the socio-economic fabric under which innovation takes place into three domains: the system of technologies ("techniques of production, nature of the products, the processes of their generation, the directions of progress, etc.", ibid., p. 102); the 'economic machine' ("economic inducements, in the form of changing patterns and levels of demand, income distribution, and relative price", ibid., p. 103); and the system of social relations and institutions ("the modes of social organization, the culture of social groups, etc. ... plus the set of international inter-dependencies provided by the international arena", ibid., p. 106 and 120).

The model also assumes that these three domains are self-regulated [34], i.e. they operate according to the following hypotheses:

1   Regardless of the powerful interactions between them, each of the three domains has a dynamic and a content of its own. The specificities of each domain's dynamic and content shape and constrain their individual impact, and the interactions amongst them, in such a way that their functional feedbacks can make possible either 'virtuous circles' or 'mismatches';

2   'Possible worlds' are limited by the number of configurations under which the three domains can operate in a relatively 'well-regulated' and smooth way;

3   Imbalance or 'mismatches' between the three domains do not necessarily lead to changes to other, more balanced or 'smoother' configurations;

4   The adaptability of the technological system to a given economic and social environment is bounded and limited. Conversely, a relatively limited

set of macroeconomic conditions and social relations are 'given' at each stage of the 'technological domain'.

3.13 Theoretical reasons for the three domains

The analytical framework proposed here for the analysis of national systems of innovation, despite the importance given to the pervasive effects of technological revolutions, is quite distant from any technological determinism. It does not see technology either guaranteeing long-term dynamic and stable growth nor adjusting the ways societies resolve conflicts over labour processes, income distribution and, ultimately, power. Furthermore, by using an analytical framework where technology is not to be dealt with in isolation from the rest of the economic and socio-institutional fabric, an attempt is made here in the direction of avoiding a 'normal' practice of economists of trying to "interpret any discrepancy as a purely casual phenomenon, more or less related to historical or sociological peculiarities, and thus without any theoretical importance." [Boyer (1988a), p. 69].

The theoretical relevance of the 'institutional domain' of a n.s.i. can be seen as a direct recognition that institutions are humanly devised constraints that structure political, economic and social interaction. According to North (1991), from an economic point of view, their evolution throughout history has been motivated by the need of agents to reduce uncertainty; to define their choice set and therefore their profitability and feasibility of engaging in economic activity; to evolve incrementally, building bridges between the past, the present and the future; and provide them with the incentive structure of the economy.

From the specific point of view of technological development, institutions can help to reduce the uncertainties which are characteristic of the innovation process. They can work as 'sign-posts' guiding expectations and helping flexible interactive learning process by providing them with stability. As for the economic domain of a national system of innovation, its theoretical relevance is related to the collective entrepreneurship that must emerge if the pervasiveness of a technological revolution is to take place [35]. The communication and interaction between firms provide important inputs to the innovation process. The national network of interindustrial 'linkages' is to be seen, then, beyond the process of exchange of goods and services in order to focus on their contribution to technical change and competitiveness which take place at the world scale and which influences the possibilities of 'learning-by--interacting' taking place between single NSI and its counterparts in other countries.

By focusing on the untraded interdependencies amongst sectors and firms, the theoretical framework pursued here emphasizes the 'public' characteristics of technology and the possibilities for the emergence of technological complementarities, 'synergies', flows of stimuli, and constraint which do not entirely correspond to commodity flows. It is obvious that in a world where competition is the driving force of company behaviour, the cooperation process behind non-commodity flows is not an act that emerges from a moral principle of companies. Identifying these flows, pursuing and exploiting them in the context of a national system of innovation become crucial policy issues in the context of associated-dependent countries.

3.14 Summing up

The analytical framework that has been established for the book in this chapter emphasizes the need to understand changes of techno-economic paradigms as a process where mismatches between economic, institutional, and technological structures take place. Indications from history of innovations have been presented to back the proposition that the emergence of information and telecommunications as the 'core' of a new wave of economic development goes beyond the introduction of new products and/or processes, and changes in the cost structure of the production process. Their impact is expected to be more pervasive and to affect the way the economy and institutions perform their roles in the world system.

Descriptions of previous changes in techno-economic paradigms were also presented in order to emphasize the diverse impact that these changes have on different socio-economic formations. The 'creative destruction' which takes place during shifts in techno-economic paradigms can both open 'windows of opportunities' to new comers and foster changes in the relative position of industrialized countries. The degree to which different countries benefit most from the opportunities which arise at times of change in techno-economic paradigm bear close connections with the degree to which 'learning-by--interacting' take place amongst agents. Furthermore, the chances of different countries to benefit from these opportunities are not established by 'deus ex machina' forces but are better understood through the analysis of internal aspects of each country.

For that reason the analytical framework established here draws on the concept of national systems of innovation in order to stress the importance of the interplay between economic, institutional, and technological forces at the national level. By doing so, the focus of the analysis not only moves from individual to collective entrepreneurship but it also avoids any sort of determinism, be it economic, technological, or institutional.

Part II examines the Brazilian national system of innovation. The analysis bears in mind the extent to which a change in techno-economic paradigm affects the relative position of countries in the international division of labour.

Despite this external constraint, greater importance is given to the reaction of internal forces - be they economic, technological or institutional - to these changes. Moreover, given the associated-dependent characteristic of the Brazilian socio-economic formation, special attention is given to the ways changes are taking place in the economic, institutional and technological domains in order to cope with the challenges of the new paradigm.

Notes

1. Rosenberg (1976) makes an assessment of Marx as a student of technology.

2. See Orsenigo (1989) for further discussions on the characteristics of the innovative process.

3. For a comparative analysis of 'creative destruction' in Marx and in Schumpeter, see Elliot (1980).

4. Even if the learning process were to be confined to 'learning-by-doing' within the firm, the whole idea of a firm with definite boundaries could not be maintained intact. As pointed out by Arrow (1973), there are direct information flows from customers in the forms of complaints, requests for product alteration or special services, or threats to change to another firm, in addition to the anonymous alterations of demand at a given price which constitute the sole information link between the firm and its market in neoclassical theory.

5. Lundvall (1992a) stresses that "actually interactive learning is undermined, seriously, when parties act, exclusively, from the view-point of calculation and maximizing. Both individual actors and organizations less rational (instrumental) in this sense, acting according to sets of social norms, including, for example, mutual respect and mutual trust, might be more successful than the purely calculated one." (ibid. p. 47).

6. This is not to say there is no room for 'leap-frogging'. As is shown in Part II, technological discontinuities may open 'windows of opportunities' for new entrants.

7. Compare Freeman (1984 , Perez (85), and Haustein (1987).

8. Based on the analysis by Devine (1983), Freeman (1989) calls special attention to the fact that "the full expansionary benefits of electric power to the economy depended, therefore, not only on a few key innovations in the 1880s, but on the development of a new paradigm of production and design philosophy. This involved the redesign of machine tools and

much other production equipment. It also involved the relocation of many plants and industries, based on the new freedom conferred by electric power transmission and local generating capacity. Finally, the revolution affected not only capital goods but a whole range of consumer goods, as a series of radical innovations led to the universal availability of a wide range of electric domestic appliances, going far beyond the original domestic lighting systems of the 1880s. Ultimately, therefore, the impetus to economic development from electricity affected almost the entire range of goods and services." (ibid., p. 48)

9. The reasons why Diebold believed that the diffusion process of computer automation would take longer than most computer enthusiasts believed in the 1950s can be thus summarized: the amount of R&D, design and investment in new machinery and instruments necessary for the new technology to be fully diffused; the radical changes that would be necessary both in the configuration and organization of every factory as well was those concerning the skill composition of the work-force. Besides these, Diebold recognized the importance of the economic aspects of diffusion, i.e. computers would not be diffused only if they were technically advantageous; they would have to be also cheap. With respect to this latter point, Freeman (1989) reminds us that "it was only with the advent of micro-electronics in the 1960s and the micro-processor in the early 1970s that computerization took off in small and medium-sized firms, as well as in large firms, and in batch production as well as in flow process industries such as chemicals. Moreover, computer technology could only realize its potential outside a few 'leading-edge' industries when computerized systems became relatively cheap and accessible." (ibid., p. 45).

10. It is interesting to notice that Dosi (1983) has been pursuing the analogy mainly in the sense of specific technologies, whilst Freeman and Perez have made it broader in order to take into account a change in the pattern of economic growth as a whole.

11. See Masterman (1970) for a discussion of the twenty-one different ways Kuhn describes a paradigm, her grouping them into metaphysical paradigms, or metaparadigms; sociological paradigms and artifact paradigms or construct paradigms.

12. The cases of the automobile and of telecommunications comprise good illustrations of the difference between the existence of technologies and their abilities to perform the role of 'core' industries of a techno-economic paradigm. Even though they have been 'available' since the latter part of the last century, automobiles only became a main 'carrier branch' in the

fourth Kondratieff and such a role has been performed by telecommunications in the newly emerging IT Kondratieff.

13. Kaplinsky (1988) and Cohen (1987) present discussions of the 'labour process' issue.

14. Historical accounts of elements of the different paradigms from 1770/80 to present days can be found in Landes (1969), Freeman and Perez (1988) and Kennedy (1988).

15. According to Kleinknecht (1987), not much has been added to the debate about regular fluctuations in economic life since the breakthrough of van Gelderen at the beginning of the twentieth century. In fact, it is not hard to identify - "the most important factors underlying the long wave process, according to van Gelderen (1913), summarized under the following headings

   · the leading sector (innovation) hypothesis;
   · the hypothesis of periodic over- and under-investment of capital;
   · credit expansion and financial crisis;
   · periodic scarcity and abundance of basic materials;
   · opening of new territories and migration waves;
   · gold production. (ibid., p. 4)

   with some recent long wave theories. Thus, the role of innovation has been identified by Delbeke (1983), as crucial to the work of Schumpeter (1939) and Mensch (1977); capital theories with the work of Mandel (1980) and Forrester et al. (1977); the labour theory with Freeman (1977) and the raw material and food-stuffs theory with Rostow (1978).

16. "Thus, in terms of broad historical generalization, whereas the first industrial revolution involved the substitution of machines for labor (from manufacture to machinofacture in Marx's terminology) the current period may well be witnessing the transition from machinofacture (production centered at the optimization of the machines output) to systemofacture." [Kaplinsky (1985), p. 433].

17. That is not to disregard, though, the importance of first-line managers as agents of change. See *The Economist*, February 1st, 1992, p. 85.

18. This view is shared by many research works carried at the levels of single countries [of which Dertouzos et al. (1989) is an example] and at a wider scope [of which O.E.C.D. (1991) is an example]. That doesn't mean, though, that the institutional innovations will inevitably take place as they are seen 'needed' by these works.

19. An alternative that gives a different interpretation to the reasons for the latest structural crisis and to the possible remedies to it, is provided by

neo-liberal thinking through the 'institutional sclerosis' approach. For this approach post-World War II political processes led to severe rigidities in the economic system due to growing government sectors and trade union powers. Under this perspective the response to the crisis is built into its diagnosis, that is, in order to cure the disease, a movement must be made towards flexibility. Moreover, the best way to achieve flexibility is through an institutional framework as close as possible to the ideal of the pure, and perfectly competitive market. For a review of the 'institutional sclerosis hypothesis' see Dunleavy and O'Leary (1987) and for its critique see Johnson and Lundvall (1991).

20. Following Schumpeter, the neo-Schumpeterians place innovation at the centre of their theoretical system. Moreover, they emphasize the importance of history in such a way that in their interpretation of economics technical change and institutional change really matter.

21. For Elam (1989) the adjectives point at essential differences in the basic argument, viz.: changes in the technological base of capitalist accumulation; and the dialectics of techno-economic and political/institutional forces, for the neo-Schumpeterian and the neo-Marxist approaches, respectively.

22. Boyer (1988) provides a general description of the French regulation approach and Stavros (1991) a general critique of the approach.

23. Marxist analyses provide a wider range of alternative periodizations of capitalism development of which Vasko (1987) has the technological feature in common with the neo-Schumpeterian approach. Nevertheless, it is important to notice that within the Marxist tradition the debate is wider than periodizations within a mode of production, in order to incorporate elements that are to be taken into consideration when analyzing periodizations of modes of production. See Fine and Harris (1979).

24. Elam (1990) provides a first syntheses and Nielsen (1991) expands on it.

25. Even though the periodizations used in my earlier work do not exactly match (because of the data available) the one used for describing the different techno-economic paradigms, it seems a good illustration of successful 'leapfrogging' as well as failure to 'catch-up' of countries like Japan, Korea and Brazil as well as Argentina, Ireland and Chile, respectively.

26. Lundvall (1992b, p. 49) emphasizes that his analytical framework is mainly concerned with "interactive processes where both parties are professional units (private or public organizations)". The main reason for this restriction is that user-producer relationships involving interaction

between agents with different modes of behaviour become a more complex matter.

27. CATI (co-operative agreements and technology indicators) is a databank put together by MERIT (Maastrich Economic Research of Innovation and Technology) which contains worldwide information on over 7,000 co-operative agreements take place worldwide and involving a large number of technologies and several thousands participating companies.

28. Based on psychologists' acceptance of the learning process as being the result of experience, Arrow (1962) advanced the hypothesis that "technical change in general can be ascribed to experience, that is the very activity of production which gives rise to problems for which favorable responses are selected." (ibid. p. 156). One of the evidences that he gives in support of his hypothesis is that of the 'Horndall effect': the Horndall iron works in Sweden had no new investment (and therefore presumably no significant change in its methods of production) for a period of 15 years, yet productivity (output/man-hour) rose on the average close to 2% a year.

29. Lundvall (1992b) stresses the differences between economic space (relates to how different economic activities are located in a system of production where the vertical division of labour is highly developed); organizational space (refers to horizontal and vertical integration which under the organized market concept can be more continuous); and geographical space which can be measured in terms of distance, when activities can be assigned to distinct locations.

30. It is important to notice that given the associate-dependent characteristics of NICs, even at times of innovations along established trajectories, national systems of innovation is an important category of analysis. This is not so obvious in the case of countries in the centre because the technological gap that might exist amongst them takes a different dimension from that which exist between NICs and core countries.

31. Compare Johnson (1992) which also points out that the search for diversity of national systems of innovation obviously does not imply ruling out other space configurations such as supra-national systems or the possibility of innovation taking place in a more footloose manner.

32. It is recognized, nevertheless, that "rather little is known about just how borders affect the flow of technological information and capabilities, (...) or the patterns of interaction between upstream and downstream firms, (...) or university industry connection. It seems clear that borders matter but not clear how much, or in what ways." [Nelson (1988), p. 310].

33. Compare with the definition by Lundvall (1992a, p. 2) according to whom "... a national system of innovation is constituted by elements and relationships which interact in the production, diffusion and use of new, and economically useful, knowledge and that a national system encompasses elements and relationships, either located within or rooted inside the borders of a nation state.".

34. "The self-organizational approach to dynamic modeling proceeds from the observation that complex interdependent dynamical systems unfolding in historical, i.e. irreversible time, economic agents, who have to make decisions today, the correctness of which will only be revealed considerably later, are confronted with irreducible uncertainty and holistic interactions between each other and with aggregate variables. The a priori assumption of an 'equilibrium' solution to this problem to which all agents ex ante can subscribe and which makes their actions consistent and in some sense dynamically stable is a leap of methodological faith. Instead we propose employing some of the recently developed methods of evolutionary modeling to show how the interaction of diverse capabilities, expectations and strategies with the thereby emerging selective pressures can drive a capitalist economy along certain definite patterns of development." [Silveberg et al. (1988), p. 1036]

35. The concept of collective entrepreneurship proposed by Lundvall (1992a) departs from other neo-Schumpeterians who focus the analysis of the innovative process as emanating form the single firm in isolation. In this respect, Lundvall's contribution to the economics of innovation can be seen as one step beyond that of Schumpeter. As is known, in his earlier work Schumpeter (1934) pointed to entrepreneurs, acting individually, as the most important economic agents, bringing innovations into the economic system. Later Schumpeter (1942) revised his theoretical scheme in order to give a critical role to the collective work in R&D laboratories.

Part Two
THE BRAZILIAN NATIONAL SYSTEM
OF INNOVATION

Introduction

Based on the theoretical framework established in Chapter 3, this second part will examine the Brazilian national system of innovation. The historical framework for the analysis is the political economy of the country's industrialization process which was reviewed in Chapter 2. Given the characteristics of the emerging information techno-economic paradigm and of the associated-dependency of the Brazilian socio-economic formation stressed in the previous chapters, two difficulties arise with respect to the analysis of the BNSI. The first one is related to the loose boundaries that exist between the technological, economic and institutional domains at times of change in paradigms. The importance given by the approach used here to the innovative interactions that take place between different agents makes harder the task of placing each of them consistently in one of the three domains examined here. For this reason, a degree of arbitrariness is inevitable when deciding in which domain to consider elements of the search [1] and learning [2] processes that take place in the system as a whole.

The second difficulty is related to what elements to take into account in the analysis. Given that the learning approach used in this book is closely related to an evolutionary perspective under which technological change is looked upon as an-open ended sequence of events, an important feature of the elements to be taken into consideration must be their contribution to the diversity and complexity of the system as a whole. Moreover, the broader understanding of innovation under the techno-economic paradigm concept implies that besides the economic-oriented factors such as diversity of products, production and trade patterns, attention must be given to institutional diversity which can affect the searching and learning capabilities of the NSI.

Thus, it is assumed that the inter-industrial relations that take place within the national system cannot be seen simply as a means of exchanging goods and services but also as a potentially important determinant for technological development and competitiveness. At times of changing techno-economic paradigm and under the peculiarities that involve development in associated--dependent socio-economic formations such as Brazil, the importance of this assumption cannot be overstressed.

An important feature of the elements to be considered in the analysis of the BNSI will be their contribution to bringing disequilibria to the system as a whole. In other words, the elements to be considered in the analysis must fulfill the requirements set-up by concepts such as Perroux's (1955) 'growth poles', Hirschman's (1958) 'linkages', Dahmen's (1988) 'development blocs', and Stewart and Ghani's (1989) 'dynamic externalities'.

Despite their different emphases, these concepts bear in common the key role played by innovation in the Schumpeterian sense ('doing new things or old things in a new way') and which is stressed under the techno-economic framework. Thus, a major feature to be sought in Perroux's 'growth poles' is the dynamic element that contributes to further development through a higher propensity for innovation. More important than the contribution to total economic growth in the short-term are the structural conditions that these poles establish for greater economic development in the medium- and long-runs [3].

Despite his own questioning concerning the way newness can be defined, Hirschman's 'linkage' exists whenever an on-going activity gives rise to economic or other pressures that lead to the taking up of new activities. In the context that is sought for the analysis of the BNSI at a time of changing techno-economic paradigm the pressure bearing linkages that will be sought are of the type which can work as 'midwives' of the new paradigm in the Brazilian national system of innovation [4].

According to Dahmen (1988) his concept of 'development block' belongs to a kind of analysis which fall under the category of what he calls 'Schumpterian dynamics'. "It refers to a sequence of complementarities which by way of a series of structural tensions, i.e. disequilibria, may result in a balanced situation." (ibid., p. 5) [5]. From the perspective of most interest to this thesis, the 'development blocs' that will be sought in the BNSI are those that combine 'immature' and 'well-established' contents in such a way that the blocs' development power is strengthened.

Departing from the concept of externalities developed by Viner (1931), Meade (1952) and Scitovsky (1954), Stewart and Ghani (1989) conceptualize 'dynamic externalities' as another class of real (technological) externalities related to economic growth. The spatial dimension of these externalities (changing attitudes and motivation; skill formation; and changing knowledge about technologies and markets) is relevant because "policies are normally focused on a spatial subdivision - e.g. concern may be with regional development, or rural development, or national development, but is rarely with 'world' development where the spatial dimension can be ignored." (ibid., p. 6).

One general criticism which is usually made of these concepts is that despite the many illustrations that can be found in techno-economic history [6] they are not easy to cope with theoretically [7]. In addition, in most cases they are used as a framework for the analysis of phenomena directly related to production and/ or exchange of goods and services.

Bearing these criticisms in mind, in the selection of elements of the BNSI to be analyzed in the next three chapters, approximations to the concepts of 'growth poles', 'linkages', 'development blocs' and 'dynamic externalities' will be made. These approximations are justified because the major objective to be pursued in the analysis of the BNSI is to capture the contribution that can be made by each element chosen in the three domains. In order to be 'selected' each element must potentially lead to a shift in the degree of disequilibrium of the system as a whole, thus starting a sequence of structural tensions and their partial resolutions. That is, they must be capabable of creating social and economic networks that can transform opportunities under the newly formed techno-economic paradigm to Brazilian development [8].

This second part comprises three chapters. Chapter 4 concentrates on three aspects of the economic domain. Firstly, attention is given to the 'development blocs' represented by the informatics and telecommunications (known to form the 'motor' of the new techno-economic paradigm) as well as capital goods industries. Secondly, the chapter analyzes the existing 'triple alliance' between local, multinational and state-owned enterprises in order to examine its possible implications for linkages between the BNSI and the production and technological networks that are being built within the industrialized world. Finally, attention is given to the possible externalities of export activities for the system of innovation.

Chapter 5 analyzes changes in the institutional domain. It is stressed that, despite the structural changes (from a rural base economy to an industrial pluralistic society) that took place over the last 40 years, and the country's recent redemocratization process, the rules established in the 1988 Constitution still strongly reflect the state of compromise between mercantile and industrial capitalism. Nonetheless, the chapter also presents evidence that there has been a change in attitude with respect to technology and that there is awareness amongst the elite with respect to the challenges posed to associated-dependent Brazil by the new techno-economic paradigm.

Chapter 6 examines four 'poles' of the technological domain of the BNSI: its educational system; its research institutes; its science parks and the different ways formalized technological transfer takes place in the system. Different linkages of these elements are examined in order to establish their possible positive and/or negative dynamic contributions to the system of innovation as a whole.

Most of the analysis carried out in these three chapters has the 1980s as the time reference. This focus was chosen to reflect key internal and external changes which took place at that time. The 1980s was a time of economic crisis for Brazil, with economic growth falling to average rates below those seen for the previous forty years; and when neither direct investment nor loans came from abroad to compensate for the country's weak domestic savings. As a result of this crisis Brazil became an outsider in the list of success stories of capitalist development. In addition to the economic crisis, the 1980s witnessed significant changes in political structures. The loosening of authoritarian ruling and the transition to democracy reached a climax with the new Constitution written for the country.

Equally significant were the changes in external conditions confronting Brazil. The 1980s has been identified with the emergence of a new techno--economic paradigm which is being shaped through concrete changes in the patterns of production, exchange and cooperation between firms and nations.

The argument here is that it is crucial to understand how the Brazilian national system of innovation which evolved during the boom years of the 1960s and 1970s, was able to adjust itself to adverse times. Firstly, to the almost exclusive priority given to short-run economic policies in the home front. And secondly, to an external context whose feature was the building of economic and political blocs amongst the industrialized countries.

The response of organizations and industrial sectors/complexes to these new times is only of peripheral concern [9]. Although information is used here from different sectoral analyses, the major concern is with the interactions that have been taking place within and between actors of the three domains of the BNSI and between them and their counterparts in the industrialized world.

Notes

1. In general one can say that there are at least two kinds of searching processes going on in society. On the one hand, there are those search activities organized in relation to production which bear close links with the commodity logic of the enterprise sector. On the other hand, there are those less profit-oriented basic research activities of universities and research institutes. The difficulty of establishing the boundaries between these two processes is greater under the circumstances of associated-dependent countries because of the role played by science and technology in shaping their dependency ties with the core countries.

2. Johnson (1992, p. 32) emphasizes that "new knowledge is also gained from economic activities which are not explicitly or primarily aiming at its generation. Learning is often connected to the routine procurement, production and sales activities of the firm, and to normal communication between firms. It is, then, rather a by-product of activities organised towards other aims. This might be called learning-by-producing, indicating that its basic components may be thought of as learning-by-doing, by-using and by-interacting in relation to normal production activities".

3. Nilsson (1988) presents a review of the ways the concept of growth poles has been misused in regional economics and of the importance to see it from its original Schumpeterian perspective.

4. Hirschman (1981, p. 95) paraphrases Marx in order to highlight that "one of the merits of the generalized linkage or micro-Marxist approach is that it invites the analyst to be constantly on the lookout for technological

'news' that may have considerable economic and sociopolitical repercussions".

5. Dahmen (1988, p. 7) points out that "a complex of industrial interrelations is easy to understand and is also possible to identify, e.g. by input-output schemes, when viewed as a set of static interrelations. But by the use of neoclassical eyeglasses one is likely to miss a point which is crucial, namely the dynamics of the interrelations. With Schumpeterian eyeglasses, a promising but demanding task is to analyze processes whereby such interrelations evolve through time. There are here hardly short cuts, e.g. by the use of econometrics".

6. The conceptualization of Perroux's 'growth poles' and Hirschman's 'backward and forward linkages' can be seen as the theoretical inspiration for many regional development and industrialization projects both in the developed world as well as in developing countries. Dahmen draws on the examples of the steel and automobile industries, as well as on the growth of the electronics industry in Sweden in order to illustrate his 'development blocs' concept. The experiences of the semi- conductor industry in the Silicon Valley and that of agriculture and industry relations in Punjab are used by Stewart and Ghani as illustrations of their 'dynamic externalities'.

7. Andersen (1991, p. 21) points out that the "the difficulty is not only due to the basic problems surrounding the notion of innovation but also often to the fact that the notion of innovation is discharged altogether while one is still talking of 'development blocs', 'growth poles', etc.".

8. Nilsson (1988) notices that to set up such networks is not as easy as it may sound. "It involves both political problems and problems of insufficient knowledge. The knowledge of what is required to bring about this kind of growth-inducing network is limited." (ibid., p. 177). Moreover, in order to avoid optimism with regard to the possibilities of technology it is important to bear in mind that "technology alone cannot be seen as producing those qualitative transformations in the economy which guarantee long-term dynamism and stability of growth, nor adjust the modes of reproduction of societies structurally characterized by the possibility of conflict over labour processes, income distribution and, ultimately, power." [Dosi (1984), p. 69].

9. For an analysis of different industrial complexes in Brazil considering their innovativeness and competitiveness, see Coutinho and Ferraz, orgs. (1994).

4 The economic domain

4.1 Introduction

The main objective of this chapter is to examine features of the BNSI's economic domain which affect the ability of the system to make the qualitative 'jumps' that are required under the new techno-economic paradigm. To do this two complementary lines of analyses are followed. Firstly, the performances of three sectors - telecommunications, informatics and capital goods - are examined in order to assess their possibilities for playing the major role of 'growth poles' of the Brazilian socio-economic formation under the new paradigm. As was pointed out in the analytical framework drawn in Chapter 3, an early entry in the 'core' industries of informatics and telecommunications may open 'windows of opportunities' for newly- -industrialized countries to 'leapfrog' in their process of economic development under the new techno-economic paradigm. As for the capital goods industry, its importance is widely recognized in the literature [inter alia Erber (1977), Amsden (1977), and Katz (1984)] which emphasizes the key position of this industry if a late-comer is expected to change the form of its dependency.

The second line of analysis will focus on three conditionalities of the Brazilian socio-economic formation which bear directly on the reaction of its actors with respect to innovation and technological development. These are, firstly, the macro-economic situation that prevailed throughout the eighties - with special emphasis on the political economy of inflation, public deficit and external debt. These three aspects of the economy are known to affect the behaviour of agents in a way which can be negative to innovation and change; inflation, because it increases the agents' uncertainties about economic returns on investment; the public deficit, because it creates constraints on state-owned enterprises' investment and R&D expenditure; and the external debt, because it weakens Brazil's bargaining power in pursuing technological policies which might adversely affect the interests of creditor countries.

In the second place is the role of state-owned, local and multinational enterprises and the way they have been interacting in the Brazilian production system. Finally, the exposure of the production system to international competition is analyzed through the performance of manufactures in the country's export drive throughout the eighties.

The chapter begins by examining two 'given' conditions under which the Brazilian national system of innovation operated in the eighties. That is, the country's macro-economic situation; and the 'triple alliance' of state-owned, and local/multinational which has functioned as the pillar to capital accumulation in Brazil. It then analyses the role of exports in the country's insertion in the international division of labour; and the performance of three 'growth poles' - informatics, telecommunications and capital goods industries.

4.2 The Brazilian economy in the 1980s

The analytical framework used here stresses the importance of the economic environment for the innovation process. In Chapter 2 the relationship between economic development and the building up of technological capabilities in Brazil was seen from a historical perspective. It was shown that moving from production capacity into technological capability was not a 'deus ex machina' process but, much to the contrary, the result of interactions between different socio-economic forces. The main objective of this section is to provide a description of the macroeconomic conditions which prevailed throughout the 1980s in order to provide a framework for the analysis of other conditionalities for the strengthening of the BNSI under the new paradigm.

a) From debt-led growth to debt-led debt and stagnation

The analysis of the political economy of the Brazilian industrialization process made in Chapter 3 purposely ended in 1979. That was so not only because 1979 was the year when there was a change (the last one) in government under the authoritarian regime but also because it represented a turning point in the agenda of public debate concerning the country's economy. Whilst, since the 1930s, the major theme had been the country's industrialization, from 1979 onwards the main economic themes in Brazil were inflation, external debt and the fiscal crisis of the State. There were good reasons for this switch.

Inflation, which has always been a feature of the Brazilian socio-economic formation since independence, took on a new dimension in the 1980s. From an initial position of 77.2% in 1979 (the highest since 1964), the rate of inflation increased throughout the decade. The only exception was 1986 when the ephemeral success of the Cruzado Plan brought inflation down to about

60%. By 1989 the annual inflation rate had surpassed the one thousand per cent figure with clear indications of a pre-hyperinflation situation [1].

Total external debt increased from less than fifty billion dollars in 1979 to more than one hundred billion dollars in 1989. As a consequence, the debt/export ratio was about the same in those two years (around 3.2) and well above the highest it had been during the 1970s (less than 2.0 in 1978). This was despite the positive response from exports (current accounts went from a deficit of over five billion dollars in 1979 to a surplus of over fifteen billion dollars in 1988) [2].

The public sector, which was a net saver of about 3.8% of GDP in 1979, by 1988 presented a negative savings of about 1.9% of GDP. Thus, whilst in the 1970s the government was capable of achieving savings in order to pursue development goals, in the 1980s it had to increase its borrowing from the private sector, despite the low levels imposed on investment programmes in social and economic infrastructure [3]. Given the importance of the public sector for capital accumulation in the Brazilian economy, the result of government's reductions in its capital spending programmes was that investment which averaged 23 percent of gross domestic product in 1975-79 and 21.3 percent in 1980-82, averaged only 17.7% of GDP between 1984 and 1988.

Table 4.1
Some indicators of economic performance in the 1980s (%)

Year	Infl.	D/E	I/GDP	TR/GDP	Interest on PSD* Internal	Foreign	Gov Sav*
1979	77,2	327,4	23,0	2,1	0,55	0,29	3,8
1980	99,7	267,5	22,5	2,2	0,74	0,36	2,2
1981	93,5	263,6	21,0	0,4	1,08	0,29	2,3
1982	100,3	374,6	20,4	0,7	1,21	1,18	1,8
1983	178,0	371,3	16,1	(2,4)	1,65	1,57	0,6
1984	209,1	337,3	15,5	(5,6)	2,05	1,83	0,8
1985	239,1	373,9	16,7	(5,1)	2,24	1,51	0,3
1986	59,2	454,4	18,5	(2,6)	1,14	1,35	1,9
1987	394,9	409,9	19,7	(3,0)	1,15	1,44	(1,2)
1988	900,0	320,6	17,0	(5,0)	1,48	1,85	(1,0)

D - debt; E - export; I - investment; TR - net transfer of resources from abroad; PDS - public sector debt.
* - % of GDP
Sources: Central Bank, IPEA, IBGE and *Conjuntura Econômica* quoted in Bresser Pereira (1990), tables 1, 2 and 3

Earlier warnings concerning the structural dimensions of the external debt and its implications for policies concerning the country's inflation and the public sector budget were disregarded by the government [4]. Critics were considered 'pessimistis' who did not take into consideration the good rating of

Brazil in the international financial community. The numbers in Table 4.1 show, however, none of the 'pessimists' were gloomy enough when predicting the problems in which the Brazilian economy was to be involved in the 1980s.

Summarizing the strong links between the three issues and the vicious circle that was created around them: the decline in foreign loans and the large budget deficits after 1981 led to a shift towards domestic financing. This shift and the progressively larger trade surpluses necessary for servicing the increasing external debt (due to higher interest rates in the international market) pushed up domestic interest rates and inflation. The higher interest rates that made possible PSBR financing did not induce an outpouring of new savings but, rather, provoked portfolio substitution. As a result, constraints were imposed upon the investment necessary to sustain adequate rates of growth whilst underwriting expanding exports and permitting the transfer of technology required for the country to remain competitive in world markets.

Not surprisingly, the eighties became the decade when per capita income stagnated and the country faced its first ever industrial crisis [5]. Throughout the 'lost decade' growth was driven mainly by consumption demand and public sector deficits that negatively affected the balance of payments, inflation, and real interest rates. Moreover, the priority that was given to immediate macroeconomic disequilibria (mainly inflation and foreign reserves) implied very limited room for structural reforms. As a result, the only option left after each failed stabilization programme was yet another dose of stabilization and austerity [6].

It would be naive to assume that mismanagement of the economy and the top priority given to short-run policies were the result of lack of technical competence by those responsible for economic policy in Brazil throughout the 1980s [7]. Technically, none of them could dismiss that the attack on inflation in Brazil must be fought on three grounds simultaneously: monetary and fiscal austerity, and incomes policy. The lack of a solution to the problems rests, then, mainly on the fragility of the alliance in power. This left little room of manoeuvre both for the restructuring of public finances and for reductions in the transfer of resources abroad. These were measures necessary for achieving stabilization and the adjustment of the economy to the new conditions which were being shaped by the new techno-economic paradigm [8].

The restructuring of public financing was necessary, on the one hand, in order to make the tax system more equitable. On the other hand, the system of subsidies and fiscal incentives (to regions and sectors) needed to be up-dated in order to respond to the financial needs of the new stage of industrialization. The latter required greater emphasis on competitiveness based on dynamic comparative advantages in a world market whose technological base was being changed with the emergence of a new techno-economic paradigm.

The importance of reducing the transfer of resources abroad can be appraised on two grounds. From an economic point of view, it was necessary because whatever extra resources were kept in the country could help in establishing a programme of income redistribution. This could make the de-indexation of the economy easier, an essential element in curbing the inertial component of the inflationary process [9]. From a political point of view, there was little public legitimacy for the foreign debt. Most of it was contracted under the authoritarian regime and at times when interest rates in the international markets were much lower. Thus, cuts on its payments could increase the political support for the belt-tightening required by other austerity measures.

Summing up, there can be no doubt that external shocks at the end of the 1970s and early 1980s - mainly the rise in world interest rates and the decline in the relative price of primary commodity exports - played a major role in sparking the country's development crisis [10]. What is stressed here, however, are the constraints that were imposed upon the crisis' possible solutions by the lack of internal political commitment to a new stage of development [11]. This new stage should bear in mind the need to increase social equality [12] and the new forms of dependency which were being built under the new paradigm of world development.

b) From associated-development to rent-driven stagnation

The roots of the lack of political commitment to a new stage of development can be found in the divisions which took place within the 'triple alliance' from the mid-1970s onwards (see Chapter 2). It can also be associated with the loss of hegemony of the modern industrial sector (private and state-owned) and the re-emergence of mercantile capital as the leading sector within the ever changing alliance in power throughout the 1980s.

The first clear signal of shifting priorities away from an industrialization project which would be in pace with what was taking place in the core countries was given by the economic agenda established by the last government under the authoritarian regime (1979/85). The economic policies followed in general assumed that the structural changes that were taking place in capitalist development were to be faced by internal actions geared towards agriculture, export and energy [13] and a 'competent' management of the foreign debt [14].

Despite the discourse with which the first civilian government since 1964 came to power in 1985 - institutional reforms, economic growth based on a new pattern of industrialization and fighting poverty - the alliance of interests which gave it political support was too heterogeneous to build a firm commitment around the radical changes necessary to promote these new priorities. Similar to what had taken place under the authoritarian regime after

1979, under the 'new republic' (1985/1990) the modern sectors of the alliance were not strong enough to give the necessary backing for the government to challenge the external debt on its political merits [15]. Moreover, they did not hold the hegemonic power necessary to commit the 'liberal alliance' to institutional changes that would enable the government to carry on the reform of the state and an incomes policy, both necessary for the stabilization of the economy and its adjustment to the new world conditions.

As a result, the most that was 'accomplished' was the declaration of an unilateral moratorium on foreign debt in 1987 (which was suspended in 1988); the many unsuccessful attempts to curb inflation through price and wages freezing; and the strengthening of the discourse in favour of privatization. The failure of industrialists (in the private sector and within the state apparatus) to build a pact with other progressive political forces (mainly organized labour) meant that the old alliance was held together under the hegemony of mercantile capitalists. Thus, just as happened in the last five years of the authoritarian regime, during the first civilian government the definition and implementation of public policies became each time more related to the needs of gaining temporary political support. In most case these policies were drawn in response to corporatist interests of capitalists [16] and workers of the public sector [17].

The perverse results of this generalization of rent-seeking behaviour throughout the structures of the Brazilian socio-economic formation in the 1980s can be illustrated through three figures. Firstly, according to data from the national bureau of statistics (FIBGE) quoted in Quadros da Silva (1991), from an initial position of 7.8% in 1980 the share of the financial sector in the national accounts increased to about 20% in 1989. In the second place, the total amount of capital flight [18] increased from less than five billion dollars in 1979 to about sixty billion dollars on 1989 [Castro and Ronci (1991)]. Last but not least, income distribution which had slightly improved (for the first time since the 1960s) between 1976 and 1981 (the Gini index went from 0.589 in the former to 0.562 in the latter) worsened and reached its point of highest concentration in 1989 when the Gini index was of 0.635 [Bonelli and Sedlacek (1991)]. Not only concentration of income took place but the relative number of people under poverty also increased during the 1980s. By 1988 the percentage of people below the poverty line was back to the levels of 1970. The dimensions of the problems behind the numbers in Table 4.2 can be better appraised if one considers the absolute increase in population (from 90 million to over one hundred and thirty million inhabitants) between 1970 and 1988.

The increasingly hegemonic power of rent-seekers relative to industrialists in the 1980s created a vicious circle of economic and political crisis. On the one hand, the fragility of the pact of domination (the old alliance did not exist any longer as such and a new project of domination had not replaced it) did not leave room for the structural changes necessary for the economy to adjust to the new pattern of development that was being shaped in the industrialized world. On the other hand, the perverse combination of economic stagnation and instability took away whatever legitimacy the pact of domination could have ever had [19].

Table 4.2
Brazil: percentage of people below the poverty line

Regions	Years			
	1960	1970	1980	1988
Brazil	41,4	39,3	24,4	39,3
Centre-West	26,4	33,5	19,1	33,3
North	34,7	41,1	24,2	37,8
North-East	61,0	60,8	38,5	56,4
South-East	33,3	28,6	17,1	31,3
South	16,4	22,6	14,4	28,0

Source: FIBGE quoted in Romão (1991)

Furthermore, despite the different discourses against the statization of the economy what took place in reality was an increasing role of the state in the accumulation process. The major difference between what took place in the 1980s and what had been happening since the 1930s is that the major beneficiaries became land and money speculators in opposition to the previous priorities given to those activities committed to the industrialization process.

Nevertheless, in Brazil during the 1980s one cannot talk of a de--industrialization process similar to that which took place in Argentina [Katz and Bercovich (1989)] firstly, because of the internal dynamics acquired by the economy through its vertical and horizontal diversification and integration which were consolidated in the 1970s with the investment programme under the II PND. And secondly, due to the relative control of industrial policies (mainly in the areas of informatics, telecommunication, steel and energy) which was retained by industrialists and state-bureaucrats committed to the continuation of the country's industrialization project [20]. The combination of these two factors not only allowed the country to maintain the existing industrial capabilities but were also important for the country's slow and yet timid moves towards its insertion in the new pattern of economic development under IT techno-economic paradigm.

The analysis of the country's industrial structure and its role in the possibilities for, and constraints upon, its active role in the production and research networks that are being built in the industrialized world under the new techno-economic paradigm is the subject of the next sections of this chapter.

4.3 The partnership of state-owned, local and multinational enterprises

a) Introduction

Chapter 2 showed that by the beginning of the 1980s Brazil had completed a quite successful late-industrialization process. From the consumer goods emphasis of the 1950/1960s, the country embarked on a comprehensive import substitution/export promotion programme of intermediary and capital goods in the 1970s. As a result, Brazil started the new decade with an industrial base capable of internalizing the accumulation process to its full extent.

The strategy used to perform the structural change from an agro-exporter economy into an urban-industrial one in a relatively short period of time was based on the alliance of three complementary forces. The build-up of an alliance of state-owned enterprises, local capitals and multinational corporations was a successful combination of different interests with the goal of the country's late-industrialization.

Table 4.3 presents indisputable figures concerning Evans' (1979) triple alliance. The 'partnership' between the state and foreign investor appears stronger if one takes into consideration the sales of the top 25 enterprises. Nevertheless, the trend in the 1980s was of strengthening the local capitals' side both amongst the top 25 and amongst the top 500 enterprises in the country.

Table 4.3
Sales' shares of State-Owned Enterprises, MNCs and LCs

	Among the 25 largest			Among the 500 largest		
Year	SOEs	MNCs	LCs	SOEs	MNCs	LCs
1979	55,2	39,5	5,3	31,3	34,5	34,2
1984	59,4	29,9	10,7	32,9	27,2	39,9
1989	45,8	41,5	12,7	25,6	32,0	42,4

Sources: Exame (1980, 1985, 1990)

Table 4.4 shows that even though the 'partnership' is unevenly distributed in the different sectors, in the more technologically dynamic ones there is not an overwhelming majority of any one of the three allies. Thus, if in sectors such as public utilities (especially telecommunications) and automobiles the presence of local capitals is insignificant; in sectors such as chemicals/petro--chemicals, machines and equipments, electronics (especially informatics and telecommunication equipments), there is no dominant partner.

The patterns of ownership in these dynamic sectors are taken here as an indication that the BNSI can benefit from the triple alliance in order to take part in technological and production networks that are being built amongst industrial countries. This is so, firstly, because the build-up of indigenous technological capabilities in some of these sectors has increased the country's negotiation power in 'core' technologies (more on that in the sections below); secondly, because subcontracting, and user-producer relations have become common practices amongst the 'partners' in these dynamic sectors. In other words, provided that proper policies are put in place and specific targets are established, conditions exists for the BNSI to interact with other n.s.i. both through MNCs subsidiaries, and through SOEs and local enterprises.

In the increasing process of internationalization taking place world wide [21] MNCs are recognized to enjoy three combined and cumulative sets of advantages [Dunning (1981)]; firstly, those 'scale advantages' derived from size, monopoly power and better resource capability and usage which they may have over others producing in the same location; secondly, those that are related to the advantages they bring to their subsidiaries abroad by allowing them to benefit from many of the endowments - access to cheaper inputs, knowledge of markets, R&D, amongst others - of the parent company; thirdly, the 'scope advantages' they have by operating in different economic environments and which allow them to profit most of different factor endowments and market situations. Not surprisingly, then, MNCs are in a better position to profit from R&D cooperation schemes that are taking place amongst themselves and those that they can establish with local, small, highly innovative firms [22]. The access to these advantages that to a greater or lesser degree are available to MNCs subsidiaries in Brazil can be seen as an important asset of the BNSI as a whole for four reasons; firstly, because positive externalities can be achieved through sub-contracting by these subsidiaries with local enterprises; secondly, because of 'demonstration effects' that take place amongst other enterprises within the BNSI; thirdly, because the presence of MNCs in the Brazilian economy also takes place in technology intensive sectors; and, finally, because through these subsidiaries the BNSI can build links with the R&D cooperation schemes that are taking place in the core countries [23].

The first two reasons are closely related to the 'normal' contribution of MNCs subsidiaries to local production and technological capabilities. The two latter ones are emphasized here because of the importance of new forms of dependencies and interdependencies that are arising amongst firms and nations as a result of the changing techno-economic paradigm. Chapter 3 showed that the new forms of dependencies and interdependencies which are being concentrated and centralized amongst developed countries can create formidable new entry barriers to development under the new techno-economic paradigm for late-comers to the industrialization process. From this perspective, then, the interactions between local enterprises, SOEs, and MNCs within the Brazilian socio-economic formation can be seen an instrument that should be used in order for the BNSI to overcome some of these entry barriers. In order for these instruments to be effective, however, issues

82

concerning the different partners of the alliance must be addressed, as will be in the next sub-sections.

Table 4.4
SOEs, MNCs and LCs' shares in key sectors - 1989 (%)

	Sales*	Local	State-owned	MNCs
Sectors				
GREATER PARTICIPATION OF LOCAL CAPITALS				
Agriculture	4.163	100	0	0
Retailers	8.633	100	0	0
Press and broadcasting	1.306	100	0	0
Vehicles distribution	908	100	0	0
Heavy construction	10.559	99	0	1
Light construction	1.333	98	0	2
Garment	2.706	93	0	7
Furniture	368	92	0	8
Paper and pulp	3.979	80	0	20
Supermarkets	11.068	80	2	18
Textile	2.643	80	0	20
Electronics	11.115	70	0	30
Fertilizers	962	67	27	6
Food	17.074	65	0	35
Wholesale	4.322	65	0	35
Transport servs.	3.056	64	36	0
Non-metallic minerals	2.980	56	0	44
Metallurgy	6.588	51	4	45
GREATER PARTICIPATION OF MCNs				
Automobile	13.455	1	0	99
Pharmaceuticals	410	17	0	83
Hygiene	2.858	20	0	80
Informatics	2.262	37	4	59
Tobacco and beverages	5.673	42	0	58
Machines and equipaments	2.643	40	2	58
Auto parts	4.270	43	0	57
Petrol distrib.	9.781	12	31	57
Transport. mat.	3.056	29	17	54
Plastics and rub.	3.565	47	0	53
GREATER PARTICIPATION OF SOES				
Public Utilities	n.a.	0	0	100
Steel	3.606	24	69	7
Chemicals/petro-chem.	13.222	8	63	29
Mining	1.249	32	60	8

*: of those firms which are among the 500 largest in the country (US$ million)
Source: *Exame* (1990) (my translation)

b) Local enterprises (LCs and SOEs) and technological capabilities

The different approaches taken towards technological capabilities - ranging from market reserves to 'import platforms' [24] - during the core of the industrialization process in Brazil have certainly contributed towards an increase in technological heterogeneity within the economic domain. This does not mean, however, that the major differences are to be found between MNCs and local firms. Even though Braga and Matesco (1989) show that there is a greater probability of MNCs' subsidiaries in Brazil pursuing technological capabilities than local enterprises, the difference between the foreign and the domestic partners of the alliance decreases as the sample is restricted to the larger firms (see next sub-section).

The heterogeneities that occur amongst the local industrial groups require a particularly careful analysis. Contrary to other NICs, the differences in technological capabilities within different industrial complexes do not diminish if one considers the big private groups in the country. Suzigan, coord. (1989) has shown that there is no correlation between the financial wealth of the ten largest Brazilian economic groups and their R&D expenditure or the areas in which these expenditures are concentrated. It also points out that there is no correlation between group size and strategies of diversification. In other words, it is not the financial capability of these big local groups that determines, by itself, their diversification towards technologically more sophisticated sectors.

The lack of concern with the development of technological capabilities throughout most of the industrialization process in Brazil, when highly concentrated economic groups emerged as a consequence of different policies sponsored by the government, has resulted in a situation where at most 5 of its 10 biggest groups are engaged in some type of hi-tech activity. Amongst these five groups it is important to highlight that two are from the banking system whose immediate interest in informatics has resulted in the BNSI's accumulation of technological capabilities in nanking automation [25].

As for the state-owned enterprises, they have been caught since the late 1970s by the ambiguities that exist between their public sector content and the expected 'private approach' to management efficiency. Tigre et al. (1989) point out that the use of SOEs as instruments of macroeconomic stabilization programmes has been so perverse that in 1989, tariffs were 30% behind the inflation rate for PETROBRAS (oil), 40% for the SIDERBRAS (steel) system, 70% for the TELEBRAS (telecommunications services) system and 100% for the ELETROBRAS (electricity) system.

The continuous cuts in SOEs investment programmes - either because their revenues have been forced by the government to lag behind inflation, or because their ability to borrow in the financial market diminished with the fiscal crisis of the Brazilian government, or both - cause two kinds of concern with respect to the BNSI. The first regards the impact that these cuts in investment programmes have on the ability of key SOEs to meet increasing demands in essential services such as telecommunications and energy. The second concern is the up- and down-stream effects on technological capabilities in the private sector. This is so because of the close links between SOEs investment programmes and R&D programmes carried out by R&D centres, universities and by the private sector (see Chapter 6).

The compounded result of a weak position of state-owned enterprises on the BNSI cannot be overstressed. Their role in the process of increasing technological capabilities will be analyzed in the chapter concerned with the technological domain. Their structuring importance within the economic domain is also widely recognized. Nevertheless, a new configuration of this role has to be sought, as will be discussed in the last chapter.

For the time being it is worth remembering that 'the windows of opportunities' which are opened to associated-dependent Brazil when changes in paradigm occur, "cannot always be taken by the private sector, due to risks and the need for pioneer type of investment. Deep-water petroleum exploration; the exploration and development of new uses for new materials such as anatasio; research work in areas such as micro-electronics and biotechnology, are examples of some specificities of Brazil (... for which) the state has an important role to play, both as a long-run investor and as structurer of industrial and technological development)" (Tigre et al. (1989), pg. 17].

Summing up, the 'no policy as a policy' which prevailed throughout the 1980s has increased technological heterogeneity amongst the largest local enterprises (private and SOES). Tighter financial control by the central government has constrained the possibilities of SOEs to pursue greater technological capabilities. With the exception of the two larger private banks, the highly concentrated financial wealth of the ten largest private has been channeled more to financial and land speculation than to investment diversification towards hi-tech industries.

c) MNCs and the Brazilian national system of innovation

Foreign direct investment is often mentioned in the literature as a way of increasing a country's technological base. Even though the flow of foreign capital to the Brazilian economy increased at falling rates in the 1980s [Correa do Lago (1987)], the numbers in Table 4.5 show that the stock of foreign capital has been concentrated in sectors for which technological innovation plays an important role.

Besides being either leaders or co-leaders of these dynamic sectors (see Table 4.4), MNCs have been playing an important role in export diversification. According to Willmore (1987), in 1980 their share of total exports was 38.3% , whilst Gonçalves (1987) indicates that MNCs' share of exports increases to 52.2% when technology-intensive products are taken into consideration.

Table 4.5
Foreign investments and reinvestments (US$million - 3/89)

Sector	Invest.	Reinvest.	Total	(%)
- Manufacture	15.176	8.201	23.377	74,7
. Metallurgy	1.803	635	2.438	7,8
. Mechanical	1.946	747	2.693	8,6
. Elect./electron	1.592	808	2.400	7,6
. Transport	3.111	1.420	4.532	14,5
. Chemical	2.746	1.601	4.348	13,9
- Food	481	989	1.470	4,7
. Others	3.494	1.998	5.492	17,7
- Services	4.457	1.753	6.211	19,9
- Others	1.345	348	1.693	5,4
TOTAL	**20.979**	**10.303**	**31.282**	**100,0**

Source: Bauman, R (1989a).

If the roots of this qualitative aspect of MNCs' share in exports is to be found in the global developments affecting the trade orientation of multinationals operating in developed countries and in NICs [26], it seems even more important to take into consideration the role of MNCs when assessing technological capabilities in the economic domain. The strong interactions that take place within the economic domain between MNCs subsidiaries and their local sub-contractors can be an important instrument of access of the BNSI to innovations taking place in core countries. One cannot overemphasize the importance of such an instrument at times of changes in paradigm, when the technological frontier is a moving target and when MNCs' R&D plays a vital role in the establishment of these frontiers [Chesnais (1988)].

d) The BNSI's local and foreign enterprises and the new techno-economic paradigm

The reactions of agents to changes in their environment is an important component of the impressionistic approximation used in this book between radical technological change and Kuhn's concept of paradigm in natural sciences. With this in mind, the findings of a survey by Salm et al. (1990) of 135 leading enterprises operating in Brazil - 88 local and state-owned enterprises and 47 MNCs [27] - with respect to their use of micro-electronic based industrial automation and of new organizational techniques [28] are an important source for identifying possible differences in responses of local and foreign enterprises in Brazil with respect to the new paradigm.

Table 4.6 shows a low diffusion of digital automation amongst the big enterprises operating in the BNSI. The general unstable economic conditions under which the country operated in the 1980s is pointed out as the main reason for such a low rate of diffusion. It should be noticed, however, that local and state-owned enterprises have performed slightly better with respect to digital automation in project and in production than MNCs. This result can be interpreted as a reaction of MNCs to the restrictions imposed by the Brazilian informatics policy (see section 4.5 below) to imports of micro-, mini- and midi-computer embodied technology. It can also be seen as a sign that MNCs believed in positive (from their perspective) results for the pressures that were being put on the Brazilian government in order to change the market reserve policy (see Chapter 5).

Table 4.6

Diffusion of micro-electronics based automation in the BNSI (% of operations controlled by micro-electronics based automation in 88/89)

	Local and SOEs		MNCs	
	Project	Prodution	Project	Prodution
. Low intensity (0-10% of operations)	57	43	71	54
. Average intensity (11-50% of operations)	35	47	19	35
. High intensity	8	10	10	11

Source: Bielschowsky and Ferraz (1990), Tables XX and XXI

The diffusion of organizational techniques (OT) associated with the new techno-economic paradigm is not much greater than that of capital-embodied new technologies. Even for those OT which have a higher rate of diffusion (internal 'total quality control' and 'just-in-time'), the numbers in Table 4.7 show a low use amongst the largest enterprises in the BNSI. The major explanation given for this low pace of diffusion were the uncertainties concerning industrial relations in Brazil which were aggravated by the debate which took place during the Constituent Congress (see Chapter 5). Nevertheless, the better level of industrial relations accomplished by MNCs subsidiaries are reflected in their slightly more intensive use of new oganizational techniques than the local and state-owned enterprises surveyed.

Table 4.7

Diffusion of new organization techniques in the BNSI (% of labour force involved in the innovation in 1988/89)

	Total Quality Control		Just-in-time	
	Local/SOEs	MNCs	Local/SOEs	MNCs
. Low intensity (0-20% of labour)	55	58	65	56
. Average intensity (21-60% of labour)	34	22	31	31
. High intensity (61-100 of labour)	11	20	4	13

Source: Bielschowsky and Ferraz (1990), Tables XX and XXI

4.4 Export drive

The commodity composition of exports has been long stressed as an important feature to assess a country's role in the international division of labour [Maizels (1963)]. The way national economies adhere to the international regime [29] indicates the opportunities and constraints imposed or offered to each country by the world system. Moreover, these opportunities and constraints are not restricted to trade in goods and services but establish grounds for advancements at the national level in abstract knowledge as well as in applied technology. In other words, "from a dynamic technology perspective it does matter whether a region or country is specialized in mushroom production or in silicon chips." [Dosi et al. (1990), p. 2].

It should not come as a surprise, then, that the non-OECD countries which are seen as better equipped to profit from the 'windows of opportunities' opened by the new techno-economic paradigm are those NICs which have engaged in the diversification of their trade links with the core countries. According to OECD (1987), by 1985 about 40% of OECD imports from NICs were in products whose characteristics were significant scale economies or extensive product differentiation. Moreover, the fact that 31 percent of the NICs' manufacturing trade with OECD cuntries were accounted for by intra-firm trade is pointed to by the OECD study as evidence that the newly-industrialized countries had also been drawn into the dynamic functions of trade.

In general, the Brazilian trade experience since the 1970s fits this description of NICs as a whole. Table 4.8 shows that Brazilian export diversification from the 1970s onwards not only occurred through a substantial increase in the share of manufactures but it did so over total exports which increased at an average rate of 16.9% a year between 1976 and 1989. More important, according to Gonçalves (1987), between 1976/78 and 1981/83, whilst other sector's exports grew at an average rate of 16.4% a year, technology-intensive ones grew at an average rate of 27.4% per annum.

Table 4.8
Brazil: Foreign trade (%)

Year	1976	1980	1986	1989
Exports:				
. Basics	64,3	43,0	32,8	27,9
. Semi-ind.	8,3	12,6	11,1	16,9
. Manufactures	27,4	44,4	56,1	54,2
TOTAL (US$ million)	10.128	20.132	22.393	34.058
Imports:				
. Basics	n.a.	30,8	35,9	36,7
. Consumption	n.a.	5,7	6,0	13,9
. Oil	n.a.	44,4	35,9	24,3
. Capital goods	n.a.	19,1	21,2	25,1
TOTAL (US$ million)	12.382	22.955	13.153	18.254

Source: CACEX/FUNCEX.

The competitiveness of Brazilian exports has been increasingly derived from dynamic comparative advantages acquired by some of the country's industrial complexes such as steel, paper and pulp and petrochemicals. Even though these sectors take advantage of low costs of local inputs, its internal demand gives them economies of scale advantages, and competition in the international market has forced them to keep their technological capabilities up to date.

Regardless of the fact that in sectors such as textiles, garments and shoes, competitiveness still relies on low wages, in more sophisticated ones such as capital goods, armaments, aircrafts, automobiles, auto-parts and consumer durables, internal technological capabilities are such that the country has been able to find niches both in the Third World and in developed countries [Erber et al. (1985b)] [30].

According to FUNCEX, most of the exports of manufactures and semi-manufactures is done to countries where there is intense competition with other exporters. Thus, the United States and Canada purchased in 1987, 40% and 30%, respectively, of the total Brazilian exports of manufactures and semi-manufactures. Given that the 1980s were times when competitiveness retained very close relationships with innovation under the new techno-economic paradigm, the export diversification towards more sophisticated goods and markets that took place in the Brazilian economy is taken here as an indication that the BNSI has used its exposure to international competition as a way of increasing its technological capabilities. A virtuous cycle was established in such a way that "the main problem faced by Brazilian exports is - as is likely to continue to be in the foreseeable future - market access rather than lack of competitiveness." [Abreu and Fritsch (1988), p.3] [31].

The framework (economies of scale, degrees of concentration, labour--ocess, etc.) under which competition takes place in the international market, however, is not a fixed one. Even more rapidly alterations in this framework should be expected when the commodity composition of international trade comes to reflect more intensively the changes in the techno-economic paradigm. If these possible changes are taken into consideration, the diversification of exports accomplished by Brazil in the past has to be seen with a grain of salt. This is so because the accomplishments of the past were not the result of a strategy in which trade was seen as an instrument of increasing industrial and technological capabilities. Much to the contrary, export promotion programmes were established by the government in order to diminish external constraints. The adherence by the industrial sector to these programmes had two basic motivations. Firstly, they were attractive to those sectors which were dependent on foreign inputs and/or wanted to modernize/ expand their production lines using imported machinery and equipment without paying high import tariffs. Secondly, they were used as competitive edge by those industries which needed to look for alternative markets at times of shrinking domestic demand.

From the perspective of most interest to this book - that of increasing internal technological capabilities at times of changing techno-economic paradigm - the major criticism [32] that can be made of the Brazilian export promotion programmes in the past is that they never moved beyond the objective of trade as a means of overcoming external constraints. In other words, they lacked the vision of similar programmes in other NICs [33] where trade was seen as an instrument of increasing industrial and technological capabilities through competition in the international market.

4.5   The production of machinery and equipment in the BNSI

a) An overview of the sector

According to Fransman (1985a), the role of machinery as one of the most important contributors to economic development can be traced back to Adam Smith who in a number of perceptive remarks foresaw the emergence of a specialized capital goods sector. However, amongst the classical economists, Marx provided the best analysis of the development of machinery and its role in accumulation. More recently, the importance of a country's ability to produce machinery and equipment has been related to this sector's role in fostering technological capabilities. Moreover, in order to cope with radical technological changes it is important that users of innovations can interact with their producers within the system of innovation. From a perspective emphasising this link, the importance of technological capabilities within the machinery and equipment sector is best assessed by the social rather than private consequences of greater technological autonomy. Such a perspective is particularly relevant in Brazil's context of associated-dependent development [Erber (1977)].

In Brazil the production of machinery and equipment had its development process sped up with the last import-substitution programme under the second national development plan - 1974/79 (II PND). According to data from ABIMAQ/SINDMAQ (1990), about 18% of the existing industry was established before 1950; another 36% were established in the 1950s and 1960s and the sector reached its peak in the 1970s when over 35% of the existing firms were established. Evidence from case studies [Cruz (1983), da Silva (1982), and Erber (1982)] show that, besides accomplishing the government targets of import substitution, the largest enterprises in the sector have also made progress in moving from the stage of copying imported machinery to developing new machinery. These studies indicate that the progressive verticalization of the Brazilian import-substitution model has contributed to the fostering of problem-resolving innovative capabilities in the country's machinery and equipment sector. This process was similar to that experienced in the early development of the more advanced countries [34].

Table 4.9
Performance of the machinery and equipment sector

| Year | Production | Exports | Employment |
	(1989 US$ billion)		(thousand)
1980	17,75	1,05	306,1
1981	16,22	1,19	296,1
1982	13,69	0,91	258,8
1983	11,54	0,89	209,0
1984	12,42	1,16	204,7
1985	15,02	1,34	234,9
1986	17,17	1,21	274,5
1987	17,62	1,43	289,2
1988	17,11	2,00	282,7
1989	16,40	2,20	275,8

Source: ABIMAQ/SINDIMAQ (1990)

In the 1980s the continuous problems with the economy (see section 4.2 above) plus the reductions of government's investment in areas such as energy, petrochemical and steel production meant drastic cuts in the demand for machinery and equipments. According to estimates made by ABDIB (the national association for the development of base industries), in 1989 the sector operated at 60% of its capacity. Under the pressure of lowering sales to the public sector, the industry diversified its market towards the private sector which in the period 1985/87 absorbed on average 70% of what was produced [35]. There was a significant increase in exports during the 1980s (Table 4.9) but, in average terms, the external market still represented less than 10% of total sales by the industry.

b) The Brazilian machinery sector and CNC technology

More important than the shifts that took place in the demand side of the industry were the structural changes in the sector's technological base with the advancement of computerized numerically controlled (CNC) technology. To these changes, the reaction of producers in the machine tools sector [36] was quite heterogeneous. As the analysis of Porteous (1992) shows, the different reactions to the new technologies can be better understood by dividing the sector's firms into three groups. The first and largest group of firms - basically local producers of relatively simple general-purpose machinery for workshops, small industrial enterprises and technical schools - concentrated their efforts in reacting mainly to the changes in demand. Thus, most of them followed a strategy of diversification over a wide range of models but remained in the more simple, universal segment of the market. In general, they refused NC and CNC as a realistic technological option.

The second group - consisting of larger local producers which in the past had made incremental progress in moving from simple models based on copies to the introduction of successive improvements as well as using licensed technology - were less fatalistic with respect to the new technologies and made explicit efforts to move into NC and CNC machinery. "Plans for entering NC and CNC amongst these firms were, however, very hesitant and often were limited to modifying existing conventional models to NC. There was little evidence of the more radical changes in approach to design, production and marketing needed to realize the full potential flexibility and precision of CNC." (ibid., p. 231) [37].

The last group - made up by foreign subsidiaries whose sales were heavily concentrated on other MNCs operating in Brazil - exploits access to the most advanced technology arising from their parent companies' designs and production know-how. Despite these advantages in access to foreign technology, the MNCs operating in the Brazilian machine tool sector do not always produce internally what their parent companies offer in the international market. Nevertheless, according to a survey conducted by BNDES (the National Development Bank) [Guimaraes, coord. (1988)] the foreign subsidiaries, in general, are amongst the sector's enterprises which show greater concern with developing better products and with training their engineering teams.

A survey conducted by the Brazilian Association of Machines and Equipment Producers [ABIMAQ/SINDMAQ (1990)] shows that there is awareness amongst the sector's enterprises with respect to what is taking place in its technological frontier. The materialization of this concern, however, has had limited impact in terms of R&D activities. Cruz and da Silva (1990) points out that more than 20% of the sector's enterprises spend nothing on R&D activities. Of the 77% which do, the majority spend less than 2% of their revenues in R&D. These figures are above the average of the BNSI as a whole (just over .6%) but are very low for a sector which plays an important role in the system of innovation and which is going through radical changes in its technological base.

c) The diffusion of CNC machinery

The diffusion of CNC machinery has been negatively affected by the general economic conditions. The major positive reaction to the new technology has come from the automobile, the auto-parts, the airplane, the armaments and the mechanical industries. These are the industries which have diversified their markets into exports and are the ones in which there is higher concentration of bigger local and foreign firms. According to preliminary data from SOBRACON (the Brazilian society of numerically controlled machinery and equipment) medium-size enterprises (between 151 and 500 workers) account for about 15% of the total of CNC machine tools in operation in the country, whilst the large-size enterprises (more than 501 workers) account for about 82%. Moreover, the above mentioned survey by BNDES [Guimarães (1988)] shows that the great majority of the users have few CNC machines per plant which reduces their impact on cost reduction and on productivity increase [38]. The diffusion of the new technology in the BNSI, then, can be seen as going through an experimental stage during which entrepreneurs want to be acquainted with it but are cautious about investing much in the new technology because of the country's economic situation.

The use of this defensive strategy has had two effects on the BNSI. Firstly, a positive learning process takes place both inside the user firms ('learning-by-using') and between users and locally established producers ('learning-by-interacting'). In the second place, and in opposite direction, the competitive edge that the new technology should confer on its users is being minimized by the limitations under which it is being used in the BNSI.

4.6 The BNSI's early start in information technology

a) The Brazilian informatics policy: an overview

Perez (1989) emphasizes the importance of early and full assimilation of the 'core' technologies if a n.s.i. is to profit most from a change in the technological base of world economic development. The combination of such an assimilation with the necessary institutional 'matches' are important ingredients of a country's development strategy aimed at maintaining (especially in the case of developed countries) or increasing (especially in the case of late-comers) its international competitiveness.

The main objective of this section is to analyze those aspects of the Brazilian informatics policy which contributed to building technological capabilities within the BNSI in a 'core' area of the new techno-economic paradigm. The emphasis here is on the capabilities which have been acquired by agents within the BNSI to interact with their counterparts in other systems of innovation in industrialized countries [39].

The Brazilian experience in informatics goes back to the 1970s when some factors converged in favour of the adoption of explicit policies towards that industry. Firstly, there was a rapid growth in the demand for electronic data processing equipment due to the fast growth of economic activities in the country, and because of the search for modernization that was taking place within the state apparatus [40]. In the second place, the use of computers in the higher spheres of the federal government contributed to the emergence of a consciousness amongst its elite with respect to the important future role to be played by IT technology. Moreover, there was increasing awareness of the constraints which could be imposed on the relationship between the users of the new technology in a country in the periphery such as Brazil and its foreign and highly oligopolized producers [41]. Thirdly, the development and diffusion of minicomputers technology in the world scene represented a technological discontinuity which opened 'windows of opportunities' to new entrants.

The combination of these factors, amongst others, raised the possibility for the country to search for a new model of import-substitution which could avoid the technological dependence which characterized the model used previously. In other words, for some agencies of development promotion in Brazil (mainly BNDES - the National Bank of Economic Development) the time was right to pursue a new stage of economic growth based on a dynamic process of self-sustained technological capabilities.

That implied that the model to be pursued should go beyond the internalization of industrial production, which had characterized other sectors in the past, in order to encompass measures that would enable local producers to develop greater technological capabilities also. The latter would take place, it was assumed, through both the controlled import of foreign technology and the support to the development of R&D activities in the country. Above all, the content of the new strategy being pursued made it necessary that the control over the new technology should be kept in the hands of Brazilians, i.e., that the new industry was to be owned by Brazilians [42].

The policy instrument that was created in order to make feasible the emergence and the development of a Brazilian computer industry was that of market reserve. Its main characteristic was the managerial and technological control by Brazilian industrialists. To them was reserved the segment of data processing equipment which was emerging with computers based on microprocessors and standardized operational systems [43]. Given that the country's existing technological capabilities were able to master that base and to develop from it, it was possible to think of protecting the infant local industry from the competition of foreign enterprises.

The market reserve policy followed earlier policies of Brazil in breaking with any orthodox subservience to market forces. In the case of the computer industry, however, the involvement of the government was greater because the market reserve implied restrictions both on foreign producers who could neither sell nor produce through subsidiaries in Brazil, and on users who could not choose their equipment freely. Furthermore, the restrictions imposed by the government meant that local users were to bear technological gaps between local produced equipment and those available in the international market [44].

The government's involvement in every stage of the process of market reserve was of a wide and deep scope. It ranged from the creation of conditions for the emergence and development of local enterprises to the establishment of organizational procedures which could guarantee and control the access of local producers to foreign technology as well as motivate them to develop capabilities in design and production. Furthermore, the aim of the policy in breaking with technological dependence meant that it was necessary to build conditions for the intensification of the process of absorption and diffusion of the industry's scientific and technological knowledge. This was sought through the intensification of cooperation schemes with the country's university and research centre systems [45].

b) The performance of the BNSI' informatics sector

Despite the changes that took place in the country's economic and political environments (see Chapters 4 and 5, respectively) throughout most of the implementation period of the market reserve policy, it sustained momentum with its adaptation to these changes without losing sight of its original aim [46]. Table 4.10 shows that the informatics industry went through the 'lost decade' attaining high growth rates (the annual average was above 22%) and increasing the participation of local producers in its total revenue (from less than 1/3 in 1980 to just about 3/4 in 1990).

Table 4.10
Gross revenues of the informatics industry (1980/90)

(US$ million)

Ownership	1980	1983	1985	1988	1990(*)
Local	280	687	1.400	2.948	4.332
(%)	(32,6)	(46,2)	52,3)	(66,6)	(75,0)
Foreigner	580	800	1.287	1.480	1.444
(%)	(67,4)	(53,8)	(47,7	(33,4)	(25,0)

(*) - Estimated
Source: Nogueira and Nogueira (1990).

Given that the market shares of local and foreign enterprises reflect the clear division in the policy implemented - to the former was allocated the market of micro-, mini-, and midi-size equipments whilst the latter was to deal with mainframes - it becomes clear that there was a positive response by local producers in terms of supplying the market with the sort of equipment which is at the centre of the 'IT revolution'. Moreover, the combination of locally developed technology (including 'reverse engineering') and the licensing from foreign producers enabled the Brazilian informatic industry to reduce the gap between its technological base and the international frontier [47].

Despite the many criticisms that are made of the results of the informatics policy followed from the beginning of the 1970s to the beginning of the 1990s [48], some of the results achieved by the BNSI with respect to this 'core' industry of the new paradigm are quite remarkable when compared with other NICs. This is true both with respect to other industrial countries in Latin America (Table 4.11 below) and with respect to the successful case of South Korea. For the latter, Evans and Tigre (1989b) show that up to 1986 the number of data processing equipment (of all different types) installed in Brazil (12,388) was much larger than that in the South-Asian 'tiger' (4,374). This situation was already expected to change rapidly (as it actually did), however, because of the extraordinary performance of the South Korean informatics industry [49].

Mammana (1989) points out that the informatics industry since the mid-eighties has become the most important sector within the electronics complex [50]. Thus, whilst in 1979 the consumer-goods electronic sector accounted for 60.7% and informatics for less than 13% of the complex, by 1986 informatics was already accounting for 43% and consumer-goods for 37%. Such a trend in the Brazilian electronic complex was in line with what has been taking place in the electronic complex in industrialized countries.

Table 4.11

General comparison of the informatics industry in

	Argentina	Brasil	México
GDP (US$ million)	84.100	337.700	198.400
Informatics	300	3.000	550
(% of GDP)	0,30	0,9	0,28
Employment			
Total	n.a.	42.000	2.100
University level	n.a.	11.400	500
in R&D activities	120	2.700	140
Imports (US$ million)	122	n.a.	142

Source: Inter-American Development Bank quoted in Mammana (1989)

Table 4.12

Sales of the top-ten informatics enterprises in the World, the Brazilian and the South Korean markets

(US$ million)

World (a)		Brazil (a)		South Korea (b)	
IBM	50,000	IBM	1,123	Sansung Elect	2,229
DEC	10,400	UNISYs	470	Golstar Co.	1,755
UNISYS	8,700	G. Brad.	143	Daewoo Elect.	606
Fujitsu	87,00	ITAUTEC	136	SST	447
NEC	6,300	SID Inf.	106	Sansumg E. Dev.	315
Hitachi	6,300	G. Iochpe	93	IBM Korea	222
Siemens	5,700	COBRA	85	Golstar Sem.	196
NCR	5,100	G. Docas	77	Daewoo Tel.	152
H-P	5,000	G. ABC	60	Oriental Prec.	121
Olivetti	4,600	Proceda	44	Hynduai Elect.	104

(a) - sales in 1988
(b) - sales in 1986
Sources: World and Brazil: de Mello, coord. (1990), Tables 3.3.5. and 3.4.9, pages 89 and 114, respectively. South Korea: Evans and Tigre (1989b), Table 8, p. 561

Some of the achievements of the Brazilian informatics policy - especially with respect to indigenous R&D capabilities acquired and to the capability to negotiate technological transfer [Schmitz and Hewitt (1992)] - are quite significant. Nevertheless, the small size of the Brazilian market and the scale of its enterprises in the informatics sector do not guarantee an 'automatic' access of the BNSI to the 'learning-by-interacting' which is taking place in the industrialized world.

As emphasized in Chapter 3, the establishment of R&D and production networks is a major characteristic of inter-firm relations under the new techno--economic paradigm. Despite the good performance of the informatics sector in Brazil throughout the 1980s, it still represents less than 2% of the sector's world sales [de Mello, coord. (1990)]. Table 4.12 shows that the scale of its largest enterprises is still quite small when compared with both the world market and other NICs such as South Korea. Thus, despite the boost given to local enterprise by the informatics policy, the major Brazilian informatics enterprises are significantly smaller than the multinational which operate in the country. This compares poorly with what took place in South Korea where the top 5 companies are local and amongst the top 10 only one is a foreign multinational. Moreover, the largest Brazilian group (Bradesco) has total sales smaller than the eighth largest producer in the South Korean market.

c) The informatics sector, user-producer interactions and automation in the BNSI

Despite the small scale of the Brazilian informatics sector when compared to other industrialized countries [51] - which is a constraint to the attainment of economies of scale and scope necessary for the development of new products - its importance for the prospects of the BNSI under the new techno-economic paradigm cannot be overemphasized. Such an emphasis becomes even more relevant when it is recognised that the diffusion of IT technology which can be attributed to the sector occurred when the poor performance of the economy created an unfavourable environment for change in its technological basis. The internalization of most of the sector's production processes meant that at times of balance of payments constraints, as Brazil went through in the 1980s, the industry's growth has not implied any significant burden on the trade balance [52].

Furthermore, the existence of local technological and production capabilities in IT meant that the diffusion of the 'core' of the new paradigm could take place in other sectors of the economy without the constraints that would have been imposed by the balance of payments if the sources of new machinery and equipment were abroad [53].

The internalization of the informatics industry in the Brazilian production sector has also contributed to increase the technological and production capabilities of BNSI through its network of technical support to users. The survey conducted by Baptista et al. (1990) shows that most producers in the informatics sector have strengthened their pre- and post-sales relations with users. Furthermore, these interactions have gone beyond price quotation and technical assistance upon request, in order to encompass direct cooperation in organizational and operational matters.

The latter has contributed to the diffusion of microelectronic based automation. This strategy used by producers has, for instance, enabled a faster diffusion of CAD (computer-aided design) equipment. Sá (1989) points out that the fast diffusion rate of CAD in Brazil (sales grew from US$4,5 million in 1985 to US$38,3 million in 1988) is due to close user-producer linkages which in many cases made producers license foreign technology in order to cope with users' needs. Thus, under the circumstances of a 'moving technological target' on the international scene and deteriorating internal economic conditions, the performance of the 'infant' informatics industry minimized the technological gap between the BNSI and the world frontier. In this sense, the importance of the sector can be attributed more to the links that it builds between the 'core' of the new paradigm and the country's industrial structure than the inter-sectoral linkages that are usually stressed in input/output analysis.

The linkages that the informatics industry has built between the 'core' technology of the new paradigm and the BNSI as a whole are reflected in the diffusion of industrial automation equipment. Industrial automation equipment's sales went from US$87 million in 1984 to more than US$270 million in 1988 [SEI (1989)]. Table 4.13 shows its diffusion throughout the economy. The way SEI presents the data, however, underestimates the diffusion within the industrial sector because the sales to state-owned--enterprises are taken as being due to government.

Table 4.13
Sales of industrial automation equipments (%)

Year User	1984	1985	1986	1987
Government	23.7	27.6	30.9	27.4
Commerce	1.3	.9	4.5	3.9
Industry	70.6	69.0	60.8	63.9
Banks	.7	.8	.3	.5
Services	3.7	1.7	3.5	4.3

Source: SEI (1989)

Table 4.14 shows that there has been a continuous increase in the production of both process controls and CAM (computer-aided manufacturing) equipment. The latter's contribution to the sector's sales went from 7.54% in 1984 to 26.66% in 1988.

According to Ferraz (1989), the production of computer-aided automation systems in Brazil has followed a pattern quite similar to what happened to the production of personal computers in the early 1980s. Thus, in the structuring process it has been going through, (i) it is highly dependent on foreign technology which means that its products are highly compatible with international ones; (ii) there is still a high number of entrants to the industry and its output is highly diversified, which means that full economies of scale have not yet been reached; (iii) the learning process is still taking place which implies that prices can become lower and quality can increase.

Table 4.14
Brazil: Production of CA automation equipment (units)

Year	Process control	CAM	Total
1984	1.098	174	1.272
1985	5.692	482	6.174
1986	5.512	2.033	5.512
1987	8.679	3.337	12.016
1988	8.090	4.239	12.329

Source: SEI (1989)

d) Automation and 'defensive strategies' in the BNSI

Besides the fact that the low cost of labour inhibits automation in many sectors [54], the major constraints on the development of the sector reflect cost and demand matters [SEI (1989)]. These problems are related to the high cost of borrowing money; the scarce availability of human resources and of training programmes; import restrictions; and the slow growth of the industrial sector as a whole. It has been estimated [Sá (1989)] the sector's demand will increase from US$429 million in 1988 to more than US$1,532 million in 1992. More than 60% of existing and projected demand is concentrated in the mechanical engineering, steel, chemical/petrochemical and paper/pulp sectors, most of which have recently undergone modernization and/or expansion processes.

Two factors are important to take into consideration when assessing computer-aided (CA) automation in Brazil. The first is based on what has happened in the petrochemical industry and is highlighted here as an illustration of the crucial difference between industrial and technological capabilities within an n.s.i. and the problems facing the diffusion of IT technology. The absence of a prior concern with technological capability during the establishment of the petrochemical industry in Brazil has resulted in a situation where most firms have become capable of increasing efficiency of plant operation and of making minor process improvements but have not developed technological capabilities necessary for substantial process innovation [55]. As a result of the limited knowledge that most petrochemical firms in Brazil have of their core technology, they have not been able to specify their needs to automation equipment producers and, consequently,

100

have become underutilizers of automation technology. In other words, the investments they have made in the 1980s "...pursued a passive strategy of modernization, in which the adoption of the new technology is primarily determined by the need to replace obsolete or faulty existing control systems. Within such an approach, the introduction of new technology is regarded as equipment replacement and digital control systems are used mainly to perform conventional control strategies." [Quadros Carvalho (1992, pg.135)].

The second point which must be taken into consideration with regard to the process of CA automation in the BNSI is the diffusion of new organizational techniques. The apparently fast rate at which some of these techniques (especially quality control circles) were adopted in the early 1980s, was followed by an equally fast decrease. Fleury (1988) points out that this was because most enterprises realized that the new pattern of organization would imply further and deeper changes than they were ready to embrace.

A possible reason for this cautious attitude is the fact that a large number of enterprises in Brazil fail to see the importance of bringing together organizational improvements along with capital embodied technological changes. According to a survey done by Neder (1989), in São Paulo state (largest industrial concentration in the country) only 10% of industries see technological development as an integral matter with organizational changes. Most of these industries are in informatics and industrial automation. Another 20% make some attempts to adapt new technologies to the cultural environment and to the characteristics of the workforce. The remaining 70% use technology as a 'closed package'. In the latter case, then, the results of acquiring new machines and equipments are undermined. Given that the adoption of new organizational techniques such as 'just-in-time' and 'kan-ban' come hand-in-hand with CA automation, this attitude from managers either inhibits or minimize the impact of the latter, or both [56].

4.7 The Brazilian telecommunications sector

a) Introduction

Most research concerning the emerging IT techno-economic paradigm emphasizes the role of telecommunication infrastructure in facilitating the changes that are expected to take place under the new paradigm. Telecommunication networks and services are seen as essential elements for both the organization and usage of information and the coordination and management of production systems. Moreover, telecommunications is seen as a basic requirement for industries' competitiveness and for countries to build dynamic comparative advantages in the ever more complex production networks that are being boosted in the industrialized world.

Despite the relevance that is given to the sector - "the most critical area for influencing the 'nervous system of modern society" [CEC (1987)] - the new roads that the microelectronics-based digital 'revolution' opened to telecommunications from the 1970s onwards have presented new challenges. These challenges affect both the manufacturers of telecommunication equipments and the ever more heterogeneous and complex systems of publicly and privately operated components of telecommunication services industry. As for the telecommunication equipments sectors, the change from an electromechanics to a microelectronics technological base has opened opportunities for new entrants and the search for synergies through stronger relationships with other sectors of the electronics complex. With respect to the telecommunication services industry, the profusion of opportunities that have been opened by technical solutions in telecommunications under the new paradigm have not always been 'matched' by institutional solutions in pace with the ever changing qualitative and quantitative changes that have been taking place in the sector, both locally and internationally [57].

In Brazil the major changes in telecommunications took place with the implementation of the the second national development plan - 1974/1979 (II PND) [58]. Under the general framework of that plan, the government committed itself to three main objectives with respect to the country's telecommunications system. Firstly, it was to accelerate the expansion of a dependable, efficient and comprehensive telecommunications infrastructure. Secondly, the ownership of the supply of telecommunications equipment was to become increasingly dominated by Brazilians. Finally, the dependence on foreign technology sources was to decrease radically through the provision by a government's R&D centre of a technological base in line with the latest digital technology.

This section examines the changes that took place in the BNSI's telecommunications sector from the perspective of the first two areas that were emphasized under the II PND and which have in many ways shaped the sector's performance since the 1970s (the R&D part is examined in Chapter 6). The analysis privileges not only the provision of telecommunication services itself, but also the production of telecommunication equipment. The importance of the supply of telecommunications services has been compared with the 'highways of the new techno-economic paradigm' because of their role in providing the necessary infrastructure for the flow of information services which characterizes the production networks which are being built around the world. As for the production of telecommunication equipment, its importance is related to the capability of the BNSI to interact with its counterparts in the industrialized world in an industry which is 'core' to the new paradigm.

102

b) Telecommunications services in Brazil

The nationalization of CTB (a subsidiary of Canadian Traction Light and Power Company which by 1960 accounted for over 70% of existing telephones in Brazil) and the creation of the Ministry of Communications in the second half of the 1960s are two landmarks for the country's provision of telecommunication services. Both measures took place with strong political backing from the military bureaucracy (telecommunication was seen as a matter of 'national security') and from their nationalist civilian counterparts.

Despite this government commitment to the sector in the 1970s, Brazil still ranks poorly against other countries. Table 4.15 shows that whilst it took twenty years to improve the country's telephone density by 50% between 1948 and 1968, in the six years between 1974 and 1980 that density increased more than 200%. Nevertheless, Brazil's telephone density (number of telephones/ 100 inhabitants) is about 60% of that of South Korea and less than that of other Latin American countries like Mexico, Argentina and Colombia [AFCPqD (1991)].

Table 4.15
Telephone services in Brazil in selected years

Year	No. of telephones (1000s)	Telephone density
1948	484	1.30
1968	1.660	1.88
1974	2.917	2.70
1980	7.535	6.20
1983	9.300	7.80
1990	9.879	6.50

Sources: Hobday (1985) and TELEBRASIL, Jan.-Feb./1992

According to TELEBRAS, the demand for new telephone lines was throughout the second half of the 1980s, on average, 20% higher than the supply [59]. Table 4.16 shows that the poor performance of the supply of telecommunications in the 1980s is due to the combination of three factors. Firstly, investment per year in real terms dropped from an average of 3.3 billion dollars between 1973 and 1980 to an average of less than 1,8 billion dollars between 1981 and 1989. Secondly, the anti-inflationary policies followed by the government imposed on the telecommunications system price controls which deteriorated the tariff collected by the system in more than 70% between 1972 and 1988. Thirdly, the telecommunication tax which was created in the 1960s in order to supply proper funding for the system, was diverted to the general budget of the federal government and little of it was applied in the telecommunications system. As a result, the percentage share in

GDP of investments in telecommunications dropped from 1.08% in 1976 to .43% in 1990 [Botelho et al. (1992)].

Table 4.16
The Brazilian telecommunications system: investment, tariff and the 'telecommunication tax'

Year	Investiment(a)	Tariff(b)	Telecom. Tax (US$ 1000) Collected	Used
1976	3,589	102,6	227,9	171,7
1977	3,202	100,9	289,8	205,8
1978	2,763	92,0	488,9	303,6
1979	2,319	85,0	419,2	164,1
1980	1,402	63,2	414,5	177,0
1981	1,814	55,9	512,9	204,1
1982	1,958	51,0	631,8	278,8
1983	1,180	41,5	401,4	94,5
1984	1,031	36,6	366,6	39,1
1985	1,059	30,4	317,5	61,6
1986	1,410	24,3	364,0	zero
1987	1,581	24,4	373,4	zero
1988	2,081	26,3	389,6	zero

(a) - In constant US$1000
(b) - 1972 = 100
Source: TELEBRAS quoted in AFCPqD (1991)

The under-funding of the sector has not only slowed down the pace at which the country was improving its telecommunications infrastructure but has also decreased the reliability of the services. Thus, "over the second half of the eighties, the quality of telephone services declined considerably. The number of failed local calls, which was below average by international comparisons in the beginning of the last decade, was 25 per cent of all calls in 1990. The number of crossed lines and wrong numbers also continued to increase. Pundits joke that TELEBRAS invented the free conference call." [Botelho et al. (1992), p. 30].

Despite these set-backs, the telecommunications infrastructure of the BNSI has been diversified and made its services available to an ever larger geographic area of the country. In 1990, over 13,000 localities were serviced by telephone lines, 20% of them with long distance access and about 10% with international access. There were over 120 thousand telex subscribers, and more than 17,000 data communication equipment leased. Moreover, EMBRATEL [60] in recent years has been increasing its investment in the development of an intelligent network and related services. In 1990, for example, over US$900 million were invested in packet data transmission, private data communication, telex, and electronic mail networks. Its investment programmes also provide for the complete installation of a new fiber-optic cable between Brazil and the United States by 1995 and to finish installation of a long distance fiber-optic network linking the country's two main metropoles (São Paulo and Rio de Janeiro). New satellites are also being planned to be launched by 1995 which will more than double (from 48 to 104) the number of broadcasting channels. This is meant to meet the rising demand created by the expansion of new information technologies and facsimiles [61].

c) The Brazilian telecommunications equipment industry

The full nationalization of telecommunication services in the 1970s came hand-in-hand with industrial and technological policies which had a radical impact on the structure of the sector's manufacturing side that until then was completely dominated by multinational corporations.   According to Hobday (1990) the presence of foreign enterprises in telecom activities in Brazil evolved in three stages. In the first one - that of transfer of production site - major foreign companies (Siemens, Ericsson, Phillips, and ITT) began by establishing assembly plants in the country in the 1940s. Most of these assembly plants were transformed into manufacturing sites in the 1950s and 1960s. The second stage was that of transfer of ownership to Brazilians which took place in the 1970s. During the implementation of the second national development plan (II PND - 1974/1979), the Brazilian government used its purchasing power in order to force foreign manufactures to come into partnership with local financial groups. A third stage took place along with the transfer of ownership when, in the case of Ericsson, unlike previous technology contracts, the agreement with the parent company in Sweden involved a substantial transfer of the core technological elements of the central exchange system.

The adoption of explicit industrial and technological policies was used by the government in order to take advantage of the 'windows of opportunities' that were being opened to late-comers due to changes in the sector's technological base.   Besides the creation of new sources of financing for investment in the sector, state-owned TELEBRAS (the Brazilian telecom) used its monopsonist's purchasing power [62] to pursue both increasing control over production by local enterprises and their greater technological autonomy. The former was made easier by the changes in the technological base of the sector - from electromechanical technologies to the more flexible microelectronic networks - which implied that the multinationals which were already established in the country (the four mentioned above plus NEC) did not have any specific technological advantage over new-coming local producers.

The government followed two strategies in order to strengthen local production. In the first place, it took the burden of high risk investments in R&D and human resources formation. Secondly, the government promoted local industrial capabilities through its preferential acquisition of local enterprises' production. The result of the complementing strategies is that the sector by the mid-1980s presented a completely different configuration to that of the late 1960s/early 1970s. The market structure changed in favour of greater local production, less concentration and increased technological autonomy.

The degree of diminishing internationalization of the sector, however, depends on which definition of local producer is used. As shown in Table 4.17, the more restricted definition used by SEI (the special secretariat for informatics) makes the results pledged by MINICOM's (Ministry of Communications) accounts less impressive. Another critical aspect of these achievements is rooted in the strategy used. That is, local producers became financially dependent on TELEBRAS (since there was no export promotion policy for the sector) and technologically dependent of CPqD (the telecommunications R&D centre established by state-owned TELEBRAS).

Table 4.17
Revenue sharing in the telecom equipment industry

			Participation of local enterprises			
Year	Larger 4	Larger 10	Larger 4 Criterion*		Larger 10 Criterion*	
			SEI	MINICOM	SEI	MINICOM
1974	90%	n.a.	0%	0%	0%	0%
1980	65%	97%	0%	77%	4%	56%
1983	61%	93%	16%	100%	20%	100%
1984	59%	86%	15%	100%	26%	100%
1985	51%	69%	10%	100%	29%	100%
1986	50%	69%	19%	100%	37%	100%

* The major difference between the criteria adopted by SEI and MINICOM is that whilst for the former Brazilian nationals must hold at least 70% of total shares and 100% of voting shares in order for a firm to be considered local, for the latter a minimum of 51% of voting capital in local hands is required.
Source: Moreira (1989)

An important implication of the policies aimed at fostering local industrial and technological capabilities in the telecomm sector is the proliferation of local firms (more than 120) supplying inputs for the TELEBRAS system. According to Hobday (1985) local firms have progressed from the production of relatively simple equipment and technology for HF and VHF used in transmission to more sophisticated areas of transmission equipment together with terminals for telephone and telegraph. Moreover, "today local Brazilian firms play a very important role as an alternative source of products and technology for TELEBRAS. Some of the larger Brazilian firms are actively engaged in technological investments and have built up their own R&D departments." (ibid., p. 52)

These positive results achieved by the sector between 1974 and 1984 made the Ministry of Communications under the government of the 'new republic' (1985/90) move away from more interventionist policies. The justification given by officials of the new government for a shift in the intent of industrial policy was that local enterprises had already achieved a 'certain degree of maturity'. Decisions concerning the key issue of the new 'purchasing model' to be adopted, however, were postponed for two reasons. This was, firstly because of problems that arose between producers and state-owned TELEBRAS with indexation of invoices under the heterodox stabilization programmes (specially the 'Cruzado Plan' in 1986 and the 'Bresser Plan' in 1987); secondly, because the discussions concerning the definition of what was to be considered local producers became the focus of much attention during the debates on the Constituent Congress of 1987/88.

In this sense, it can be said that the sector moved from a policy which was strongly in favour of establishing local production capabilities in the 1970s/ early 1980s to a no-policy in the second half of the eighties. This is in great contrast with what took place in major industrialized countries (Germany and France, for example) and in NICs (South Korea, for instance) where there were explicit policies towards the strengthening of their telecommunications equipment industry due to the central role played by the sector as a whole in the shaping of the international division of labour under the new paradigm.

4.8 Summing up

The analysis of the BNSI's economic domain carried out in this chapter puts into perspective the perverse effects that the country's unstable economic situation has had on agents' reaction to the challenges and opportunities under the new techno-economic paradigm. In this respect, it is not only the deteriorating economic conditions that matters. The short-term policies implemented to 'combat' inflation, and the debt and fiscal crises, not only made each of these problems worse but they also undermined agents' confidence in the country's future economic perspective. This deterioration of agents' confidence was a major set-back for the BNSI at a time of a changing paradigm.

A second 'given' economic condition under which the BNSI operated throughout the 1980s was the way the country's industrial base is structured on state-owned, local, and multinational enterprises. The analysis of this triple alliance stresses that, even though one can say that past policies have been quite liberal to foreign capital and/or strongly statist, they have, in general, ensured a significant interaction scheme between MNCs, SOEs and their local partners in the country's production system.

It is not an easy task to establish under which rules the interactions between MNCs-LCs-SOEs can have a more positive impact on the rate at which diffusion of technological capabilities should take place under the new techno-economic paradigm [63]. The associated-dependent character of the Brazilian socio-economic formation, however, makes unreasonable the use of neo-liberal 'recipes' for industrial development. Their postulate that new technological capabilities occur 'naturally' through competition in the international market can be rejected on the grounds of dynamic comparative advantages which concentrate and centralize economic growth amongst few countries and technological development amongst few enterprises [64]. As emphasized in Chapter 2 the emergence of a new techno-economic paradigm can increase even more these processes of concentration and centralization. The recognition of this phenomenon is an important indication that the role of the state is not to be taken for granted. New forms of regulation and new tasks for SOEs and local private enterprises have to be sought in order to strengthen the system of innovations of the associated-dependent Brazilian socio-economic formation.

Similarly, it is naive to appraise the MNCs' contribution in the BNSI simply by comparing their R&D expenditures with those of their headquarters or those of domestic firms, private or state- owned [65]. This more nationalistic approach underestimates the 'collective entrepreneurship' triggered by the 'learning-by-interacting' process and the importance of MNCs in it at times of changing paradigm.

The diversification of the country's exports was also presented in this chapter as a sign of strength of the BNSI. The diversification of exports into manufactures were interpreted as an instrument for the BNSI's economic domain to keep in close relation with changes that are taking place - even in 'traditional' industries - due to alterations in the techno-economic paradigm. Nevertheless, emphasis was given to the dynamic nature of international competition and the role played by technology on the different countries' positions in the international division of labour. Moreover, attention was drawn to policy-makers' inability in the past to use the country's export promotion policies as explicit means to strengthen its competitiveness in technology-intensive goods and services.

Another aspect of the analysis of the BNSI's economic domain highlighted in this chapter was its machinery and equipments sector. The chapter presented evidence that this key industry of the system has been keeping in touch with its technological frontier. Despite the heterogeneous way by which new technologies have been diffused within the industry, the use of technology from parent companies by foreign subsidiaries and the licensing of foreign technology by some local enterprises have been complemented by in-house R&D in such way that a continuous learning process has been taking place.

The pace at which the machinery and equipment industry is following what is taking place in the world frontier, however, has been inadequate mainly because of the country's economic conditions. Moreover, the lack of industrial and technology policies has left the sector's enterprises and its users no other alternative besides following a defensive strategy with respect to what is taking place on their technological frontier. The sufficient conditions, then, for the Brazilian machinery and equipment sector to take part in the production and technological networks that are being built amongst industrialized countries depend on political and economic commitments which go beyond the response to market forces. The need for political and economic commitments is not new to the industry. After all, under Brazil's pattern of associated-dependency, the build-up of production and technological capabilities in the machinery and equipment sector have been the result of long-established industrial policies rather than the response to market signals.

The importance of industrial policies established in the past has also been emphasized with respect to two 'core' industries under the new paradigm, i.e. informatics and telecommunications. The country's early entry in these two strategic industries has created technological and production capabilities in the BNSI which may enable Brazil to change the form of its dependency under the new techno-economic paradigm. Adverse macroeconomic conditions and the weakened position of industrialists in the power alliance during the eighties, however, have driven these industries into a 'survival' strategy.

In the informatics industry the 'survival' strategy was made easier because the 'market reserve' gave local enterprises a time-span under which they could build up technological and production capabilities without suffering from international competition. As a result, throughout the 'lost decade', the industry expanded and diversified its technological and production base. Moreover, it functioned as a 'motor' for the technological up-dating of the BNSI's industrial base. The diffusion of computer-based automation in the BNSI strongly benefited from closer user-producer relations which were made easier by the existence of local production and technological capabilities in IT. Furthermore, the learning process which took place in the BNSI thanks to the country's early acquisition of these capabilities has also strengthened its capacity to negotiate technological transfers under the new techno-economic paradigm.

A 'survival strategy' in the telecommunications industry was also possible in the 1980s thanks to past policies. These policies took advantage of technological 'windows of opportunities' that were opened in telecommunications in the 1970s in order to establish a more autonomous technological and production base in Brazil. As a result, the country has today a well-established telecommunications equipment industry, and the technological capabilities necessary to up-grade its telecommunications services in line with the requirements of the new techno-economic paradigm.

Summing-up, despite the economic crises in which the country was involved throughout the 1980s, and the short-sightness of the policies pursued to overcome them, evidence was presented in this chapter which indicates the strengthening of technological and production capabilities in the BNSI's economic domain. Having said that, it is important to bear in mind that these technological and production capabilities by themselves cannot be seen as sufficient to ensure the country's participation in the networks which are being built in the industrialized countries under the new paradigm. This is so because changing the form of dependency at a time of shifts in the technological base of world development is not a matter that can be dealt with just by economic forces and technological capabilities. The challenges that are posed to institutions in Brazil if the country is to take advantage of 'windows of opportunities' under the new paradigm are the subject of the next chapter.

Notes

1. The increasing importance of inflation in public debate in Brazil was followed by major contribution of academics concerning the main features of the inflationary process under the specificities of the Brazilian socio-economic formation. Simonsen (1990) presents a summary of the main theoretical contributions of Brazilian economists in the subject whilst Lara Rezende (1990) and Modiano (1990) summarize the major attempts to curb inflation in Brazil during the 1980s.

2. Cardoso and Fishlow (1990) and Velloso, ed. (1990c) discuss key aspects of the relationship between foreign debt and development in Brazil throughout the eighties.

3. Bresser Pereira (1990) discusses major aspects of the linkages between external debt and the fiscal crisis in Brazil.

4. See, for example, Malan (1978/1982).

5. The only exception being the fall in industrial output during the first years of the 1930s due to an international crisis. Nevertheless, by 1933, industrial production was already at the levels of 1929.

6. The fragility of the many orthodox 'pacotes' (economic stabilization programmes under the authoritarian regime) can be illustrated by the fact that seven letters of intent were sent to the I.M.F. between 1983 and 1984. The economic teams of the first civilian government (1985/90) were even more 'creative'. Four heterodox anti-inflationary shocks (two

in 1986, one in 1987 and one in 1989) and one orthodox attempt in 1988 were tried. For an analysis of these programmes up to 1987, see Cardoso and Fishlow (1990). For a summary of the heterodox shocks, see Castro and Ronci (1991) and Rebouças (1990).

7. This is not to minimize the fact that between 1979 and 1989 the Brazilian cabinet had six different ministers of the exchequer and five different ministers of economic planning and an even larger number of chairman of the Central Bank.

8. The way the majority of the Brazilian economic elite tried to avoid any confrontation with the international community with respect to the problems of the country's external debt is another facet of its associated-dependent development. "The Brazilian debt problem has not had a sovereign solution because the country's elite has been afraid to challenge the interests of international capitals with which it wants to be integrated." [Bresser Pereira (1989), p. 58, my translation].

9. For a theoretical contribution regarding the inertial component of inflation, see Arida and Lara-Resende (1985).

10. For a theoretical discussion of the ineffectiveness of domestic policies in situations of persistent external imbalances, see Paloni (1992).

11. That is not to imply that the Brazilian elite has not been capable of designing its development project. The challenges that were imposed to the country's development process by the structural changes that were taking place in the world economy as a whole could be felt already in the mid-seventies. Gomes and Leite (1978) summarizes the positions of industrialists, government officials and leaders of the opposition party regarding the necessity to search for a new phase of industrialization as the import-substitution one was about to finish with the investment programme sponsored by the second national development plan (II PND - 1974/79).

12. Berg and Sachs (1988) point out the difficulties that are imposed by income inequality on budgetary control. According to them, these difficulties occur because income inequality raises the pressure for redistributive policies toward the poor and working class; enhance the power of economic elites to resist taxation; decrease the political legitimacy of governments that defend the existing distribution of income; contribute to direct labour militancy; more generally, impede the development of a social consensus around policies that promote development in the long term, but which might impose costs on some social groups in the short term.

13. One can see in these priorities the re-emergence of the liberal ideas which opposed so fiercely the Brazilian industrialization project since its beginning (see chapter 2). The chairman of the Central Bank in the beginning of the 1980s, Carlos Langoni (whose academic links have been with Getulio Vargas Foundation the fortress of liberal ideas under the guidance of Eugenio Gudin and his heir Mario Simonsen) started to point to the priorities for agriculture and minerals as a response to the country's 'legitimate comparative advantages'.

14. Malan (1982) was one of the first to criticize the belief of the country's economy 'czar' under the authoritarian regime. For the latter (Delfin Neto), the roll-over of Brazil's foreign debt was guaranteed by the high liquidity in the international market and/or by the level of indebtedness which the country had already reached by the end of the seventies. In response to the fact that foreign debt had jumped from US$ 49.9 billion in 1979 to US91.1 billion in 1984, Delfin Neto used to be apologetic of the thought according to which 'beyond a certain level, debt is not a problem of the debtor but should be a concern of the creditors'.

15. The political dimension of the Brazilian foreign debt is often mentioned by mainstream economists such as Sachs (1987), Dornbusch and Cardoso (1989) and Cohen (1991). The importance given to a political discussion of the debt (which most recognized would imply some sort of reduction in the stock of the debt and its rescheduling) gradually faded as it became clear that the government was not capable of carrying on the internal counterparts of a broader stabilization and adjustment programme which needed to involve a reform of the state and its financing.

16. In this respect, the major difference between my analysis and that by Bresser Pereira (1989) is that he avoids emphasis on the continuum in social and economic policies throughout the 1980s. That might be so because of his early political commitments to the possibilities of the 'new republic' representing a possible new wave of political and economic democracy in the country. Nonetheless he agrees with Welffort (1984) that what took place in Brazil was a 'conservative transition' in the sense that it was not capable of incorporating a larger popular base in its pact of domination.

17. According to Velloso (1990) in 1987 explicit subsidies and fiscal incentives (to sectors and regions) amounted to more than 3.3% of GDP. Furthermore, the wage bill of the federal government was increase in real terms between 1984 and 1988 in 101% in the executive, 132% in the legislative and 198% in the judiciary.

18. "Capital flight refers to the accumulation of foreign assets by the private sector of an economy, often at the same time that the public sector is incurring sharply rising external debts." [Sachs, ed. (1990), p. 13].

19. Opinion polls showed degrees of popularity for the civilian government in 1988 (11% good and 64% poor) worse than those achieved by the military-ruler when the 'Diretas Já' (popular movement pressing for direct elections for the Presidency) was at its highest in 1984 (10% good and 40.5% poor) [*Folha de São Paulo*, 13-3-88 and 18-3-84, respectively].

20. This is not to say that they have all followed the same strategy of property control and technological capabilities.

21. According to Chesnais (1988) the notion of internationalization designates "the wide set of economic mechanisms and relationships whereby previously fairly separate national economies become increasingly interrelated and interdependent with one another in all areas of economic activity." (ibid., p. 497).

22. Hagerdoorn and Schakenraad (1990) provides an account of these cooperation schemes taking place in R&D intensive areas such as IT, biotechnology and new materials. Freeman (1991) discusses both the historical content of networks of innovators and the main features of those networks that are being built for new technologies. Whilst seeing similarities between the networks which took place under the 'electrical and heavy engineering techno-economic paradigm' and under the 'fordist mass production t-e p' and those that are happening with new technologies, Freeman calls attention for the fact that "IT not only greatly facilitates various forms of networking, but has inhereted characteristics, such as rapid change in design, customization, flexibility and so forth, which, together with its systemic nature and the variety and complexity of applications, will lead to a permanent shift of industrial structure and behaviour. This will assign to networking a greatly enhanced role in the future." (ibid., p. 511).

23. According to Chesnais (1988) inter-firm cooperation schemes can fall in a wide range whose 'limits' are markets and hierarchies. Amongst the types identified by Chesnais, it is worth emphasizing the following agreements which have been used by firms with a view to producing, acquiring and/or commercially exploiting technology in common: university-based inter-firm cooperative research projects; government-industry cooperative national or international research projects; research corporations (private joint-venture companies focused on generic technologies).

24. For a discussion of the market reserve for informatics see Schmitz and Hewitt (1992). Baptista (1987) makes an assessment of the 'import platform' established for the electronic consumer goods sector in Manaus.

25. The involvement of these banks in informatics (which has resulted in the accumulation of technological capabilities in banking automation), follows an international pattern of big enterprises diversifying their investment programmes towards hi-tech activities. Andreff (1984) exemplifies this tendency with the cases of Schering and Standard Oil of California in biotechnology; of Exxon in micro-processors and office technology.

26. From a situation where the delocation of production within a country replaced the exports previously made to that country from the MNCs' home base, to a position where MNCs use affiliates to ship products (generally intermediary goods) to the parent company or to other affiliates.

27. The sample surveyed represent about 17% of sales of the 500 largest enterprises in Brazil; 68% of local and state-owned enterprises and 81% of MNCs surveyed have more than 500 employees.

28. The use of new organizational techniques comprise both those OT internal to the firms ('quality control circles', 'total quality control', 'just-in-time' and 'group of technology') and with relation to suppliers ('external just-in-time' and 'total quality control').

29. According to Boyer (1988a) the concept of international regime is defined by "the set of rules and conventions which organize the exchange of commodities, the location of production units (via direct foreign investment) and the financing of external disequilibria." (ibid., p. 74).

30. In this sense, the technological capabilities and competitiveness of these sectors provide further evidences for the reasoning of Teitel and Toumi (1986), according to which export-diversification is a 'natural' consequence of the import-substitution industrialization process.

31. For an assessment of Brazil's competitiveness in six industrial complexes, see Araujo Jr. et al. (1989).

32. Bauman (1989b) provides a critique of Brazilian export programmes from the perspective that they increased the profitability of participant enterprises in a way that resulted in barriers to new entrants in their industries and to higher concentration in the domestic market. Clements and McClain (1991) criticize export promotion in Brazil on the grounds that they increased the veto power that MNCs collectively could exert on

the country's export sector in times when public policy is perceived to affect adversely the interests of the community of MNCs.

33. For an analysis of the South Korean experience, for example, see Amsden (1989).

34. For an analysis of the response of the capital goods sector to the demands for increasingly specialized machinery in the early stages of industrialization in the developed countries, see Rosenberg (1976).

35. Such a performance has to be seen with caution because this was an 'atypical' period during the 1980s in the sense that the economy grew.

36. The importance of looking at the reaction of the machine tools industry is related to the fact that it is both user of the new technologies and producer of machinery incorporating the new technologies.

37. Porteous (1992) reports on an exception to this general rule by presenting the case of the largest local enterprise in the sector which has been setting the standards for local production of universal machine tools. Given its previous efforts to acquire and master foreign technology in order to establish itself in the production of CNC lathes, and its conviction that its ability to maintain its leading position in the local market would depend on having strong capability in CNC machinery production, this local firm took three steps towards strengthening its technological capabilities. Firstly, it decided to manufacture the electronic controls in-house. Secondly, it imported CNC units and made considerable efforts in order to build up component suppliers reliability which would allow it to assembly the hardware. Finally, it brought a foreign expert to direct the development of an in-house team to ensure sound basic software skills. Besides being far-sighted with respect to software, the enterprise also "installed over a hundred of its own CNC machine into its plants in order to maximize the opportunities of learning at first hand the potential of CNC." (ibid., p. 232).

38. The greater usage of CNC machine tools allows easier shifts in the production process by making possible the formation of 'cells of working stations' in which all operations are concentrated.

39. For more recent appraisals of the Brazilian informatics policy, see Baptista et al. (1990), Rosenthal and Moreira (1991), Meyer-Stamer (1992), and Schimitz and Hewitt (1992).

40. According to Piragibe (1988), imports of electronic data processing equipment increased more than 60% between 1969 and 1974.

41. Rosenthal and Moreira (1991) points out that in the early 1970s there was already the perception amongst some segments of the country's military

and economic elite about the importance of the computer if the country was to pursue its development goals with political and military autonomy.

42. The market reserve policy was not to be applied to mainframe computers which continued to be sold by the subsidiaries of IBM and UNISYS already operating in the country.

43. The market reserve scheme was later extended to other sectors of the informatics industry in order to encompass peripherals and equipment of banking and services automation.

44. Rosenthal and Moreira (1991) stress that up-to the passing of the Informatics Lay by Congress in 1984, no deadlines had been established with respect to the prevalence of the general concept of market reserve in the Brazilian informatics industry.

45. For an analysis of the mobilization of ideological and institutional resources towards the goal of technological autonomy in the Brazilian computer industry, see Adler (1988).

46. For a review of the different strategies used during the 'CAPRE period' (1972-1979), the 'SEI period' (1979-1984), and the 'CONIN period' (1984-1990), see Rosenthal and Moreira (1991).

47. Baptista et al. (1990) show that, whilst in the first phase of licensing foreign technology for the internal production of superminicomputers, Brazilian firms were only able to have access to technology which had been available in the international market for over 2-4 years, by the late-1980s the gap had been shortened to less than a year. For a review of cases where the ability of the Brazilian informatics industry to keep-up with the world frontier is questioned, see Meyer-Stamer (1992).

48. The major criticisms of those who see room for improving the existing policy refer to the high degree of vertical integration [Baptista et al. (1990) and Cassiolato et al. (1992)]; to the 'mismatches' between the informatics policy and those of other sectors in the electronic complex [Baptista (1987); Pessini (1986); and Rosenthal (1987)]; and the gap between 'hardware policies' and those which refer to software [Gaio (1992)]. As for those who oppose the policy, the main criticisms refer to the high price charged for locally produced equipment 'vis-`a-vis' those prevailing in the American market [Frishtak (1990)]. The strength of this criticism diminishes, however, when the comparison is made with prices in other industrialized countries. Meyer-Stamer (1992) points out that the price differential fall from 2/1 to 1/.65-.75 when the comparisons changes its base from the USA to Germany. Furthermore, price differentials between Brazilian producers and those of core countries is

116

not a specificity of the informatics industry but a perverse characeristic of the Brazilian industrial sector as a whole.

49. The high growth rate of the Brazilian informatics industry (annual average of 23% between 1981 and 1986) was still small when compared to that achieved by the South Koreans (95% per year in the same period) [Evans and Tigre (1989b)]. Moreover, whilst in the second half of the eighties the South Korean government strengthened its political commitment to the industrialization process under the new techno-economic paradigm [Amsden (1989)], in Brazil the perverse combination of economic crisis (see section 4.1) and the lack of institutional 'sign-posts' (see chapter 5) was taking place.

50. The electronics complex comprises the electronic consumer-goods industry, the informatics industry, the microelectronic industry and the telecommunications equipment industry.

51. This characteristic of the Brazilian market is not specific to the informatics industry but is a result of the country's income distribution emphasized in Chapter 2 and in section 4.2.

52. According to data presented by Baptista et al. (1990), between 1981 and 1988 imports by local informatics producers represented in average less than 15% of their total gross revenues.

53. During interviews I had with directors of small- and medium-size enterprises in 1990, one point that was stressed was that they would hardly have taken the risk of making even minor technical changes in their production processes if they were to depend on foreign technology. That was so because, firstly, the uncertainties brought by the new technology were diminished because "the local supplier was close by and spoke the same language". This sort of reasoning reinforces the importance of national identity in user-producer relations stressed in Chapter 3. Secondly, they felt they did not depend on the situation of the balance of payments in order to be allowed to buy repair parts and services from abroad when they were needed. It is obvious that both constraints diminish when referring to bigger companies because they are better staffed and have closer and easier links with the government's bureaucracy.

54. Tigre et al. (1989) suggest that one of the main reason why automation in the Brazilian steel industry is so behind other countries (the technological gap is estimated between 45% and 90%) is the low cost of labour in Brazil.

55. That is not to say the complex has not invested in R&D. Even though the level of R&D expenditures in the complex (between 1% and 2% of sales),

is below what is spent in the industrialized world, it is higher than the national average. Suzigan coord. (1989) have pointed out that technological capability within this complex has been accomplished mainly through learning-by-using the existing plants.

56. A survey done by Salm, coord. (1990) with 135 leading enterprises (88 domestic and 47 MNCs), shows that despite the fact that more than 80% of both local and foreign companies use automation in project, production and planning, the percentage of domestic firms adopting new organizational techniques is smaller than MNCs in all three areas.

57. An important reason for such a 'mismatch' between the technological possibilities and some of the institutional 'solutions' found so far is the fact that telecommunication is still seen as an infrastructure which generates externalities for other activities. Mansell (1990) emphasizes that this infrastructure analogy must be overcome because networks are not simply conduits for information. In her view, they are integral to activities that are 'glued' together by software applications.

58. That is not to deny that the development of telecommunications in Brazil has its institutional roots in the establishment of the National Code of Telecommunications in 1962; in the creation of EMBRATEL (state-owned enterprise encharged of international communications) and the National Fund of Telecommunications (FNT), both in 1965; and in the establishment in 1972 of a state-owned holding company - TELEBRAS - which was to supervise the operation of telephone services and to manage the FNT.

59. The repressed demand was even higher in the early 1980s due to the stabilization policies followed by the government which in most cases implied in cuts in the investment programmes of its enterprises.

60. EMBRATEL is a state-owned enterprise created in 1965 and charged with the implementation and exploitation of national and international telecommunications trunk operations.

61. The diversification of telecommunications services has also attracted private investors. They already operate mobile cellular phone services with a total of 12,500 lines in the pilot operational services implemented in Rio de Janeiro and Brasilia. Botelho et. al. (1992) estimate the 1995 potential market in one million terminals and report on the interest of major international telecommunications enterprises in bidding in partnership with Brazilian firms for mobile cellular phone contracts in the metropolitan areas of São Paulo, Fortaleza, Recife, Salvador, Belo Horizonte, Campinas, Curitiba, and Porto Alegre.

62. According to data presented by Moreira (1989), between 1977 and 1986 more than 80% of the sales of telecommunication equipments was done to the public sector in Brazil. In the later part of the 1980s there was a slight change in this pattern due to (late started and slowly moving) office automation and to private ventures in the transmission of voice and data. As for exports, they comprise less than 5% of the sector's sales. There are two complementary explanations for such a poor performance. On the one hand, the technologically more sophisticated equipments produced in core countries are more demanded by third world countries even though their needs do not necessarily require much sophistication. On the other hand, Brazil's international debt has not allowed a more aggressive sales with financing market strategy often used by industrialized countries.

63. A research project to assess the different experiences (market reserve, 'joint venture', 'import platform') in hi-tech sectors would certainly contribute to the design of policies more adequate to times of changing paradigm.

64. Cassiolato et al. (1992) point out the contribution of foreign computer firms to the building up of specialized supplier in Brazil. "Not voluntarily, though, but because government policy ('law of similars') forced them to buy locally. Thus the two bigger multinational subsidiaries making mainframes in Brazil have around four hundred different internal suppliers of parts and components. Such parts integrate products which are exported and have had their technical quality certified by agencies and associations responsible for technical standards in the US and Europe." (ibid., p. 283-84).

65. Braga and Matesco (1986) estimated that MNCs' contribution to R&D expenditures by the productive sector in Brazil was 8.4% in 1978, 5.4% in 1980 and 10.4% in 1982. Since their share of total sales is around 30% of the total, it is obvious that their R&D expenditure/sales ratio is much lower than that of domestic firms. This is not specific to Brazil, or for that matter to LDCs and/or NICs. After all, "even in larger European countries (...) governments had to rely on measures such as the use of real or threatened trade barriers and access to public purchasing (particularly in computers, telecommunications and semiconductor components) for getting MNCs to perform R&D locally." [Cassiolato et al. (1992), p. 292].

5 The institutional domain

5.1 Introduction

The main objective of this chapter is to present the institutional context within which the Brazilian national system of innovation is inserted. The analysis will present some basic differences between the institutional domain of national systems of innovation in core countries and those of a late-comer in the industrialization process.

Whilst most countries in the developed world have long-established legal frameworks under which stable relations between state and society can prevail, in the case of Brazil the long rule under an authoritarian regime brought these relations to deadlocks which had to be overcome politically in the 1980s. This has meant that, whilst in the core countries the centre of the institutional debate in the 1980s was concerned with the building up of new forms of interactions amongst firms, between capital and labour and amongst nations, in Brazil the major issue was how to build political institutions which could bridge the gap between an authoritarian regime and the long-awaited democracy. Moreover, whilst in the core countries part of the debate was concerned with building supra-national institutions that could strengthen their position in the emerging order under the new paradigm, in Brazil the major issue in public debate was how to bridge the gaps between the 'isles of economic modernity' and the 'continent of social needs and political instability' which have co-existed for more than 50 years. If in the core ountries the debate centred on the different forms of capitalist development [Albert (1991)], in Brazil the main discussion had not yet overcome aspects of the content under which its capitalist model should be built.

These constitute some of the reasons for the focus on the institutions at the centre of the country's political agenda rather than on any specificities of the debate concerned with technological development under the new techno-economic paradigm. Despite the evidence that is presented in this chapter that a concern with technological development exists amongst the country's economic and political elites, the major institutional change analyzed is that given by the debate during the Constituent Congress of 1987/88. That was the privileged forum of discussions concerned with two major aspects of the Brazilian socio-economic formation; firstly, with the institutionalization of forms of State/Society relations which are to be shaped under the recently established democratic regime; and secondly, with respect to the social dimensions of the country's development and with the still blurred approximations with respect to the economic model to be pursued.

The new Constitution has covered substantial ground in matters regarding the political rights of Brazilian society 'vis-à-vis' the State, and has established new grounds for inter-governmental relations which might affect the ways political support for technological development and its funding will take place in the future. Furthermore, ambiguities in the new Constitutions with respect to the roles to be played by the State, and by local and multinational enterprises in the country's economic process are presented as an illustration of the 'mismatches' between its institutional framework and its economic and social possibilities.

As in the analysis of the other domains, here there is not a 'prescription' that can be followed. The strength of the conceptual framework used in this book is exactly to search for singularities in local processes. These singularities make each national system of innovation more or less compatible with the interactions which are taking place amongst the other systems of innovation in the industrialized world. For this reason, besides the changes in the institutional framework that can be ascribed to the letter-of-intent of the new Constitution, the analysis of the institutional domain of the BNSI will privilege the perceptions of different agents with respect to the way they see the new techno-economic paradigm and the challenges it poses to the country's socio-economic formation.

The section that follows this introduction discusses the role of institutional rigidity and flexibility in providing a framework for innovation and change. The third section analyses aspects of Brazil's institutional path-dependence which widened the gap between economic and socio-political development. Section 4 highlights the new elements in Brazilian polity [1] due to its economic modernization and their tensions with the old institutional forms. Section 5 discusses these tensions as they were expressed in the Brazil's Constituent Congress of 1987/1988. The sixth section looks at the legislation which emerged from the new Constitution and examines some of its implications for the BNSI. Section 7 examines the perception that different actors - entrepreneurs, workers, politicians, bureaucrats, etc - have of the new techno-economic paradigm. The last section discusses how changes in the debate on technological development can contribute to the strengthening of the BNSI.

5.2 Institutions and modes of societalization

The concept of institutions has been defined in many ways. They regulate the competition for power (political institutions); they are concerned with the production and distribution of goods and services (economic institutions); they deal with the religious, artistic, and expressive activities and traditions in the society (cultural institutions); and they focus on the questions of marriage and the family and on the rearing of the young (kinship institutions) [Bullock et al. (1988)]. Consisting of both informal constraints (sanctions, taboos, custom, traditions, and codes of conduct) and formal rules (constitutions, laws, property rights), institutions in general terms "are humanly devised constraints that structure political, economic and social interactions." [North (1991), p. 97].

A basic feature of institutions is that they are informational devices drawn to reduce uncertainties. By reducing the amount of information needed for individual and collective action, institutions make society possible and are a fundamental building blocks in all societies [2]. As emphasized by Johnson (1992) institutions make society possible because they make it unnecessary to start life from scratch every day by being widely accepted as guidelines for social life, regardless of whether each member of society accepts them ideologically or politically.

From an economic point of view, the institutionalist tradition has stressed the time and place dimensions that characterize regularities of social behaviour. Economic behaviour is instituted, then, not because of some universal human characteristics, but rather through a process of enculturation. Moreover, by identifying learning and innovation with 'habits of thought' Veblen (1919) emphasized the role of institutions in shaping them both.

In a world characterized by innovative activities, uncertainty is an important aspect of economic life, and the existence of institutional set-ups at the different levels (of a specific firm, of a group of firms or of a country as a whole) become a central component of a system of innovation. In such a world, then, institutions move beyond the above mentioned characteristics of routines, and guiding every day life in order to work also as a framework for change.

The duality between stability (in order to make routines possible) and flexibility (needed to make changes feasible) which must characterize institutions if they are to perform their role in socio-economic life, poses a basic question. That is, which institutions and what aspects of them should be privileged at times when changes become necessary in order to overcome a situation of crisis. For the neo-Schumpeterians the scope for institutional changes is wider and more complex than the market solution prescribed by orthodox economics [3]. Thus, for Freeman and Perez (1984) the need for institutional changes ranges from those in the pattern of skills; to those governing industrial relations and worker participation; and to changes in social, political and legislative priorities [4]. For Lundvall (1992b), emphasis must be given to cooperation amongst actors which makes institutional flexibility a fundamental aspect of intra- and inter-firm relations, and of the different ways intra- and transnational political processes take place.

For the 'regulation approach' the major question regarding institutional stability/flexibility is how social cohesion and economic stability can be achieved and maintained despite the unremitting pressures of disrupting cleavages [5]. By linking economic stability and social cohesion in a more dynamic and integrated framework, the 'regulation approach' avoids the compartmentalization of the institutional issue into two spheres (economics and politics) as if they were separable [Elam (1990)].

As a consequence of the integration of political and economic institutions, causal powers are allocated to specific cultural and political forms. Under these circumstances, emphasis may be given to qualitatively different impacts of the same techno-economic forces in time and in space. Thus, the way the 'regulation approach' stresses the different institutional arrangements that exist amongst developed countries in response to changes in techno-economic forces [6] is similar to the emphasis given by Cardoso and Falleto (1979) to the peculiarities of national capitalism in the context of the undeveloped world.

Amongst the key concepts used by regulationists in order to stress the importance of the specificity of national contexts - such as accumulation regime, mode of regulation, industrial paradigm, mode of growth and mode of development - one that is particularly suitable for the analysis of the institutional domain of the BNSI is that of 'mode of societalization. It is defined by Jessop (1990) as a pattern of mass integration and social cohesion in such a way that when societalization is successful, there is both a 'historical bloc' and an 'hegemonic bloc', in Gramsci's terms (ibid., p. 43-44).

5.3 Some roots of Brazil's institutional path-dependence

The concept of 'mode of societalization' helps to understand the institutional framework under which the BNSI works because in the 1980s Brazil was still searching for a pattern of mass integration and social cohesion. This is a significant contrast between the Brazilian socio-economic formation and that of most industrialized countries. In the centre during the 1980s the major concern was with the breakdown of the 'growth compromises' and the dissolution of the 'protective frameworks' established in the post- II World War period [7]. In Brazil, however, the basic debate was centred on the ways to reconcile State and society in the transition from authoritarianism to democracy and on the alternative routes to build a 'capital-labour nexus' which could bring together politics of the masses and economic development.

In the centre the structural crisis was identified, amongst other tendencies, with growing social expenditures and with consumption patterns of the 'affluent worker' which could not be satisfied by conventional means of standardized production [Boyer (1988b)]. In Brazil the crisis was associated with a growing social debt in a situation where the great majority of the population had not yet known the true meaning of mass consumption [8]. The percentage of the work force covered by social security is still very low [less than 20% according to estimates made by Draibe et al. (1991)] and the 'safety net' provided by the Brazilian welfare state has concentrated about 40% of its benefits in less than 17% of the population which are in the highest income strata (Table 5.1).

Table 5.1
Brazil: Social benefits and income (1986)

Minimum wage per capita	Percentage of Total population	Percentage of Benefits
20 and more	0.3	0
10 to 20	1.0	4
5 to 10	3.0	14
2 to 5	12.0	21
1 to 2	18.0	21
1/2 to 1	24.0	22
1/4 and less	19.0	7

Source: World Bank, *Report of the Public Social Expenditure*, quoted in Draibe et al. (1991)

With respect to the ways the welfare state works in most core countries 'vis-à-vis' its development in Brazil, then, the institutional 'innovation gap' that exists between those countries and late-comer Brazil is greater than that which prevails in the economic domain. This is not just because the socio-political innovations have taken different forms in Brazil from those in countries of the industrialized world. These differences in forms also take place amongst the countries in the centre [9]. The problem is that in the case of Brazil - with close to 40% of the population people below the poverty line (see Table 4.2) - a pattern of mass integration and social cohesion has not been achieved yet in such a way to provide a stable framework for institutional innovations in areas such as capital/labour and inter-capital relations.

North (1991) points out that the institutional matrix of any country consists of an interdependent web of political and economic organizations characterized by massive increasing returns. From this perspective, then, the best way to look at the BNSI's institutional domain is through its path dependence.

Drawn from an approximation to the concept of path of technological change [David (1985) and Arthur (1989)], that of institutional path-dependence points to "historical structuring processes by which social developments become locked-in to relatively stable pathways or 'dynamic disequilibria'. ... [given the possibility of both positive and negative local feedback in a network context] ... A particular sequence of choices at the beginning of a process may lead to a self-estimulating mechanism which 'encloses' the development in a growth equilibrium that 'locks out' alternative development possibilities." [Hohn and Schneider (1991), p. 112].

Like the 'mismatches' stressed by Freeman and Perez (1988), under the path-dependence perspective, the content of institutional development does not necessarily follow a path in harmony with the socio-economic development which they are meant to support. That is, rigidity and flexibility of the institutional matrix is a possibility but not an inevitable process. The dichotomy between possibility and inevitability implies that making the most of the possibilities must be strongly related with breaks that take place with past institutional paths. The more is inherited from past institutional forms, the greater the constraints imposed on present choices and the less inevitable becomes structural changes [10].

Ferraz (1990) and Graham (1990), amongst others, emphasize that the low initial institutional set up costs of the Brazilian modernization process [11] have resulted in an institutional matrix in which pre-modern structures have both survived and become chronic. Moreover, these pre-modern structures have strengthened their position in the institutional matrix by perpetuating and expanding their practices in the country's political arena.

As a result, the institutional framework under which the BNSI is to face the challenges and opportunities of the new techno-economic paradigm must take into account three modes of political action which are embedded into Brazilian institutions: 'coronelismo', 'populismo' and 'autoritarismo' all three tempered by different degrees of nationalism [12]. For Camargo (1990) each mode has left a heritage that in many ways limits present options. This is even more so because Brazilian society and polity are strongly characterized by relationships and simultaneities rather than by sequences and interruptions [da Matta (1989)] in the sense that there are not 'breaks' but 'co-habitation' amongst different modes. That is, 'creative destruction' is not a common feature of Brazilian society and polity.

These characteristics of relationships and simultaneities are strongly reflected in the way different tiers of the elite are superimposed on the country's power structure. Camargo (1990) exemplifies that with the case of the Ministry of Industry and Trade (MIC). Under MIC's administration co--exist IAA (the federal institute of sugar and alcohol) representing the interests of an industry which dates back to the XVIII century; IBC (the federal institute of coffee) which represents the dynamic activities of the last part of

XIX century and beginning of the XX century; and SIDERBRAS (holding of state-owned steel companies) which represents the interest of the 'engine industry' of the 1950-1970s. For a short period of time during the 1980s MIC was also responsible for supervising the implementation of the informatics policy.

5.4 New entrants in Brazilian polity

The co-existence of different forms of institutional action in Brazil has been blamed as the main reason for the existing gap between the country's economic performance and its institutional matrix. Moreover, 'coronelismo', 'populismo' and 'autoritarismo' contribute to the fragility of the country's political parties and organizations. That is, a lag has been built between the country's economy and society and its institutional framework.

It is obvious that this does not mean that nothing has changed in the country's institutional framework. Despite all the set-backs of a system which has not been able to get rid of 'old' interests, institutional changes have taken place which have enabled the emergence of new arenas of disputes between 'old' and 'new'. The state apparatus has been shaped by a multitude of public organizations at the federal, state and local levels [13]. The political and social forces both within the state apparatus and in civil society in Brazil are giving shape to a regime which goes far beyond the still timid strengthening of party representation which has re-emerged with the democratic wave of the 1980s.

Some of these new social forces have been established in direct confrontation with old practices. Populism, for example, has been faced by the emergence in the 1970s and consolidation throughout the 1980s of a new labour movement which drives itself quite independently from the labour union structure that was first established by the government in the 1930s [14]. Centralism in the definition and implementation of government policies is being gradually replaced by the emergence of politically and financially stronger municipal and state governments [15].

Direct confrontation between 'old' and 'new' practices has also taken place in the sphere of entrepreneurial representation. The complexification and diversification of the Brazilian economy has pushed forward the establishment by entrepreneurs, side-by-side with the archaic political representation ensured by government rules, of new channels of socio-political representation for new industrial activities in the country [16]. ABICOMP (the association of industrialists in the computers and peripherals business) is an example of an association of entrepreneurs specifically connected to issues of technological development and industrial capabilities under the new techno-economic paradigm. Created in 1979, it played an important role in the establishment of the 'Informatics Law' which gave political legitimacy to the 'market reserve'. ABICOMP was also a key actor in the many negotiations which took place in the Constituent Congress with respect to the strengthening of indigenous technological capabilities [Mendes (1988)]. Its membership went from 64 members in 1989 to 80 in July 1990 which shows its representativeness at a time when the market reserve was under heavy pressure by the neo-liberal ideas of the new government.

The establishment in 1984 of ANPEI - an association of entrepreneurs particularly concerned with matters of technological development - is also an illustration of the emergence of BNSI-related pressure groups in the country's institutional matrix. Amongst its objectives, ANPEI stresses those of "representing the interests of industrial enterprises with respect to technological development; and studying and proposing solutions to the problems which hold back technological innovations in the industrial sector" [ANPEI (1988), p. 4]. Besides its wider objectives, ANPEI differs from ABICOMP in that whilst the latter presents strong 'nationalistic' content, the former has its membership spread amongst local (68%), state-owned (18%) and multinational companies (14%) [17].

More recently, at the end of 1989, the institute for the study of industrial development (IEDI) was created. Despite the fact that it is an association of 'thirty modern Brazilian industrialists', IEDI is not directly interested in matters regarding local/multinational; private/state-owned enterprises. IEDI's Executive-Director emphasizes (interviews) that these entrepreneurs decided to join their political efforts in order to make explicit the agenda for action needed for a new stage in the country's industrialization process. Moreover, these industrialists believe that the new stage of development in Brazil will have to be established in pace with the new frontiers of world development which are being opened by the new techno-economic paradigm. Since all IEDI's industrialists are also members and hold positions in the old system of corporatist representation sponsored by State legislation (of which FIESP - São Paulo state's confederation of industries - is the strongest politically), its creation in itself can be seen as another example of da Mattas's (1989) 'relationships and simultaneities' which permeate Brazilian socio-economic formation.

Amongst workers there has also taken place the emergence of associations which represent the specific interests of what dos Santos (1985) calls a special section within the Brazilian middle class. This is formed mainly by those who work for the government at technical and scientific positions. They are lecturers, technicians and researchers who occupy high positions in the education and formation of a new Brazilian elite [18]. They also play an important role in the

> production and maintenance of technology upon which the Brazilian industrial sector depends so much for its dynamic expansion. ... Gradually in Brazil is

taking place the movement which was at the core of the industrial revolution last century. That is, the junction of scientific and technological dynamism to the dynamics of wealth accumulation. Even though this relation cannot yet be seen as strong, which makes it vulnerable to scientific and technological colonization, it is impossible to deny that a stock of labour force has been formed (which used to be statistically insignificant), whose gestation and on-going maintenance has been financed by the State. [dos Santos (1985), p. 291, my translation).

Throughout the eighties, besides the continuation of this development of a network of organizations that articulate and give collective identity to social agents, shape their behaviour and voice their demands, an important re-entry to the institutional matrix also took place. As that was the decade of elections [19], politics was brought significantly to the scene and ended up by providing a symbolic substitute for the former 'legitimacy-through-efficacy' formula of the authoritarian regime.

Despite the perverse effects of the re-emergence of old practices (populism and new forms of coronelism), the reencounter of the country with electoral practices is significant, to say the least, for its quantitative magnitude. This can be illustrated by the fact that whilst in the 1962 election (the last time the country's President was elected before the 1964 coup) there were less than 16 million voters; when the country went back to the polls in 1989 to choose its new President freely under civilian ruling there were over 80 million voters. Not only had absolute number increased, but so had social composition. A signal of 'new times' can be seen in the fact that a leader of the new labour movement came in second place in that electoral race.

5.5 Institutional dependence-path and the change in the political regime

The increasing diversity and complexity of Brazilian society and economy in the post-1960s, were hard to contain within the rigidities which characterize an authoritarian regime. Some of the regime's leaders, amongst whom President Geisel and his government's political coordinator General Golbery were the most outspoken, were conscious of it. The country's transition from authoritarianism to democracy, though, had two elements which are important to highlight in order to summarize the major questions that permeated the country's institutional matrix in the 1980s [20].

Firstly, the Brazilian authoritarian regime was able to achieve high rates of economic growth for quite a long period of time. Thus, despite the high costs of social exclusion, the regime was legitimized by deepening the country's modernization process which was accomplished through a new form of state intervention in the economy (see Chapters 2 and 4).

Secondly, the transition from authoritarianism to democracy took much longer in Brazil than in most other countries. The starting point was in 1974 when President Geisel inaugurated the process of 'slow and smooth opening of the political system'. The slowness and smoothness of the process was designed to allow time for different political segments to disengage progressively from the military regime; and to facilitate their inclusion into a coalition of an array of divergent interests, loosely articulated and with conflicting priorities. As a result, when the first civilian government took power in 1985 it did so through a coalition which included a Vice-President who had been until a few months earlier the chairman of the party which gave political support to the outgoing regime [21].

More important, from the point of view of those interests strongly linked to the 'old' in Brazilian society and economy, the combination of economic and social exclusion [22] and the above mentioned re-arrangement of forces guaranteed to the 'old' a Constituent Congress (elected in 1986) which was very far from a forum in which interruptions with the past could take place. The analysis of data on election trends, political representation, the principal occupations and economic activities of those elected to write the country's new Constitution show that co-option and resistance to progressive change still retain the upper hand in the Brazilian political system [Graham (1990)].

Fleischer (1990) brings evidence of the persistence of co-option and resistance to progressive change in the country's institutional matrix. Out of the 559 members of the Congress elected in 1986, 217 were affiliated with Arena (the old regime's party) in 1979. Thus, even though the old regime's political party (re-named PDS) won only 30% of the seats in Congress, the 'migration' of some of its members to other parties had guaranteed their continuing influence in the country's political system.

From the point of view of representation, the situation in the Constituent Congress was even more revealing of the 'mismatches' between the country's socio-economic diversity and complexity and its institutional configuration. Table 5.2 shows that, out of the five most important activities performed by members of the Constituent Congress, three were connected with agriculture, commerce and finance-banking business. The numbers presented by Fleischer (1990) show that 37.7% of the Congress' members were capital-owners, 24.9% were managers; 36.3% were white-collar and only 1.1% were manual workers [23]. Moreover, amongst the 211 capitalists, 91 came from agriculture, 48 from the banking-financial sector and 23 from the commerce-insurance-service sector (ibid., p. 240).

According to Goes (1990), the almagam of interests in the Constituent Congress revealed the weakness of the political parties in Brazil [24]; the lack of political and ideological homogeneity amongst the many 'parliamentary blocs' that were formed at different stages and which disappeared very quickly; and the resulting strength of corporatist lobbies. All the strong groups

- both amongst capitalists and amongst organized labour - worked above and beyond the political parties and without any ideological line of action.

Table 5.2
Occupations of Constituent Congress members by order of importance, 1987 (in %)

Occupations	First	Activity by Order of Importance (a)			
		Second	Third	Fourth	Cumulative (b)
Agriculture	16.3	8.0	3.1	0.0	23.8
Comm.-Serv. Ins.	7.2	6.7	4.5	3.2	14.5
Fin.-Bank-Bus	12.2	12.2	9.8	1.6	25.8
Media (owners)	2.3	0.7	0.4	3.2	3.4
Industry-Transp.	5.4	2.8	2.7	0.0	8.6
Lawyer-Judge	9.1	25.3	29.9	46.0	46.0
Medicine	6.4	2.5	1.8	1.6	9.3
Dental-Pharmacy	0.5	0.7	0.4	0.0	1.3
Engineers	4.7	6.9	9.4	6.3	14.5
Teaching	9.3	11.7	12.9	17.5	25.6
Religious	1.1	2.1	2.7	0.0	3.8
Journalists	9.1	4.1	5.4	4.8	15.0
Economists	2.1	4.1	8.5	6.3	9.5
Social Sciense	0.5	1.6	1.8	0.0	2.5
Public Servants	12.9	9.9	4.9	7.9	23.4
Military	0.9	0.7	1.8	1.6	2.3
TOTAL (%)	100.0	100.0	100.0	100.0	100.0

(a) Importance defined by larger proportions of income
(b) Cumulative total of constituent members in each respective activity over the total of 559 member; thus, these percentages do not sum to 100.0
Source: Fleischer (1990), Table 11.10, p. 233

A strong feature of the Congress consistent with the pendular movement that historically typifies Brazilian federalism was the move, once again, towards decentralization. The large redistribution of political power - from central government to state and municipal ones; from the executive to the legislative and judiciary - which took place in the Constituent Congress is the result of both the crisis of centralism which was exarcebated by the authoritarian regime, and the new pattern of organization and political awareness which permeates Brazilian socio-economic life today.

Governors and state assembly members, as well as mayors and city councillors, freely elected by the population shortly before the Constituent Congress [25], exerted strong pressure to ensure that the new constitution would grant greater political powers and increase the shares of states and municipalities in total government revenues. Viewed in a wider period, this meant that the federal share came down from 50.5% in 1974 to 45% in 1985 and to an estimated 36% in 1993; whilst state share came from 36% in 1974 to 37% in 1985 and then to an estimated 42% in 1993; and the share of the municipal tier of government which rose from only 13.5% in 1974 to 18% in 1985 will increase to an estimated 23% in 1993 [Resende (1990)] [26].

5.6 The new Constitution and new institutional frameworks

A reallocation of functions amongst the three tiers of government is expected from the ways states and municipalities had their financial and administrative powers strengthened by the new Constitution. Thanks to the adopted doctrine of federal 'concurrent responsibilities', besides the usual co-responsibilities in areas such as health and social administration; cultural affairs; and education, the new Constitution introduced that of science and technology.

The concurrent responsibilities regarding science and technology are subscribed in the new Constitution in two ways. Firstly, towards decentralization as the new Constitution allows member-states to tie resources to science and technological development [27]. The second one is less objective and rules that "the internal market is part of the national endowment and will be encouraged to make feasible socio-cultural-economic development, the well-being of the population and *the technological autonomy of the Nation, as to be referred to in federal law.*" (Title VII, Chapter IV, Article 219 of the 1988 Constitution, my translation - emphasis added).

The ambiguities of the two rules are, once again, the result of the amalgam of interests represented in the Constituent Congress and the ways these interests were channeled. Thus, whilst pressures carried out mainly by research institutes and university faculty members were granted the possibility of tying state resources to science and technology (more on that in the next section), those carried out by both nationalists and liberals had their disputes transferred to the debates which will surround a future federal law.

The transfer of the debate from the Constituent Congress to the negotiations of a federal law is a compromise between two strong blocs which were formed around issues of technological autonomy, neither of which was strong enough to push its way through. On the one hand, there was the group formed mainly by the academic community, segments of the military establishment and local entrepreneurs directly involved with informatics, whose legislative representation was based mainly on parties of the left (PT - the Workers Party, PDT - the Labour Party, and the PCs - the two Communist Parties) and on the progressive wing within PMDB (the party that succeeded the only opposition party allowed to exist between 1967 and 1981).

On the other hand, there was a bloc formed mainly by multinational corporations, the domestic firms with close ties in the international market and the big industry's federations of São Paulo, Rio de Janeiro and Rio Grande do

131

Sul. It was represented in the Constituent Congress by the so-called 'centrão' (literally, the big bloc of the centre) - a coalition of conservative MPs of PDS and PFL (both heirs of the one party which gave political backing to the authoritarian regime between 1967 and 1981) and of PMDB [Mendes (1988)].

Thus, the roots of the two blocs can be found in the diverse 'nationalistic approaches' that have been sought by the different development projects in Brazil. On the one hand, there is the 'nationalism' of the 1950s which - as emphasized in Chapter 2 - opened the internal market to foreign capital for the sake of promoting industrialization. On the other hand, there are those nationalists of the 1970s and 1980s which experienced the possibilities of greater technological autonomy with the short-term results of the policy for informatics.

The former bloc kept its more liberal approach to technological capabilities and was strongly influenced by pressures from the American government which signaled trade retaliations if Brazil kept a 'nationalistic' approach in informatics and other hi-tech areas [28]. The general feeling amongst those in favour of legislation for greater technological autonomy was that "the case of the Brazilian policy for informatics was a success story which core countries (mainly the U.S.A.) did not accept to take place in the periphery." [29].

The formation of the above mentioned two parliamentary blocs, though, go far beyond the discussions regarding technological development. In fact, they encompass much more controversial issues regarding the role of the State, of local enterprises and of multinational corporations in the process of economic development. In the first stage 'comissões temáticas' - theme subcommittees - of discussions of the Constituent Congress, those in favour of a stronger role for the State and explicit differentiation between local and foreign capital made the Sub-Committee on Science and Technology their stronghold. Their vision with respect to technological autonomy was guaranteed by the presence in the sub-committee's chairmanship of Cristina Tavares, an MP with longstanding positions in favour of protection for locally-owned enterprises.

The forces strongly linked to the interests of foreign capital, of the big local enterprises, and of financial capital made the Sub-Committee on Economic Order into their fortress. It was chaired by former 'csar' of the Brazilian economy - MP Delfin Neto (Minister of the Exchequer between 1967 and 1973 and Minister of Planning between 1979 and 1985) - and had amongst its members Roberto Campos (known for his longstanding liberal ideals) and Francisco Dornelles (head of the Internal Revenue Department for over ten years under the authoritarian regime). This subcommittee proposed strong limits to State intervention in the economy and treated as very small the differences between local and foreign capital. The trick used was the proposition of considering as Brazilian or local enterprises all those whose headquarters were located in Brazil.

The deadlocks between the two positions throughout the works of the Constituent Congress are reflected in the wordings of the new Constitution. Thus, on the one hand, the text guarantees the role of foreign capital in the Brazilian economy ("Based on the national interest, the law will discipline foreign capital investment, will promote re-investments and will regulate profit remittance" - Article 172 of the new Constitution). On the other, it differentiates between enterprises which have their headquarters in the country from those whose effective capital control is handled by residents in the country and allows for privileges to the latter (Article 171 of the new Constitution).

As for the role of the State, those who advocated its greater intervention gained the assurance that "the State will promote and give support to the scientific development and technological capabilities" (Article 218 of the new Constitution). For those who wanted to curb the role of the State in the economy there was the assurance that "the direct exploration of economic activities by the State will only be allowed when necessary to the imperatives of national security or when relevant to collective interests, according to what will be defined in law." (Article 173 of the new Constitution).

Summing up, the conflict of interests which exists in the complex and diverse Brazilian socio-economic formation were brought into the Constituent Congress. In it the gap between the country's socio-economic formation and its political representation was made explicit. As a result, the country has a new Constitution whose main characteristic is a lack of clear directions. Above all, it lacks both the flexibility and the rigidity which should be expected of its institutional role. In other words, "the new Constitution is ultra-liberal as far as political rights is concerned; it is socially interventionist and protective; and economically undecided. The impact that this amalgam of different principles will have upon the country's modernization process is clearly upredictable." [30].

As a result, side-by-side with the accomplishments regarding redistribution of constitutional powers from central government to states and municipalities, and from the executive to the legislative and judiciary, the new Constitution is hesitant and contradictory with respect to the economy. Above all, it does not provide the grounds for the drawing up of a hegemonic project regarding the country's development. It does not indicate what sort of economic interaction (both internal and external) the country should be heading for. The many cases in which the Constitution transfers the discussion of economic matters to future ordinary legislation indicates that the Congress opted to "subordinate the institutionalization of the economy simultaneously to the logic of the market and to political-ideological competition." [dos Santos (1990), p. 166].

5.7 Economic agents' perceptions of the new paradigm

The lack of clear indications by the new Constitution with respect to a hegemonic project for the country is not in tune with the perception that political and economic agents have of the challenges that must be faced by the Brazilian economy. Much to the contrary, some of these agents perceive the frontiers that the new techno-economic paradigm sets [31]. Moreover, they feel the need for actions towards greater integration between "the new paradigm's engines - such as informatics and micro electronics - and more traditional sectors." [IEDI (1990), p. 7].

These perceptions are not confined either to top industrialists or to well-intentioned research people doing work in universities' laboratories. Based on a survey with 450 entrepreneurs, labour leaders, association leaders, intellectuals, journalists, politicians, military and high-ranking government officials, Lamounier and Souza (1990) show that over 80% of the sample identified the need for State intervention in science and technology if the country is to keep up with what is taking place in the core countries. A more specific survey with 550 entrepreneurs by the National Confederation of Industries [CNI (1990)] shows that their interpretation of their colleagues' perception is that: (i) - more than 80% give strong priority to the need for catching-up with technological change; (ii) - more than 90% plan to increase their R&D expenditure; (iii) - close to 80% intend to use new technologies in the creation of new products and in the search for new processes.

This is evidence that there is a positive attitude amongst industrialists concerning the changes towards the new paradigm of economic development. Bielschowsky and Ferraz (1990), using data from the CNI's survey, show that these attitudes towards future modernization are quite similar in both domestic and multinational companies. What might be even more significant evidence of concern with the challenges of the new paradigms is that both multinational and domestic enterprises - regardless of the efficiency improvements they achieved in the 1980s - feel that what has been done so far is not enough to catch up with international capabilities.

A qualification of these positive attitudes must be made, though. In a survey with 135 leading Brazilian industries (88 domestic and 47 MNCs), Salm, coord. (1990) show that "approximately half of those interviewed feel lack of information to be a barrier to diffusion [of industrial automation (IA) and new organizational techniques (NOT)]. ... If this is the situation amongst the Brazilian industry's elite [most of whom already use IA and NOT, AV], the lack of information on the nature, costs and possible impacts of these technologies has to be taken as a more serious problem amongst those industries which are not yet users of these innovations." (ibid., p. 60, my translation).

These broader intentions of using modern technology in the future 'vis-à-vis' what they have been able or willing to do so in the past is a social asset of the BNSI. Nevertheless, it is a social asset which presents divisions on how the country's technological capabilities should be developed in the future. A survey done by *Gazeta Mercantil* (a leading Brazilian business newspaper) in July 1990 shows that amongst 766 entrepreneurs of all sectors of the economy, 51.6% feel that there should be less regulation/barriers to the use of foreign technology; 45.7% think that fiscal incentives should be given to local enterprises to develop new technologies; whilst 4.6% feel that market reserve should be used in strategic sectors. Moreover, the latter should be considered as priorities by the government in its investment programmes.

Data on workers' perceptions of the new technologies [Neder (1989)], show that, even though all the interviewed had some knowledge about the new technologies, only half of them were able to distinguish microelectronic-based automation from the conventional one. The great majority of them have acquired their knowledge about the new technologies either by in-the-job interactions or through political interaction in the labour-unions. "The majority of those interviewed showed a favourable position regarding negotiations with employers with respect to 'robotization' and 'automation' in general." (ibid., p. 28). Nevertheless, they point out that possibilities of negotiating these matters have been facing resistance on the employers' side.

It should be of no surprise that these attitudes of employers are different in those industries where there have been changes in industrial relations policies in order to diffuse organization techniques associated with technical innovations such as 'just-in- time' and 'quality control circles'. It is also relevant to notice that "there is no homogeneous identification by those interviewed with respect to the actions to be taken as far as the new technologies are concerned. The discrepancies in attitude are caused by different factors: exposure of the interviewed to work environments with industrial automation; interactions with other workers who have knowledge of the new technologies; and technical support given by labour organizations." (ibid., p. 31) [32].

The results of the different surveys that have been used above in order to illustrate social capabilities towards technological development in the Brazilian national system of innovation have to be treated with caution. To begin with, they have used different samples and have been done in times of distinct political and economic pressures on the people being interviewed. Above all, they do not intend to show any 'real' reaction in terms of effective decision making. Despite this, they have been used here in order to give an 'impressionistic approximation' of the attitudes business, labour and political leaders have to the changes in techno-economic paradigm and of their perceptions of the routes that the country should follow with respect to technological capabilities.

It is also interesting to notice that all those who I interviewed in Brazil in August/September 1990 regarded the credibility of institutions as a very important factor if the country is to develop its technological capabilities. Some were emphatic in saying that research and development survived in Brazil throughout the 1980s thanks to the interactions between individuals in the public/private sectors; bureaucrats, business leaders in state-owned and local companies; politicians and research people. But it was recognized by them as well that this 'survival strategy', of new alliances based on individuals' commitments to technological development, is too precarious if the country is to face the challenges of changing paradigm.

5.8 Technological development and the public debate

The setting-up of new alliances and new institutional arrangements have been taking place as the government in the 1980s failed to fulfill its longstanding (Chapter 2) role of signaling the directions of changes in the accumulation process. In particular, the political debate concerning science and technology was elevated from the status of what Adler (1988) calls 'guerrilla groups within government, universities and R&D laboratories' to the rank of focus for open political debate.

This increase in the scope and intensity of the political debate concerning science and technology in Brazil started in the late 1970s. By then it had become already clear to the forces behind the market reserve for local producers of segments of the informatics industry that the policy needed political support from Congress. That was needed because strong pressures were emerging from the big multinational computer companies with the political backing of the American government. Moreover, a local counterpart of this pressures was being voiced by local entrepreneurs who were afraid of trade retaliation from the U.S.A., the major market for Brazil's exports.

The stage that followed the passing of the Informatics Law by the Brazilian Congress in 1984 was of a wider scope. Firstly, because the 'Campaign in Favour of Indigenous Technology', staged throughout the works of the Constituent Congress, took the political debate further than the informatics sector. The idea was to gain political support for an explicit policy of greater technological autonomy. In the second place, because the grass roots of the campaign also pushed for greater involvement of local governments in matters regarding science and technology.

The result of the first goal have been discussed above. As for the involvement of local governments with science and technology, twenty member-states have tied resources specifically to those ends, ranging from 0.5% of local taxes to 3.0% of total revenues. According to preliminary estimates [33], in 1990 money approximately US$350 million dollars would be allocated for science and technology in those 20 member-states.

This was a victory of the academic community which had for a long time tried to repeat in other states the success story of São Paulo where since the 1950s there has been a special funding system for scientific development. Such an accomplishment, however, has to be seen with caution. Firstly, despite the state laws which establish them, these resources are never automatically transferred by the state governments to the agencies charged with giving financial support to science and technology [34]. Moreover, the political support that the academic community got for the new legislation is rarely matched by political commitment to expenditures in science and technology. This is especially so when S&T are competing for scarce resources with areas of higher social priorities and greater political sensitivity such as education, health and housing. Under the new Constitution these areas are also subject to 'concurrent responsibilities' between the three tiers of government.

Secondly, the initial intention of using these local resources to leverage other sources - mainly from the federal government - runs the risk of not being fulfilled. Greater control on the levels of expenditures by the federal government - due to its deficits - has meant substantial decrease in resources allocated to science and technology. Table 5.3 shows that, despite the increasing demand, the resources available to FNDCT (the federal government's fund for the scientific and technological development) decreased dramatically between 1978 and 1990. Furthermore, the prospect for any reversal of this trend is slim. The federal government has in fact used the 'concurrent responsibilities' established by the Constitution as a pretext for transferring any financial commitments relative to science and technology to the state governments [35].

Media coverage has been important influence on public awareness of issues on science and technology. It has helped promote a context susceptible to institutional flexibility. The increasing coverage in the press took place both during the political debate on the informatics law and during the discussions about science and technology at the Constituent Congress. Moreover, there has been given increasing space in newspapers, television and radio for the discussion of issues regarding scientific achievements and technological development. Besides specialized magazines [36], all major newspapers and television networks have weekly features and programmes on S&T.

Since the country's educational system performs poorly, the mass media plays a vital role on two counts. It helps in the diffusion of innovations and in the discussion of fundamental aspects of scientific findings; and it also contributes to building political awareness with respect to an area which is not 'naturally' on the agenda of public debate in the periphery. As a result of mass media coverage, big companies have established S&T prizes as part of their public relations package, whilst the scientific community see in these p.r. motivated campaigns "the possibility of building new political ties with enterprises" [37].

Table 5.3
FNDCT - number of contracts (constant values, 1978=100)

Year	Number of contracts	Financial suport
1978	201	100*
1979	207	64
1980	177	48
1981	302	42
1982	415	38
1983	693	32
1984	663	26
1985	682	38
1986	917	47
1987	745	40
1988	719	38
1989	n.a.	24
1990	n.a.	10

* - The total financial support given in 1978 was of
approximately US$220 millions.
Sources: FINEP quoted in *Cadernos de Política
Tecnológica da AFCPqD*, February 1992, p.
2, and Gondim (1992).

It is obvious that these informative systems and institutional flexibilities are necessary but not sufficient conditions for the institutional support the BNSI needs to promote the development of technological and economic capabilities under the new paradigm. Nonetheless, they are a sign that there is more taking place in the institutional domain of the Brazilian national system of innovation than is generally assumed under the 'lost decade' claim.

5.9 Summing up

Evidence presented in this chapter stresses the path-dependence of Brazilian institutions. This has contributed to their difficulties in performing two major roles in the context of innovation and development; that of providing stability which makes the action of innovative agents less vulnerable to opportunistic behaviour of other agents; and that of being flexible in such a way that disruptions are minimized at times of radical changes.

Many of the inherited characteristics of Brazilian institutions have taken organized interest close to paralysis. Especially in the 1980s, this was in flagrant contrast with other countries where the "potential dilemma is overcome through accumulated mutual trust and common conceptions of economic reality, and the procedures for regulation of conflicts and mediation of disputes." [Nielssen (1991), p. 7].

Institutional path-dependence in Brazil became more clear in the 1980s. Low rates of economic growth, increasing poverty, high inflation, mounting public debt and the fiscal crisis of the state, took away what was left of legitimacy in the authoritarian regime. The re-democratization of the country took the political struggles between forces behind its socio-economic formation to the more open forum of Congress debate. 'Prisoner's dilemma' situations emerged when policies had to be sought to face the country's crucial socio-economic problems. The political responses in most cases were characterized by postponing the solutions to deadlocks.

This was clearly the case of many decisions taken during the Constituent Congress. Elected in 1986, its role in public perception went beyond re-establishing democratic institutions in the country. Expectations were high also with respect to crucial socio-economic issues such as land reform, social security, capital-labour relations, education, health, science and technology, etc. Not surprisingly, then, the Constituent Congress became a privileged battle ground for pressure groups of the most diverse origins and with the most divergent objectives.

Despite the improvements in areas such inter-governmental relations, the new Constitution has not provided the country with institutions which can work as a framework for its future development. Crucial decisions were transferred to ordinary legislation and a sense of 'lost opportunity' can be felt amongst those who thought that a 'national project' should emerge with the new Constitution.

Not surprisingly, the directions given by the new Constitution with respect to science and technology are dubious. On the one hand, it mentions technological autonomy as a goal to be pursued through the strengthening of the internal market as part of the national endowment. On the other, it fails to provide the means through which this endowment can be built under the circumstances of deeply rooted income inequalities. It also leaves for future legislation basic definitions of how to pursue technological autonomy at times of increasing transformations in the way nations interact in science and technology.

Despite the deadlocks which are embedded in the country's institutional path-dependence, evidence has been presented that there is growing perception amongst BNSI's agents with respect to the new techno-economic paradigm. The transformation of these perceptions into institutions which can work as stable and flexible frameworks for innovations and changes under the new techno-economic paradigm is a great challenge. In order to face them, the BNSI will certainly need to overcome bottlenecks in the other domains and to pull together their strengths. Both have already been stressed with respect to the economic domain.   Constraints upon, and possibilities for the technological domain are the subject of the next chapter.

Notes

1. Polity is meant to express the "state apparatus that has taken form in Brazil (with its multitude of public organizations at the federal, state, and local level) and the political and social forces within the state and outside (made up of groups and individuals) that are giving shape to a new regime (consisting of a constelation of actors quite different from the Brazil of a decade ago)." [Graham (1990), p. 2].

2. North (1991) summarizes the need to constrain human interaction with institutions by using a game-theoretic context.   "Wealth-maximizing individuals will usually find it worthwhile to cooperate with other players when the play is repeated, when they possess complete information about the other player's past performance, and when there are small numbers of players.   But turn the game upside down.   Cooperation is difficult to sustain when the game is not repeated (or there is an endgame), when information on the other players is lacking, and when there are large number of players." (ibid., p. 97).

3. The basic reasoning of orthodox economics is that excessive regulations of goods, labour, land and money markets create rigidities that impair the search for new equilibrium positions.   Such a diagnosis has built into itself the cure of the disease, i.e. a movement towards flexibility is assumed to demand the restoration of an institutional framework closer to the ideal of the pure, and perfectly competitive market economy.   For a critique of the 'institutional sclerosis hypothesis' see Johnson and Lundvall (1991).

4. The necessity of such changes according to Freeman and Perez (1988) has initiated a growing search for new social and political solutions in areas such as flexible working time; shorter working hours; re-educating and retraining systems; regional policies based on creating favourable conditions for information technology (rather than tax incentives to capital-intensive mass production industries); new financial systems; possible decentralization of management and government; and access to data banks and networks at all levels and new telecommunication system.

5. Elam (1990) stresses the fact that the 'regulationists' perspectives is close to Gramsci's' focus on the containment of capitalism's inherent 'animality' which results in the indefinite postponement of the 'impeding catastrophe': "the history of industrialism has always been a continnuing

140

struggle ... against the element of 'animality' in man. It has been an uninterrupted, often painful and bloody process of subjugating natural (i.e. animal and primitive) instincts to new, more complex and rigid forms and habit of order, exactitudes and precision which can make possible the increasingly complex forms of collective life which are the necessary consequences of industrial development." [Gramsci, A (1971), quoted in Elam (1990), p. 23].

6. For the 'regulationist' [see Boyer (1990), for instance] the dissimilarities cannot be confined to different paths followed by marketeers in the U.S.A. and Great Britain 'vis-à-vis' interventionists in Japan and Germany. They are also present in long-thought 'homogeneous' social-democracies such as those of the Nordic countries.

7. De Vroey (1984) points out that for most countries in the developed world, the golden age after World War II was a period of social consensus, interrupted only by short phases of social upheaval. Although capitalist societies in the centre had not foregone the system's invariable features (exploitation and domination), employers and wage-earners had come to a mutually advantageous compromise. Stronger institutional and political collective position of workers secured them regular increases in wages which gave them access to ever higher consumption patterns. "Unemployment was low, while workers provided with insurance systems and a network of collective goods and services. ... For the capitalist class, the advantages were obvious: the attainment of social peace and class collaboration, minimizing halts in production and gaining outlets for the increased production." (ibid., p. 56).

8. That does not mean that welfare benefits are not significant in Brazil. According to Draibe et al. (1991) the main problem is that - given the way social expenditures are financed - they work in a pro-cyclical manner. That is, they decrease when the economic growth decelerates and increase when the economy booms.

9. Many authors [Freeman (1988), Freeman and Perez (1988), Dertouzos et al. (1989), Boyer (1990)] point out these differences as a question of substance regarding the present position and the perspective of developed countries in the international division of labour under the new paradigm.

10. For an analysis of the Brazilian case 'vis-`a-vis that of the German and Japanese modernization processes, see Fiori (1990) and Ferraz (1990). For indications of the roots of the institutional dependence path of Latin American countries 'vis-à-vis that of the United States, see North (1991).

11. As is stressed in chapter 2, the Brazilian industrialization process was achieved through political compromises between the existing agro-

-exporters hegemonic power and the emerging industrialists and segments of urban workers. This feature of the Brazilian modernization process has meant that the country's institutional matrix has never broken with its pre-modern roots but has incorporated them into the 'new' system.

12. 'Coronelismo' is an institutional form originated in the pre-republican period through which the landed class obtained bureaucratic appointments, sinecures, livings, and commissions for their family and for the vast network of dependents and clients in exchange for their 'pork-barrel' political support for government's policies. 'Populismo' has been a style of doing politics since the thirties through which benefits are granted to the lower middle and working classes without passing on real power. 'Autoritarismo' in Brazil is rooted on the 'national security doctrine' which argues that all interests, values, and principles in political, social and economic life must be sacrificed to those of national security. Graham (1990) stresses that "nationalism could be used for a while to paper over the widening cleavages between diverging interests. Official nationalism was not directed against foreign investors (except for a few who had prospected for petroleum), but against the importation of foreign-made goods. Under populism the growth of industry, even if foreign owned, could be hailed as a nationalist achievement." (ibid., p. 11).

13. The importance of some of the new-coming institutions for the technological and economic domains of the Brazilian national system of innovations are also stressed in chapters 4 and 6.

14. Graham (1990) provides an analysis of the ways coronelism, populism, and authoritarism is being challenged and is finding new ways to fight emerging social organizations.

15. According to Medeiros (1986) this is a phenomenon which increased after direct elections for state-governorships were re-established in 1982 but which is rooted in the need of the military governments to build new channels of legitimization for the authoritarian regime.

16. dos Santos (1985) points out that between 1964 and 1984, 67 associations of entrepreneurs were created.

17. In 1991 ABICOMP changed the rules of membership in order to allow MNCs as members (*Gazeta Mercantil*, 18/06/91). This is a clear indication of its adaptation to the country's new political environment.

18. The number of scientific and technological associations in Brazil has gone from 225 in 1984 [IBICT (1984)] to 381 in 1990 (interviews at IBICT).

19. There were elections in 1982, 1985, 1986, 1989 and 1990. The general elections of 1982 were significant because for the first time since 1962 state governors were freely chosen. The 1985 election was called specifically for choosing the mayors of state capital-cities which had not happened since the 1960s. As for the 1986 general election they were significant because the Congressmen who were elected then were to perform the role of writing the new Constitution in the first half of their four year term.

20. Rouquie et al., eds. (1985) and O'Donnel et al., eds. (1986) present a comparative analysis of political transition in Brazil, Argentina, Portugal and Spain, amongst others.

21. This is not to say that the transition took place in accordance with what had been planned by the authoritarian regime's strategists. The long and pervasive pro-democracy movement of popular pressure which culminated with the 'Diretas Já' in 1984 certainly changed, to say the least, the timing of the 'opening process' planned by the authoritarian regime. For an analysis of the old within the 'new' republic, see Fernandes (1985).

22. In the sense that social and economic exclusion leave little room for political conscience amongst the masses.

23. The emergence of organized labour as the most important new force in Brazilian politics was recognized by the Constituent Congress through significant reform of Brazilian labour law. Many provisions in the new constitution such as the reduction of the work-load per week to 40 hours; 50% increment for overtime work and paid vacation with supplements were not achieved through the workers' representation in Congress but through their organized pressure on the majority of its members. For an analysis of the ways the new constitution recognizes that a militant and independent unionism has become a political reality in Brazil, see Swavely (1990).

24. "With the exception of PT (the Workers Party which had only sixteen members in Congress, AV) no other party worked in the Constituent Congress according to any political or ideological commitment." [Goes (1990), p. 198, my translation].

25. Mayors and municipal councillors were elected in 1984 (with the exception of state capital mayors' who were elected in 1985) and state governors and assemblymen were elected in 1986 together with members of Congress who were to write the new constitution.

26. For an analysis of the political implications of decentralization in Brazil, both during the authoritarian regime and as a result of the new Constitution, see Medeiros (1991).

27. Education was the only other exception to the general rule of not allowing public resources being 'ear-marked' to specific activities.

28. For a discussion of the negotiations between the USA and Brazil regarding informatics policy, see Bastos (1992).

29. A senior member of ABICOMP I interviewed in September 1990.

30. Prof. Wanderley Guilherme dos Santos in a interview I had with him in August 1990. He also pointed out that the new Constitution can be looked at for negative indications rather than a positive economic agenda. "There is much more that cannot be done - foreign capital cannot perform in the petroleum and mining industries; bank cannot charge more than 12% of real interest - rather than to what sort of development model the country should be heading for. The concern is more with what the State is not to do - in response to the wave of neo-liberal thinking - rather than what should be its new role in the stage of economic development the country ought to be looking for." (ibid., interviews).

31. Kuznets (1989) points out the importance of this perception. He also recognizes the need to identify a socio-political component "that encourages the continuous production of a variety of new knowledge relevant, directly or indirectly, to problems of economic production; that contains an entrepreneurial group perceptive of such new knowledge, and capable of venturing attempts to apply it on a scale sufficient to reveal its potential; and that can generate without costly breakdowns, institutional changes and group adjustments that may be needed to channel efficiently the new technology - with its distinctive constraints." (ibid., p. 10).

32. This support has increased since 1985 when CUT (the unions federation which was created as part of the new labour movement) established in 1985 its committee on technology and automation whose main concern has been to "propose policies that both safe-guard the workers' interests 'vis-à-vis' the new technologies and promote technologies which are of the workers's interests." [CUT (1987), p. 5].

33. This estimate was made by different sources during interviews I had in August/September 1990.

34. The most mentioned example is that of the Rio de Janeiro state where the governor fails to make the transferral of resources unless they are to be managed by someone of his personal trust.

35. The only exception to this rule has been the negotiations of funding from agencies such as the World Bank and the Inter-American Development Bank.

36. *Ciência Hoje* a magazine published by the SBPC (the Brazilian society for the progress of science) was aimed at the general public and sold more than one million copies in the 1980s.

37. Prof. Enio Candotti of SBPC who I interviewed in September 1990. The effectiveness of this strategy is questionable because the mass media coverage of science and technology is closely related to the possibilities of increasing publicity revenues. Another critical aspect regarding mainly the coverage by television networks is that the broadcasting of science and technology programmes takes place at very odd hours - specially early Saturday and Sunday mornings when the number of viewers is very limited.

6 The technological domain

6.1 Introduction

The objective of this chapter is to assess elements of the technological domain which can contribute and/or impose constraints upon the Brazilian national system of innovation at a time when the technological base of world development is going through radical changes. The usual starting point for this kind of assessment is to appraise the financial support given to the system of innovation measured by the ratio of R&D expenditure over gross domestic product.

From this perspective, the 1980s can be characterized as a critical period for science and technology in Brazil. The R&D expenditure as percentage of GDP increased from .24% in 1971 to .68% in 1980, fell to less than .60% in 1989. Besides being a break with a positive trend that was being established in the country, the slowdown in R&D expenditure in the BNSI compares poorly with what was taking place in other industrialized countries. Table 6.1 shows that Brazil's per capita expenditure in R&D is not only substantially below that of all the core countries, but is also behind that of other NICs, such as South Korea [1].

Moreover, the total amount spent in R&D in Brazil in 1989 [US$2 015 (CNPq 1990)] does not match even what IBM spent in 1985 [2.7 billion dollars (Hewitt (1992)]. These are strong indications that the short-term economic policies followed by the country throughout the 1980s have had a negative impact on the BNSI at a time when the norm amongst industrialized countries was to increase their R&D (by themselves and/or in cooperation with others) in order to cope with the changes that were taking place in the techno-economic paradigm.

The importance of these comparisons is based on the generally accepted correlation between GDP per capita and R&D expenditure. It is relevant to note, however, that even those [like Fagerberg (1987)] who find that close correlation as an explanation of why growth rates differ, acknowledge that "when the non-OECD countries, and later USA and Japan, are removed from the sample, the explanatory power of the technology variables, especially growth in innovative activities, diminishes." (ibid., p. 87).

Table 6.1
R&D expenditures in selected countries

Country	Year	%GDP	Per capita (US$)
Brazil	1982	0.6	13.37
Canada	1984	1.4	183.15
France	1979	1.8	194.10
Germany (W)	1983	2.5	272.47
Italy	1983	1.1	69.41
Japan	1983	2.6	254.14
Korea (S)	1983	1.1	19.98
Spain	1984	0.5	19.30
United Kingdom	1983	2.2	178.10
United States	1983	2.6	376.10

Source: de Mello (1990), Table 1.4.1, p. 40

Besides, the approach used here stresses the importance of examining different elements of a national system of innovation which may reflect its strengths in learning processes that go beyond the existence of formal research institutions and laboratories [2]. In chapters 4 and 5 special attention was given to some of the learning processes which are taking place in the context of the economic and the institutional domains. In this chapter some fundamental aspects of the BNSI's technological set-up are examined from a perspective which privileges the possibilities of, and constrains upon, Brazil to make positive changes in the form of its associated-dependency. As mentioned before, the assumption is that at times of shifts in techno-economic paradigm 'windows of opportunities' are opened which can favour such a change in the form of dependency.

The chapter begins by examining a critical aspect of the BNSI, i.e. its educational system. Emphasis is given to both, the poor performance of the system as a whole and the specialization of engineers which are emerging from the system. The two sections which follow that, examine the country's research infrastructure from a perspective which privileges their 'spin-offs' reflected in R&D activities and in the emergence of science parks. The last section examines data on technological transfers as a 'proxy' for interactions between the BNSI and its counterparts in the industrialized world.

6.2 Human resources

The human resources component of national wealth increases in importance when there is a shift in techno-economic paradigm. Good historical evidence for this is provided by the better performance of newly industrialized Germany and the U.S.A. 'vis-à-vis' that of the industrial leader U.K. when the electrical techno-economic paradigm emerged in the latter part of the XIX century. Freeman (1988) emphasizes that

> It was not just a question of 'spirit of entrepreneurship' which explained the differences in the innovative performance of British industry on the one hand or German and US industry on the other. It was a different social climate related to changes in the national system of innovation, which meant that it was possible for a new type of technical innovative entrepreneurship to flourish in Germany and USA, but not the same degree in Britain. Those European countries, such as Sweden and Switzerland, which imitated the German educational and institutional innovations, also began a rapid catching up process, which enabled them too, to overtake Britain in the new technologies and to develop strength in specialized industries related to local resources and user interactions (ibid., p. 9).

Bearing that in mind, many national governments and international agencies have started to address the issue of whether existing systems of education and training are adequately equipped to meet increasing international competition and the particular challenges posed by new technologies. The knowledge-intensity which characterize these technologies makes of skilled, highly trained scientific, engineering and technical labour power one of its most important assets. "Without such labour, even access to adequate financial resources and material inputs would not be a decisive advantage in a country's effort to develop an indigenous industry." [O'Connor (1985), p. 325]. Taking this line of reasoning one step further, OECD (1990) and Dertouzos et al. (1989) stress that neither the technical nor the economic potential of the new techno-economic paradigm can be fully realized without concomitant, even anticipatory, changes in the different country's education and training systems.

a) The Brazilian education system: a broad view

In general the performance of the Brazilian educational system has been very poor. Table 6.2 shows that if public expenditure in education is taken as a 'proxy' for comparing different countries performance in the area, that of Brazil is at the lowest level amongst the countries listed. Moreover, Brazil still has a very high illiteracy rate (about 18% in 1989, according to the Ministry of Education; 23% according to less optimistic sources), and enrolment in primary school has been increasing at a lower rate than the growth in population. The efficiency and the efficacy of the system are also highly questionable. Students remain in the primary schools for many years (over 7.5 years) but progress through the grade sequence at a very slow rate. Only 58% of those who complete the first grade go beyond the fourth grade and only 16% of the same group go on to secondary education [Barreto et al., coords. (1990].

Table 6.2
Expenditure in education in selected countries

Country	Year	Total expenditure (US$ bi)	%GDP
Brazil	1984	5.63	2.9
Canada	1982	23.75	7.2
France	1982	31.68	5.8
Germany (W)	1984	28.38	4.6
Italy	1983	19.90	5.7
Japan	1983	65.95	5.6
Korea (S)	1985	4.06	4.9
Spain	1985	5.39	3.3
United Kingdom	1984	22.23	5.2
United States	1983	226.50	6.8

Source: de Mello (1990), Table 1.4.1, p. 40

In the secondary school system, the experiment of the 1970s, of trying to copy the model provided by the American comprehensive high schools and to expand on the country's successful technical schools system, has failed [3]. As a result, of a total of 3.4 million students enrolled in secondary schools in 1989, less than 3% attended the highly demanded system of technical schools sponsored by the federal government. What can be seen as an irony in the quality of these 138 schools is that their high standards have worked as an incentive for most of their graduates to carry on their education to university level. Thus, the major purpose for which they were planned in the beginning of the 1950s - i.e., to increase the supply of the labour force with technical and professional qualifications at the secondary level, is only being partially achieved.

Another source of technical training is supplied by SENAI (industry financed training service) which has been the major supplier of qualified manual labour to the Brazilian industrialization process since 1942. Given its initial objectives, SENAI has geared its training programmes mostly to primary school graduates. Despite the efforts made in order to adapt its courses to the new demands of the industrial sector, SENAI recognizes that it has only been able to meet quantitative targets. The qualitative aspects of the demand of technicians with a professional training adequate to the requirements of the new techno-economic paradigm are still far from being met [4].

In higher education Brazil is also a latecomer, even when compared with other Latin American countries like Peru and Mexico. Despite the fact that the first universities in Brazil were only established in the early part of the twentieth century, political pressures emerging from the middle class has provoked a boom in the country's higher education system during the last 20 years. Enrolment increased from about 280,000 students in 1968 to over 1.5 million in 1988. This quantitative change has taken place mainly through the 'liberalization' of higher education towards private single schools. Thus, in 1988, 35% of the students were attending single schools of higher education, and another 25% were at private universities.

One result of this recent trend of private schools acounting for the largest proportion of the higher education system is that there has been a predominance of courses that require less equipment and lower operational costs. As can be seen in Table 6.3 below, at the undergraduate level, about 70% of total enrolment/graduations are in social sciences; whilst engineering and technology's share is about 7% and 10%, respectively .

Table 6.3
Brazil: Undergraduate education (1988)

Area	Enrolment	Graduation
Sciences and Geosciences	133.929	19.149
Biological Sciences	20.613	3.058
Engineering	145.914	16.264
Health	172.033	29.060
Agriculture	41.585	6.119
Social Sciences	578.067	77.928
Humanities	410.173	73.233
Others	1.26	-
TOTAL	1.503.560	224.809

Source: Ministry of Education, Education Census 1988

Another aspect of the process of rapid increase in enrolment and shift towards private schools is that there has been an increase in heterogeneity of higher education standards in the country. Table 6.4 gives a general idea of 125,000 lecturers' qualifications at the different institutions. It should be noticed that 60% of the total are part-time. This figure increases to 95% in the single schools of higher education which should be sufficient to illustrate the fact that, despite the discourse of research-oriented higher education in Brazil, research work is still confined to very few areas of knowledge and few universities, predominantly at those located in the south and southeast regions of the country.

At the graduate level, enrolment increased from about 1,500 in 1969 to more than 38,000 in 1980. According to CAPES Data Bank, out of the 40,000 enrolled in 1986, 80% were on masters courses. At this level of education, the share of private institutions in 1986 was 17%, whilst federal and state universities enrolled 46% and 37% , respectively, of the students attending masters and Ph.D. courses in the country. 30% of the total were enrolled in social science courses, whilst 14% in engineering and 12% in natural sciences.

Table 6.4
Brazil: Academic background of lecturers in 1988 - (%)

	Graduate/Specializ.	Master	PhD
Federal University	55	30	15
State University	45	25	30
Munic. University	80	15	5
Private University	77	16	7
Private Single Schools	83	13	4

Source: Ministry of Education's Educational Census 1988

It has been pointed out in the literature that a major characteristic of the Brazilian educational system is its high heterogeneity [see, for instance, Barreto et al. (1990)]. According to Moura Castro (1985), "there is the co--existence of very poor local and private institutions with very expensive and sophisticated public schools. There are higher education institutions charging fees lower than nursery schools, whilst the University of São Paulo has a budget that compares with that of Harvard University." (ibid., p. 4, my translation).

The general state of the education system, as should be no surprise, has consequences for human resources performing R&D. According to CNPq data, in 1989 there were about 17,000 (5) people involved exclusively with research work in the country. The numbers in Table 6.5 speak for themselves. Of the numbers shown below, the Southeast region concentrates more than 50% of researchers with Ph.D. and about 50% of the total number of human resources involved with R&D activities.

There has been substantial pressure from the scientific community regarding this situation. The response has been an increase in financial resources allocated which has helped to boost the number of grants awarded by CNPq from a total of 6,707 in 1980 to over 25,000 in 1989. Nevertheless, the number of requests has always been at least twice as big as the ability of the agency to meet them from the available resources.

The distribution of these resources according to the different areas of knowledge (Table 6.6) simply reflects the political weight of the different groups within the academic community and the way the system of higher education is structured.   In general, it implies that very little of the resources available have been used to build cooperation schemes amongst the different universities which could strengthen their research and teaching activities. The

151

pressure groups follow two complementary strategies. Firstly, the corporative lobbies which try to maintain (and whenever possible to increase) the level of resources allocated to the different areas of knowledge. In the second place, the state lobbies which pressure on behalf of the 'centres of excellence' 'vis-à-vis' the 'emerging centres' and vice-versa. As a result, there is little room of manoeuvre for those who want to engage into cooperation either at the local level (interdisciplinary research groups) or at the national level (inter-university cooperation schemes. [6].

Table 6.5
Brazil: R&D human resources* (1989)

	Undergrad./Especial.	Master	PhD
Government	7.785	3.659	1.614
State-owned enterp.	1.332	250	36
Private instutions	1.361	598	364
TOTAL	10.478	4.507	2.014
	(62%)	(27%)	(11%)

* - These numbers do not take into account R&D performed at
   educational instituions, in order to avoid double counting
   R&D/teaching

Source: CNPQ (1990), Brasilia: CNPq, mimeo.

Table 6.6
Brazil: Grants awarded by CNPq (%) - 1989

Areas	in the country	abroad
Exact and earth sciences	19.59	17.64
Engineering	15.30	20.21
Health and biol. sciences	24.46	20.11
Agrarian Sciences	16.74	8.64
Human and social sciences	23.90	33.40
Masters	95.0	5.0
PhD	66.0	34.0
Post Doctarate	7.0	93.0

Source: CNPq/APJ/COOD (interviews)

   The adequacy of the educational system and of the human resources that it 'produces' has been rated poorly from a perspective that takes into consideration different social actors' perception of its quality [7]. A survey [Lamounier and Souza (1990)] of 450 members of the Brazilian elites (comprising entrepreneurs, labour leaders, intellectuals, politicians, amongst others), points out that 66% of them rated the accomplishments of the educational system between 1930 and 1990 at best as poor. If the period under evaluation is 1985/90, the percentage of a less favourable perception increases to 89%. A more specific survey done by the National Confederation of Industry [CNI (1990)], show that 63.6% of the 550 business leaders felt that the quality of the human resources were inadequate. More specifically, when evaluating the quality of business administration and engineering courses according to their needs, 64.5% and 58.9% evaluated them as bad, respectively [8].

Even the highly appraised technical training programmes sponsored by the federal government's technical schools and by industry's sponsored SENAI's training centres, were taken as less than adequate by 58.2% of those interviewed. It is striking that even those areas which have received special financial support along the recent industrialization process, are also considered as performing so poorly. This should be of major concern to policy-makers because it is known that under the new techno-economic paradigm new demands will arise for a better qualified labour force to perform with more sophisticated skills. These demands will be hard to meet if quality education at all levels is kept as a privilege of a few.

b) Engineers and the BNSI: some reasons for concern

The general picture of rigidities and quality scarcity of the Brazilian university system taken as a whole is also present in the specific areas of engineering and basic sciences. Despite the importance of these fields of knowledge in the process of what Kuhn calls 'changing spectacles when there is a shift in paradigm', the general structure of the engineering courses is still based on the division of the training system into the six areas (civil, mechanical, electrical, chemical, mines, and metallurgy) which were defined by the Federal Council of Education in 1976 (Resolution 48/76) [ABENGE/CONFEA (1990)].

More important, if the number of places available to undergraduate students in engineering is taken as a 'proxy' of resource allocation, the more traditional areas (civil and mechanical engineering) are more privileged than the 'new' areas of electrical/electronics engineering. Table 6.7 shows that the former areas combined take more than 2/3 of the places available, whilst the latter accounts for less than a quarter.

From a qualitative point of view, a major rigidity in the training of engineers at the undergraduate level emerges from the syllabus specified by the Federal Council of Education in 1976 for each of the areas of specialization. Because of its rigid structure, the system of engineering education fails in two senses. Firstly, it has responded slowly to shifts in the demand away from civil engineers and towards those with formal training in mechanics, electrical and chemical engineering.

Secondly, within these areas the system has failed to respond to the specificities of higher specialization. "In the case of computer engineering, for instance, there would be room for substantial improvements in its theoretical and training contents if it did not have to follow the minimum syllabus established for the electrical area from which it is derived." [ABENGE/CONFEA (1990), p. 5, my translation]. The quality of training at the undergraduate level is also down-graded by the inadequate and very poor conditions of laboratories in the majority of the existing engineering departments [9].

Table 6.7
Places available to undergraduate students in engineering (1986)

Civil Engineering	47.0%
Electrical/Electronics	21.0%
Mechanical	20.0%
Chemical	7.6%
Metallurgy	2.7%
Mines	0.9%
Others	0.8%

Source: ABENGE (the association of engineering education)

As far as the quality of engineers is concerned, there is also a mismatch between the priority given by most lecturers and the expectations of entrepreneurs who hire engineers. Whilst the former favour syllabuses which stress stronger theoretical background, the latter would rather have engineers with practical experience. As a result, enterprises are faced with two alternatives. Either they establish their own practical training programmes. Or, when given the option, they hire the few engineers who have attended one of the country's three federal centres of technological education, where practical training is stressed.

Besides these more qualitative questions, the supply of engineers in the Brazilian national system of innovation is also subject to quantity constraint. The 5 engineers / 1000 workers ratio of the BNSI compares poorly with that of the United States where there are 28 engineers/1000 workers [Freeman (1988)]. The situation becomes worse if one considers that engineers in Brazil deal with technical tasks for a period of 5 up to 10 years only. In general, after some time the engineers are bounded to assume managerial and other administrative functions. Therefore, it is estimated (interviews) that just about half of the total population of engineers are actually involved with technical activities.

Some of the criticisms that are made of the system of engineering education at the undergraduate level can be seen as partially overcome at the post--graduate level. On the one hand, in the 142 post-graduate courses offered in the country there is greater flexibility with respect to the areas of specialization which can be offered. On the other hand, the formal training of their faculties has been object of support by CNPq (the national council of scientific and technological research), by CAPES (the Ministry of Education's coordination for the improvement of higher education lecturers), and by special programmes supported by the Ministry of Science and Technology.

Tables 6.8 and 6.9 show that at the post-graduate level there has been a stronger response to the increasing demand of areas such as electric/electronics, production, and biomedical. One reason for this more adequate response is that post-graduate education is not as heavily regulated by the Federal Council of Education as the undergraduate courses. Another reason is the stronger links that these post-graduate courses in engineering have built with industry, especially with state-owned enterprises in the areas of petroleum exploration (PETROBRAS), electricity (ELETROBRAS), and telecommunications (TELEBRAS), as will be seen later in this chapter.

Table 6.8
Engineering Master's courses - 1986 (percentages)

Areas	Courses	Students	Staff with PhD
Elect./Electronics	19	26.8	27.8
Civil	17	21.3	15.6
Mechanical	18	12.7	15.9
Metallurgy/Materials	9	8.3	8.5
Production	9	8.9	6.4
Chemical	6	5.3	5.6
Nuclear	6	3.4	7.4
Transports	5	2.9	2.8
Agriculture	5	3.1	5.2
Biomedical	3	1.6	1.4
Naval	2	3.5	1.6
Spacial	1	2.2	1.8
TOTAL	100	100	-

Source: CAPES' Data Bank, quoted in Rocha Neto (1990)

Despite the better conditions of post-graduate education in engineering when compared with those at the under-graduate level, the general situation of the system is still precarious. As it stands now, most of postgraduate centres are not able to keep their staff on a full-time basis; firstly, because the wages they can offer is below what is paid in the private sector and in some state-owned enterprises. In the second place, they lack an adequate research infrastructure. Finally, the allocation of grants and financial resources for research and training follow a pattern of discontinuity and unpredictability.

The pressures on the existing postgraduate system are bound to increase in the future for two reasons. On the one hand, the education system itself has repressed demand. The implementation of changes currently being proposed by ABENGE for a more adequate (to the paradigmatic shifts that are taking place in the profession) training of engineers at the undergraduate level will require retraining of existing staff and an increase in the number of engineers with post-graduate education. On the other hand, demand is also increasing in the private sector as more enterprises are establishing and/or increasing their in-house R&D teams. At ANPEI (the association of enterprises which perform in-house R&D) I was told that about 80% of its associates are planning to employ increasing number of M.Sc. and Ph.Ds. in the future and that a similar percentage wants to accelerate their re-training programmes.

Table 6.9
Engineering Ph.D courses - 1986 (percentages)

Areas	Courses	Students	Staff with PhD
Elect./Electronics	19.0	30.75	32.78
Civil	23.6	28.50	17.80
Mechanical	19.0	17.85	18.30
Metallurgy	4.8	7.10	7.39
Naval	2.4	1.15	1.60
Spatial	2.4	2.95	2.90
Transports	7.2	3.85	2.96
Agricultural	-	-	-
Biomedical	4.8	0.05	0.06
Production	4.8	4.75	3.09
TOTAL	100	100	-

Source: CAPES' Data Bank, quoted in Rocha Neto (1990)

6.3 R&D activities

Freeman (1982) considers R&D laboratories in the big private firms one of the most important institutional innovations of the twentieth century. Despite its importance for the emergence of Germany and USA as major leaders of the industrial world [Freeman (1988)], this institutional innovation has been taking place in the BNSI at a very slow pace. According to ANPEI [10], there were only two enterprises performing in-house R&D activities in Brazil by 1950. In the following twenty years, ten more began operating research and development laboratories. It was only after the priority given by the II PND (the second national development plan) to indigenous technological capabilities that there was a quantitative change in this trend. Amongst ANPEI associates, 27 created their R&D departments in the 1970s and another 42 in the 1980s. ANPEI also estimates that another 300 firms perform in-house R&D in the country and that more than 2,000 are assumed to be performing activities more sophisticated than quality control. Despite the

156

significance of these numbers in the context of poor economic environment and lack of technological policies throughout the 1980s, they compare badly with the 1,000 R&D institutes which were established during the last decade by private industries in South Korea [Lee (1991).

a) The contribution of State-owned enterprises: four different experiences

State-owned enterprises have played a major role in establishing the need for in-house R&D amongst enterprises in the country. PETROBRAS (the state--owned petroleum conglomerate) was one of the first to give priority to in-house R&D activities. Since it was established in 1953 PETROBRAS understood the importance of training and research if it was to transform the nationalistic ideals which inspired its creation into the reality of a nationalized petroleum industry. In 1955 CENAP (the centre for training and research in petroleum activities) was created with a major task of training engineers for the specific operational tasks of the petroleum industry [11].

In 1966 CENPES (Petrobras' R&D centre) was created with the specific objective of performing quality control and giving technical support to the company's operational activities. A major shift took place in 1973 when CENPES entered a new phase of activities more involved with scientific and technological research. In its new physical installations located next to the campus of the Federal University of Rio de Janeiro, CENPES increased its laboratory facilities by more than 460%. Towards the end of the 1970s 1,000 people were working in CENPES whose main activities became petrochemical research, basic engineering and petroleum exploration and production [Tigre and Ferraz (1989)].

The experience that has been accumulated by CENPES makes it a complex and integrated centre of technological research and basic engineering. As a result of close links with the operational departments of PETROBRAS, the company today masters about 60 technologies [12], including the capability of developing basic engineering projects. In the area of refining, the company has gradually mastered technological capabilities to a degree which allows it to draw refineries to the specificities of local conditions in processing, raw materials, and marketing. In the area of exploration and production of petroleum CENPES has had to give quick technological solutions to the country's needs to explore its deep-waters reserves. As a result of its indigenous R&D activities, PETROBRAS since 1988 has been exploring petroleum in areas as deep as 492 meters, only surpassed by a few platforms in the Gulf of Mexico [Tigre and Ferraz (1989)].

A different strategy and commitment to R&D activities from that of PETROBRAS has been followed by state-owned enterprises in the sector of steel production. Despite their role of 'growth poles' of the early Brazilian industrialization process, steel-makers have been late-comers with respect to in-house R&D as well as conservative in terms of R&D expenditures. It was not until the 1970s that the first specific R&D laboratories were installed and amongst state-owned steel producers only USIMINAS has a ratio of R&D expenditure as percentage of sales compatible with that of the European steel industry [13].

Despite the accomplishments of the Brazilian steel industry in terms of mastering optimizing innovations and technological changes which adapt imported technology to local conditions [Dahlman and Fonseca (1978)], not much has been achieved in terms of autonomy in process technology. The R&D efforts made so far have only enabled the sector to acquire capabilities to diagnose more properly its technological needs and to negotiate better and cheaper contracts for technology acquisition from abroad. Moreover, there has not been much coordination of the R&D activities performed in the different steel plants of the SIDERBRAS (the federal government's steel holding company) system. As a result, the country has not been able to change its relative position in the sector's international division of labour [Tigre and Ferraz (1989)].

A third different approach to R&D capabilities was taken by ELETROBRAS (the federal government's holding of Brazilian electricity companies). Since its creation in 1972, CEPEL (Eletrobras' R&D centre) has concentrated its efforts in three main areas; firstly, that of operational research and software engineering aimed at the planning and operational aspects of electrical systems; secondly, to the development of electronic digital equipment adequate to local conditions in the areas of control, supervision and protection of substations and transmission lines; and finally, to the quality improvement of equipments produced in Brazil, mainly by local enterprises. Despite the purchasing power of state-owned electricity companies, cooperation and interaction between CEPEL and enterprises of the electrical sector have been limited. Mechanisms have not been created which could generate greater autonomy of local suppliers with respect to international cartels [Tigre and Ferraz (1989)].

A successful experience of developing indigenous technological capabilities and of building strong interactions with university and R&D centres, on the one hand, and with suppliers of equipment, on the other, is that of TELEBRAS' (the state-owned telecommunications holding company) CPqD. Since its creation as TELEBRAS' research centre in 1976, CPqD has played a major role in boosting basic research in universities and in developing the technological capabilities of local enterprises through the development of products and prototypes which are later transferred to these enterprises for production.

The importance of CPqD for boosting technological capabilities in a 'core' area of the new paradigm can be seen from two perspectives. On the one hand, according to Moreira (1989), given the financial and technological fragility of local firms, they would not have been able to increase their technological capabilities if they were to rely solely on the preferential ('vis-à-vis' multinationals) sales to TELEBRAS. On the other hand, "by subjecting the universities and R&D institutes to CPqD's overall technology planning, Brazil could also begin taking over the important 'choice of technology' decision, previously under the sole direction of the MNCs." [Hobday (1985), p. 35].

A result of the technological objectives pursued by CPqD is that, despite having started at a very low level in relation to foreign products, in some key areas, the BNSI has been able to narrow significantly the gap and even come closer to the technical performance of developed countries [14]. With a budget a little over 1.5% of TELEBRAS system's revenues [15], CPqD engages about 1,800 people in its R&D activities which also involve fifteen university and twenty-seven private enterprises research teams. Moreover, in the area of technology transfer, which in 1990 embraced eighty different products and manufacturing processes, CPqD interacts with over fifty different local and multinational companies [Rezende Neto (1991)].

Summing up, the linkages that CPqD has established with various research groups, industrial firms and other organizations have all been geared towards the strengthening of the country's technological capabilities in telecommunications and microelectronics. Thus, through its coordination and financing of R&D activities, CPqD has run a successful programme of technological capabilities in Brazil even when compared with similar programmes in other industrialized countries [16].

b) R&D Institutes

Another source of research and development in Brazil is provided by the 65 research institutes which have been created to provide services to the industrial sector. The establishment of scientific and technical institutions is often mentioned in the literature as building weak relationships with production and exchange activities in the economy [Cooper (1973, 1974)]. However poor might be the explicit results of these R&D institutes in Brazil, they are presented here because of the externalities they usually generate in terms of accumulated informal and frequently undocumented knowledge.

In Brazil, these centres of industrial R&D are mainly institutions sponsored by the federal/state governments (directly or through their enterprises and universities). "Even research centres such as CODETEC (high tech R&D centre based in Campinas) and CTCCA (a producers' cooperative-type leather and shoe technology development centre, based in Rio Grande do Sul), sponsored by private enterprises were created under the guidance and partial sponsorship of the federal government." [IPT (1987), p. 49)

The majority of the R&D institutes were established in the 1965-1980 period when the country went through a very fast industrialization process. Most of the work performed by the majority of them is of a less sophisticated content. Only 12% of the work done is of basic applied research; 10% of process development and 5% of product development [IPT (1987)].

A possible explanation for such a performance is that most of these centres (mainly the ones sponsored by state governments) have been vulnerable to pressures from local politics. At times when industrial diversification was being sought through both import-substitution and export-promotion, the basic survival strategy used by most of these R&D institutes was to move from a 'policy geared to technological relative autonomy' towards a 'policy of response' [17].

Two more factors during the 1980s can be identified as imposing further constraints upon the development of most R&D centres sponsored by the government. The first one is the increase in red tape for hiring new employees which in many cases inhibited training programmes and the establishment of new lines of research. The second is the prohibition of imports of equipment, parts and materials necessary to the operation/improvement of R&D institutes. In interviews I had at SBPC (the Brazilian society for the improvement of science) they emphasized that as a result of cuts in public expenditures and cuts in imports for the sake of improving trade balance figures, research in Brazil throughout the eighties had been as constrained as other sectors. A result of these short-sighted policies, is that "even in areas such as 'new materials' - which are said to be a top priority by government officials - most of the 102 groups performing research in the country, work under poor conditions with outdated and/or poorly maintained equipment" (a senior official at INT - the national institute of technology).

6.4   Science parks

Amongst the examples most frequently mentioned as illustrating 'dynamic externalities' and 'development blocs' are those of the emergence of growth poles around university centres with good records in research in new technologies [Stewart and Ghani (1989), Dahmen (1988)]. These synergies have also been taking place in Brazil through the consolidation of technological poles in different areas of the country. That has been mainly the result of interactions between universities, R&D institutes, local governments, and private and state-owned enterprises which have created the conditions for what Bianchi and Bellini (1991) call "a distinct regional path of development based on endogenous, entrepreneurial forces which could not emerge without a supportive social context." (ibid., p 489).

According to Medeiros et al. (1990), there are 16 such poles in Brazil. Four of them (Florianópolis and Curitiba, in the South, São Carlos in São Paulo, and Campina Grande in the Northeast) are structured under formal organization patterns (non-profit organizations); two of them (São José dos Campos, in São Paulo state, and Santa Rita do Sapucaí, in Minas Gerais), have no formal organization; whilst the rest of them are in the process of formalization (RIOTEC and Campinas) or at the implementation/evaluation stage (three in the South - Santa Maria, Porto Alegre and Joinville; three in the Southeast - BIORIO, Vitória and Petrópolis; one in the Northeast - Recife; and one in the North - Manaus).

These 'technological poles', at different stage of implementation, are the result of strong interactions between the academic world (universities and/or research institutes) and enterprises. In Brazil, there are more than 50 universities/research institutes; 250 enterprises; 10 state governments; 6 state development banks; and more than 20 different associations of entrepreneurs, involved in these poles. They range from high-technology activities to more traditional ones such as mining, food processing, clothing and shoe production.

The 'formalization' of most of these poles took place in the 1980s, with only minor institutional support from federal agencies such as CNPq and FINEP. That is by itself a break with the long established tradition of the almost exclusive role played by the federal government in new economic initiatives. Their histories show different starting points and the interaction of many autonomous initiatives.

The history of the Campinas Pole, for example, can be referred to as far back as the creation of research institutes geared towards agricultural activities such as the institute for food production technology (ITAL). Its main reference, though, is UNICAMP, a state-government sponsored university, created in 1966, with activities that today involve more than 12,000 students, in more than 75 courses, of which over 50% are of graduate studies, all of them geared towards research activities. According to Brisolla (1989), UNICAMP was able to attract Brazilian scientists who had been in exile, and foreigners as well, who brought with them the most up-to-date knowledge from Europe and the United States. "The arrival of professors from the first world made it possible for UNICAMP to achieve scientific and technological standards comparable to the best international centres." (ibid., p.4, my translation).

Medeiros et al. (1989) mention two other 'autonomous' steps which were important for the shaping of the Campinas pole as it is today. The first one was CPqD which has been described above. The second one was CTI (the informatics research centre sponsored by the federal government's special secretary for informatics).

The outcome of the close relationship (formal and/or informal) built between ITAL, UNICAMP, CPqD and CTI, and the people working within them, is a succession of events which took place in the 1980s. They have resulted in a greater political and financial commitment by the Campinas local government, and in the attraction of more than twenty high-tech enterprises to the close neighbourhood of the university campus.

Another example of relative vitality of the technological domain in Brazil, even at times of strong macro-economic constraints such as those of the 1980s, is given by the technological pole of São José dos Campos. Its landmark can be dated to 1950 when ITA (an approximation to MIT's experience sponsored by the Air Force Ministry) was created. Along ITA's stream, four other institutes were created between 1954 and 1980, which today comprise CTA (Aerospatial Technical Center), a military institution under the supervision of the Brazilian Air Force which employs more than 7,000 people.

CTA's major industrial forward linkage has been EMBRAER. Under operation since the 1960s in the production of aeroplanes, EMBRAER's sales exceeded US$650 million in 1989 (more than 2/3 in the international market) and has been presented as a success story both amongst the state-owned enterprises and in the drive of Brazilian industries to increase their share in the world market of technology-intensive goods.

A second research institute - INPE (research centre for the development of non-military space activities) - was created in São José dos Campos by the federal government in 1961. Besides its research activities geared towards the development and manufacturing of space satellites, INPE (1,650 employees) sponsors a graduate course in its area of activities which has trained more than 500 Masters and 30 Ph.Ds.

Medeiros and Perilo (1990) point out that the technological capabilities built around São José dos Campos Pole are the result of the combination of two factors. Firstly, the political commitment of the federal government, which invested in R&D institutes, to high quality teaching facilities. It used its purchasing power as an incentive for the establishment of high-tech industries in the area [18]. The second factor was the non-conventional approach used by the institutes in order to bridge the gap between R&D activities and the industrial sector. As a result of this concentrated and, to a certain extent, coordinated effort by the government, São José dos Campos Technological Pole today hosts more than a dozen high-tech industries, some of them investing as much as 30% of their sales in R&D activities.

In the São Carlos Technological Pole there are more than 50 small, high-tech enterprises, with total sales of more than US$25 million, and a workforce of more than 1,000 employees, most of them with technical or university degrees. Its roots are closely connected to the teaching and research activities at the state university's institute of chemistry and physics and at the federal university's department of materials engineering.

An interesting feature of the São Carlos Technological Pole which differentiates it from the two other mentioned above, is that there was no direct or indirect government programmes which spun-off its establishment. As mentioned by Medeiros et al. (1989), all the 'Schumpeterian entrepreneurs' (in this case mainly university lecturers with business drive) received was the institutional support given by CNPq/FINEP in the mid-1980s.

Santa Rita do Sapucaí in Minas Gerais state is another example of the successful combination of education /research activities and political determination (this time at the municipal level) in the establishment of close links between academic work and high-tech production activities. The pole began with a vocational high school started in 1959, followed by the Institute of Telecommunications of Santa Rita do Sapucaí (a non-profit private organization) which since 1970 graduates engineers specialized in telecommunications. In the 1970s, the city's close location to the main industrial centres of São Paulo and Rio de Janeiro, plus its human resources attracted small and medium size high-tech enterprises. Since 1985 there has been political support by the municipality in the consolidation of the pole which comprises more than 45 small and medium size firms, mostly related to electronics/telecommunications.

A different sort of experience in establishing a successful technological pole is the case of Florianópolis. Based on the research capabilities accumulated at the federal university's school of Engineering (mainly electric and mechanical), a 'joint venture' between state government, federal agencies (CNPq, FINEP and SEI), the university and private business (some MNCs like Mercedes Benz and Pirelli and some big Brazilian high-tech firms such as Metal Leve and Itautec), created in 1984 CERTI (Centre of Informatics Technology of Sta. Catarina). Its main task has been the implementation of cooperative-like R&D projects and of high-tech industries. There are more than 16 enterprises in operation in the areas of informatics, telecommunications, industrial automation and precision mechanics.

6.5 Technological transfer

The analytical framework used here stresses that the ability of different agents to learn-by-interacting is a major element to be investigated in the context of national systems of innovation. The importance of 'learning-by-interacting' is even greater when the objective is to assess an n.s.i.'s ability to take part in the technological/production networks that are being built under the new paradigm. In this respect, the analysis of technological transfers that follows has to be seen with caution due to its limited scope with respect to the 'core' industries of the new paradigm and because of the period for which information is available [19].

Based on a survey conducted by IA-FEA/USP in 1981 involving 4,342 industrial production units, Braga and Willmore (1990), estimated that the main sources of technology used by industries in the BNSI are as shown in Table 6.10.

Table 6.10
Brazil: alternative sources of technology (%)

Type of Technology	In-House	Local Suppliers	Local R&D Instit.	Imported
Product design	81.3	22.5	2.8	9.1
Tool design	65.4	32.1	5.6	7.2
Product engin.	86.9	9.8	4.3	5.2
Proj. engin.	75.2	17.5	13.1	5.9
Layout	82.3	11.4	9.6	4.0

Obs.: the totals are greater than 100% because of multiple sourcing.
Source: Braga and Willmore (1990) Tabela 2

Two points should be stressed about the table above. The first is the reliance on local suppliers as an important source of technology. It shows that the establishment of a fairly large capital-goods sector in Brazil has increased the possibility of broadening user-producer interactions in the BNSI. The second fact is that the data from the beginning of the 1980s are in line with earlier findings by Erber, coord. (1974) and Marcovitch (1978) on the enterprises' reaction to R&D institutes. When surveyed they complained about the quality of the services the institutes could deliver on more complex technological questions. In this respect, the more up-to-date information available concerning 'technological parks' analyzed above can be interpreted as a positive shift in attitude towards greater interactions between professional R&D centres and industries, especially regarding more advanced technologies.

Even though the definition of in-house R&D used in the above mentioned survey seems to be quite broad, the importance of this source of technology might reflect the emphasis given by FINEP [20] to the building of R&D facilities in industries. Between 1970 and 1984, 45% of the resources allocated by FINEP to the program of technological capabilities in local enterprises (ADTEN) were for that purpose [21]. As should be expected, in more recent years there has been a change in the pattern of spending of ADTEN's resources. According to Melo (1989), in the 1985/87 period, 26% of ADTEN's resources were spent on building R&D facilities, 27% on process development, 27% for product development and 5.7% for technology absorption [22].

As for the use of foreign sources of technology, the highlights in the 1980s were:

1.   out of more than 13,000 contracts approved by INPI (23), more than 80% were for trademark licenses (35%) and technological services (45%).

2.   the U.S.A. was the country which supplied most of the technology transferred (35%), West Germany coming in second place with about 15%;

3.   mechanical (13.5%), chemical (11.6%), metallurgical (10.8%) electronics and electric material (7.8%) and mining (6.1%) accounted for over 50% of all technology transfer agreements. It is interesting to note that, whilst in 1980 electric and communications accounted for less than 5% of all contracts, their participation was twice that in 1989, coming next to mechanical andchemical.

Data on technology transfer contracts are presented on Table 6.11. Note that out of 1.9 billion current dollars spent between 1980 and 1988 in payments for technology transfer (BACEN - Central Bank), over 80% were made under technical services, whilst industrial technology licenses, industrial cooperation agreements and patents/trademark responded for 8.5%, 7.1% and 3.3% of the payments, respectively.

Table 6.11
Technology transfer contracts approved by INPI (1980/89)

Country	Trademark	Patent	ITL	ICA	TS
Brazil	1.502	323	312	30	77
Germany (W)	666	160	126	390	863
France	354	51	68	63	615
Japan	100	34	126	79	630
United Kingdom	335	36	44	45	414
United States	2.154	323	312	234	2.014

Source: DIRCO/INPI. Data collected at INPI's library

6.6 Summing up

The analysis of elements of the BNSI's technological domain made in this chapter shows that the challenges that are posed to the country's educational and R&D systems are both qualitatively and quantitatively significant. Some of these systems' weaknesses are historically rooted in the little importance that has been given to education and to research activities throughout the industrialization process of the past fifty years.

Evidence has been presented in support of the generally acknowledged 'bankruptcy of the educational system'. The poor performance of the system as a whole does not provide for the better training of engineers, an area which is recognized for its importance in the needed 'change of spectacles' when there is a shift of paradigm. In general, the situation is well expressed by the words of the president of one the larger local computer firms, "...at the level of human resources, specifically engineers, the situation is catastrophic. We are paying the price of the thoughtlessness and lack of foresight of the last ten years." [quoted in Hewitt (1988)].

Regrettably, even in those industries for which there has been explicit and positive efforts towards technological autonomy, the political commitment to policies has not gone beyond the needs of the specific sector. In other words, the skills and training externalities springing from a 'core' sector such as tele-communications have moved slowly to the BNSI as a whole due to the lack of a general commitment to education and training in the country. Worse, in other cases even training and skills within the sector have been late-comers to the priority list of policy-makers. In the case of informatics, for example, it was not until the establishment of PLANIN (the national plan for informatics) in 1986 that for the first time the need for human resources was made explicit in planning the future of the industry. This is not to deny that there has been an accumulation of both knowledge by the education system and of skills by the entrepreneurial and government sectors in 'core' areas of the new para-digm. Such an accumulation of knowledge and skills can be seen as a positive externality of the country's early entry in the 'core' areas of informatics and te-lecommunications. Obviously, given the necessary political commitment, this can be of help at drawing and implementing programmes aimed at reshaping the education and training systems to the needs of the IT techno-economic pa-radigm.

An important feature of the long learning process which has been taking place within these core areas of the new techno-economic paradigm is the increasing perception of the importance of human resource if the BNSI is to face properly its new challenges. The idea that there is a risk "... in the medium term which will come about by not perceiving that protectionism in itself is not sufficient. We urgently need aggressive measures for human resources." [*Dados e Idéias*, quoted in Hewitt (1992), p. 198] is becoming common-sense not only at the level of the 'core' sectors of the new paradigm but at the level of the economy as a whole as well [24]. Even if 'perception' cannot be equated with 'getting the job done', it is certainly an important starting point.

Research and development in the BNSI has also not followed the pace of development which has characterized the industrialization process of the Brazilian socio-economic formation. In the private sector the institutional innovation of in-house R&D is recent and has been taking place quite slowly when compared with other industrialized countries. The explicit policies drawn especially in the 1970s with the aim of increasing indigenous technological capabilities were followed in the 1980s by excessive red-tape, administrative control and financial constraints by the government on its R&D institutes and on SOEs' research centres. Some of these research centres, nevertheless, have responded quite positively to the needs of their specific industries [25]. Despite the absence of explicit, comprehensive and coordinated policies towards the goal of strengthening the national system of innovation as a whole, some of these R&D centres have accumulated technological capabilities which can contribute to the country's ability to interact with other systems of innovation. Others, have spin-offs to regional networks of technology and production by providing the initial facilities for the emergence of science parks in the BNSI.

The accomplishments of these technological poles of the BNSI seem to be greater than the lack of political and financial support by the federal government would indicate. They also seem to be more relevant for the analysis of the Brazilian national system of innovation than is implied in the indifference with which they are treated by many people involved with science and technology in Brazil. This is not to deny, however, that they still lack a proper assessment that could indicate up to what point they actually have established a 'clan' of agents having a common interest in innovation. In other words, further research is needed to appraise more properly if they have gone beyond the technological learning related to basic technologies in order to build production knowledge and linkages which favour the establishment of strong interaction amongst them [26].

Many other issues, numbers and analyses could be brought together in order to characterize the technological domain of the BNSI. No matter what it has and what it has not accomplished in the past, and regardless of the relative strength or weakness of the system compared to others in developed countries or NICs, it seems that the major criticism of its past performance has been its inadequacy to respond both to the economic and to the social challenges facing the country. Its dilemmas are better characterized by two illustrative perceptions of what it actually has meant to the productive sector and to the social well being of the Brazilian population.

On the one hand, the entrepreneurs [ANPEI (1990)], talk of a "a high technological dependency ... (and) the constraints that such a dependency imposes on our growth as a exporting economy" (ibid.,pg.7) and of a historical disequilibrium that took place in Brazil "between industrial and technological development which has had as one of its consequences a weak commitment with technology. ... The lack of technological development has jeopardized both the adequacy of the productive system to local social conditions and to national sovereignty, as well as the country's autonomy in the international market, which makes it harder for the country to take part in the world economy" (ibid., p. i, my translation).

On the other hand, the workers [DIEESE (1988)] have a strong feeling that "social conditions have not kept up with the improvements in technology: working hours are amongst the longest in the world; unemployment is high; and the workers, in their day-to-day activities, outside the work place, have limited access to 'the wonderful world of science and technology'". (ibid., p. 137, my translation).

Notes

1. The policies followed by South Korea illustrates the 'wasted opportunities' which took place in the BNSI during the 1980s. Comparisons of the data for Brazil with that provided by Lee (1991) show that whilst Brazil started the decade with a better R&D expenditure as percentage of GDP (0.68%) than that of South Korea (0.64%), by 1989 the South Korean percentage (1.92%) was more than three times greater than that of the Brazilian national system of innovations (0.6%).

2. In this sense, the analysis put forward in this book bears in mind that "...the strength of R&D capabilities in a given country is not a function simply of the existence of formal research institutions and laboratories. Perhaps equally important is the accumulated informal and frequently undocumented knowledge acquiring by the indigenous work force through a protracted process of learning-by-doing and transmitted through formal and informal on-the-job training." [O'Connor, (1985)].

3. As an illustration of the total lack of political commitment to tackle the problems facing the system in the 1980s, Moura Castro (1989) points out that "although thousands of experiments with vocational curricula were conducted in the 1970s, no effort was made to take advantage of those that were successful or even, for that matter, to preserve them. Unfortunately, less affluent students having the greatest need to acquire a profession were enrolled in schools lacking both the means and know-how necessary to develop meaningful programs." (ibid., p. 279).

4. Hewitt (1992) identifies the roots of this inadequacy in existing second grade courses in electronics. "For example, of the 109 schools (public and private) in the state of São Paulo which offer courses for electronics technicians, only eleven were considered [by SENAI staff] to be of adequate quality. Even in these schools, the third year of specialization was considered to be inadequate through lack of resources for practical training." (ibid., p. 196).

5. This number is an underestimation, though, because it does not take into account those involved with research in the education system. It is

important to remember, however, that more than 60% of lecturers are part-time, which must be seen as a constraint on they performing systematic research work.

6. According to Schwartzman (1988), the struggle between the 'centres of excellency' - usually located in the south and south-east regions and with accumulated research and teaching experiences - and the 'emerging centres' - usually located in the north and northeast regions - increased in the 1980s when ANDES (the university lecturers' association) and CRUB (the university rectors' council) campaigned intensively in favour of a more equitable distribution of resources amongst the Brazilian public universities. As resources became scarcer, the conflicts between the 'high clergy' of the 'centres of excellency' (some of which in private universities) and the 'low clergy' of the 'emerging centres' (the great majority of them in universities maintained by the federal government) turned out to be one of the unresolved disputes of the 1980s.

7. For a more technical appraisal of the performance and of attempts to change the educational system at different levels, see Moura Castro (1989) and Schwartzman (1988). For an analysis of training and development of human resources for informatics in the country, see MCT (1986).

8. In the interviews I had with Ivan Rocha Neto, of CNPq, and with a member of ABENGE (the national association of schools of engineering), I was told of an on-going project to reform engineering courses' syllabus in order to keep in pace with the changes in technological paradigm.

9. In general, the situation of laboratories resembles that of Electrical Engineering Departments where "with exception of COPPE, PUC-RJ, UNICAMP, USP, UFSC, ITA and UFPb ... the experimental teaching facilities are not at all adequate. ... The situation of the private universities with respect to experimental facilities are even worse. Hence, the governmental efforts for human resources upgrading during the last three years has not been duly followed by adequate investments to improve the teaching and R&D facilities." [Rocha Neto (1990), p. 20].

10. ANPEI, created in 1984, is an association of 82 enterprises which perform R&D activities in the country. In 1989, 68% of its members were local private enterprises, 18% were state-owned and 14% were MNCs. The increasing involvement of the private sector both in the funding and in the activities of R&D is certainly a recent and positive fact for the sector. As was seen in chapter 5, more than the resources in themselves, it seems important to emphasize the political involvement of the productive sector in the discussions concerning R&D.

11. Tigre and Ferraz, coords. (1989) emphasize that training programmes sponsored by CENAP played an important role in establishing an 'organizational culture' which involved PETROBRAS' personnel as well as those working with its suppliers. Some of the personal ties which were generated by these training programmes contributed to the creation of 'bureaucratic rings' supporting R&D activities for the Brazilian petroleum industry.

12. Of which 24 are in refining; 7 in natural gas; 10 in exploration; 3 in alternative sources; 8 in petrochemic and alcoholchemic; and 6 in fertilizers [Tigre and Ferraz, coords. (1989)].

13. CST (a joint-venture of the Brazilian government, Kawasaki Steel of Japan, and Italsider of Italy) which began production in 1983 is another exception. Its R&D activities already involve more than sixty people and its ratio of R&D expenditure as percentage of sales is over .50.

14. For an appraisal of CPqD's achievements in time-switching; digital transmission; fiber optics communications; satellite communication; data and text communication; outside plant; microelectronics and product technology, see Graciosa (1989).

15. In 1990 CPqD's budget was of 73 million dollars which compares well with what South Korea carrier spent in 1987. The R&D intensity as percentage of sales of the Korean telecomm, however, is much greater (2.4%) than that of TELEBRAS (less than 1.5%) [Grupp and Schnoring (1992) and Rezende Neto (1991)]. Moreover, TELEBRAS's R&D intensity and its total expenditure in R&D are quite below the major carriers in the industrialized world.

16. For an analysis of R&D in telecommunications in France, Sweden, Italy, U.K., Japan, South Korea, Spain, the Netherlands, and Germany, see Grupp and Schoring (1992).

17. The major exceptions to this general rule have been those institutes of industrial R&D sponsored by the federal government that are part of big projects such as energy, petrochemicals, aviation and telecommunications, is stressed in other parts of this chapter.

18. For a review of the government's policies aiming at the creation of an internationally competitive aeronautical industry, see Cabral (1992).

19. An attempt was made to have access to the MERIT-CATI data bank (the Maastricht Economic Research Institute on Innovation and Technology's Co-operative Agreements and Technology Indicators information system) which has gathered information with respect to the different networks of production and technological cooperation in the industrialized countries.

Unfortunately the attempt was unsuccessful and the analysis carried out here will use data which are more concerned with property rights and their payments than with innovation itself.

20. FINEP is the federal government's agency which gives most of the institutional and financial support to the development of technological capabilities in private business and/or R&D institutes and university centers. For an appraisal of the agency's performance see Melo (1989).

21. Between 1973 and 1988 FINEP spent over US$5 billion, 20% of which on the ADTEN program. It should be noticed that FINEP's budget has gone through very rapid year-to-year fluctuations which make the agency's performance highly criticized by its users. The uncertainties about federal government's allocation of funds to FINEP has increased even more the risks and uncertainties of R&D activities in Brazil. Nevertheless, the demand for resources has been always greater than the agency's ability to meet them.

22. There has also been a shift in spending from sectors such as mining and mechanical (from 43.3% between 1970 and 1978 to 19.7% in 1986-87) to chemical and petrochemical (from 3.8% to 27.2% in the same periods, respectively). These shifts - of which the one in electronics is the most significant (from an average of 7% in 70-84 to 36.4% in 1985-1987) - reflect close relations with government's industrial policies and/or with state-owned enterprises' investment programmes.

23. INPI is a federal government agency created in 1970 to regulate technology transfer to the country. Royalties for patent licences and trademark licences can only be paid if the licenses are registered with INPI; industrial technology agreements are treated as a sale rather than a license; technical and industrial cooperation agreements depends on convincing INPI that the services are not available in the country; and technical service agreements require a detailed schedule of payment for foreign technicians. The common factor on all agreements is that they are appraised with focus on quality improvement; substitution of Brazilian products for imports; and the possibility of the licence to absorb and master technology within the lifetime of the contract.

24. That is not to minimize the slow pace at which changes are taking place in the education and training systems. "If the computer is not 'allowed' into the classrooms of our education system we run the risk of perpetuating a situation where skills are in short supply and the new technologies are an abstraction with very negative effects on the vast majority of the population." (interviews).

25. The positive outcomes of SOEs' R&D strategies is due to their direct, more autonomous actions. Despite the administrative and financial constraints which were imposed on them by SEST (the state-owned enterprises' watch-dog) in its effort throughout the 1980s to curb SOEs' autonomy, they have been able to maintain reasonably well-trained research teams and up-dated laboratories. To their credit are also the externalities they generate through the different linkages they have established with local suppliers, the latter's in-house R&D laboratories and with other research centres in the country.

26. The emphasis given here to an analysis of the Brazilian science parks along the lines proposed by Bianchi and Bellini (1991) is due to the way these poles are many times seen - by those who are apologetic about their importance - as the panacea for technological development, whose major requirements would be the cheap supply of warehouses, laboratories, and office facilities.

7 Conclusions

This book has examined Brazilian development from a perspective that takes into consideration global restructuring. The perspective is focused on changes in the techno-economic paradigm of world development and on the potential for different national systems of innovation to 'match' these changes, or not, through their own appropriate technological, economic and institutional arrangements.

Interpreting Brazilian economic performance

i. The lost decade diagnosis: Recent interpretations of Brazil's economic performance [Sachs (1990) and Dornbusch (1991), amongst others] have revolved around the diagnosis of a lost decade. They compare the Brazilian stabilization programmes unfavourably with those pursued by other Latin American countries (especially those which followed the IMF/World Bank 'recipes' - such as Chile and Mexico) [1].

The approach used here points to oversights and biases in this approach. Focus on debt management, unbalanced public sector accounts, and price instability puts emphasis on policy failures without recognizing more positive structural changes. The roots of the biases are to be found in the way academics and international development agencies focused on Brazil's economic performance up to the early eighties but failed to recognize world institutional and technological conditions which allowed that economic performance.

From such a neo-liberal perspective, Brazil's economic achievements were concrete manifestations of the reduction in distortion which allowed the economy to find a 'correct' position within the international division of labour. Moreover, these economic achievements were viewed as signaling a new era in North-South relations, as NICs - such as Brazil - gained the opportunity to upgrade their niches in the international division of labour. As Brazil's economic performance deteriorated throughout the eighties, the neo-liberal ideology defined the 1980's as a 'lost decade' arising from the country's failure to respond adequately to the prescriptions of more market and less government [Castro and Ronci (1991)].

With regard to the achievements of newly industrialized countries (especially in the 1960s/'70s), elsewhere [Villaschi (1991)] it is shown that the claim for their apparent convergence towards the growth structure of developed countries has to be treated with caution. Market based explanations fail to recognize that in that period there was a fruitful combination of (i) political commitment towards industrialization by those countries' governments; and (ii) 'windows of opportunities' in industries whose technological trajectories were well-defined and realizable under the 'fordist techno-economic paradigm' [2].

The major objection made here to the 'lost decade' diagnosis is that it focuses on a number of the most immediate symptoms of economic difficulties whilst neglecting the underlying determinants of economic performance. Crucial problems such as high inflation, inefficient management of government bureaucracies, and over-protection of local producers from external competition undoubtedly need to be addressed. However, it is the contention of the present analysis that these problems should be placed in the context of global changes. In other words, framing the Brazilian crisis within the neo-liberal perspective of internal conditions and management disregards important features of the country's associated-dependency. The diagnosis of the 'lost decade' addresses economic constraints to the country's development (mainly those regarding inflation, external debt, and public deficit) rather than the possibilities that the IT techno- economic paradigm opens for the transformation of its associated-dependency.

ii. Looking beyond inflation, external debt, and public deficit: in order to provide an analysis of the Brazilian political economy in the 1980s which goes beyond the narrow focus of the 'lost decade' diagnosis, two concepts have been appropriated and extended in this book. Firstly, the concept of associated- -dependency was broadened in its analytical scope in order to take into consideration changes in techno-economic paradigm and the way it raises new constraints and/or opens windows of opportunities for transforming technological dependency.

The characterization of the IT techno-economic paradigm (Chapter 3) implies that today it is more important to be aware of the possibilities from, and the constraints imposed by, greater 'technological interdependency', than it is to search for 'technological autonomy'. Whilst a degree of technological autonomy was necessary to escape from dependency under the regime of inter- -firm competition which prevailed during the 'fordist' techno-economic paradigm [3], technological interdependency is crucial if the transformation of dependency is to be achieved under the networking regime prevailing under the IT techno-economic paradigm (Chapter 3).

The analysis of elements of the 'economic domain' (Chapter 4) shows that, despite the wasted opportunities (due to lack of coherent industrial and technological policies), the Brazilian industrialization process did move in the 1980s beyond the transformation of its dependency on trade of agriculture and semi-industrialized products. It finalized the 'forced march' conceived by the II PND (Chapter 2) and accomplished industrial and technological capabilities [4] in 'core' industries of the IT techno-economic paradigm. In particular, the analysis has shown that in the 1980s the BNSI continued to build industrial and technological capabilities appropriate to the new techno-economic paradigm through interactions amongst local, multinational, and state-owned enterprises; between R&D institutes and users of technology in the production system. Empirical material presented here (mainly those in Chapters 4 and 6) indicates that, provided proper mechanisms are put in place, these capabilities can increase the potential of the BNSI to play an active role in the production and technological networks which are being built amongst firms, industries and countries in the industrialized world.

The major evidence for the development of technological and industrial capabilities is in the 'core' areas of the IT techno-economic paradigm - informatics and telecommunications (Chapters 4 and 6). As was pointed out in the analytical framework established in Chapter 3, the sooner firms and countries master a techno-economic paradigm's core industries, the greater are their chances to sustain their position or even 'leap-frog' in technological and, hence, economic capability. The 'lost decade' diagnosis overlooks these key aspects of technological capabilities and, consequently, draws incomplete conclusions on the performance of the Brazilian economy in the 1980s.

The more optimistic analysis of Brazil's economic performance in the 1980s, derived from the technological focus of the book, recognizes the constraints which are imposed upon development outside the OECD countries. In particular it recognizes changes in the international regime and how these changes can create obstacles for development outside the 'core' counties. International investment today is driven by a different logic from that prevalent up until the late 1970s. Previously, the main carrier of interdependence was international trade, whilst foreign direct investment was a mere extension to the international arena of national oligopolistic rivalries. This international regime was favourable to the creation of foreign affiliates serving overseas markets, and Brazil took advantage of it (Chapter 2). Nowadays, investment has been increasingly taking over from trade in current globalization patterns [5]. Moreover, innovation and production under the IT techno-economic paradigm have increasingly been taking place through cooperation agreements and strategic partnerships between companies from and within the 'Triad' of USA, Japan and Western Europe.

As a result of this new pattern of interdependence, "firms of the smaller industrialized states, and the countries with weaker technology base, (...) face particular constraints with respect to international technological cooperation." [Chesnais (1988), p. 112]. Since these technological cooperation schemes also inform production networks (Chapter 3), different thresholds are confronted by new entrants both in technological and in production networks.

In today's economic environment, the availability of abundant, low-cost raw materials and a pool of cheap labour is no longer enough to ensure growing markets for NICs such as Brazil which can sustain a process of industrialization and social progress.

Extending the n.s.i. concept

The concept of national system of innovation has been adopted and extended in this book in order to highlight features of Brazil's conservative modernization (Chapter 2). Moreover, evidence for the lack of institutional stability and flexibility, provided in the analysis of the economic and technological domains pointed to the need to focus institutional analysis beyond those aspects which are usually treated in sectoral studies.

Chapter 5 showed how the system's rigidities created barriers to institutional changes. The new Constitution of 1988 offers an example of failure to provide clear institutional 'building blocs' for new directions for the country's economic and social development. The analysis of the BNSI's institutional domain showed that in the 1980s political forces emerged in the Brazilian polity which could be favourable to the BNSI. Thus, regardless of the continuing lack of coherent technological policies, active political debate emerged around the theme of technological development (Chapter 5).

The political debate went beyond the specificities of the market reserve law for informatics in order to make explicit in the new Constitution that, "the State will promote and give support to scientific development and technological capabilities", (Article 218). Further, in the state apparatus, intense debate concerning technological development took place at the local level, as regional governments tied resources in their constitutions for the funding of science and technology projects.

Despite the conservative characteristics of Brazil's industrialization process (Chapter 2), the analysis of the BNSI's institutional domain in the 1980s revealed the emergence of strong pressure groups committed to science and technological development. These pressure groups amongst entrepreneurs is seen here as the seeds of 'collective entrepreneurship' which arises from the 'learning-by-interacting' which lies at the centre of a national system of innovation (Chapter 3).

The emphasis of some of these pressure groups is not restricted to technological development as a tool for increasing productivity but is also explicitly directed to the task of drawing a 'national project' for science and technology. Above all, these groups recognize that this project must move beyond the institutional arrangements made for the industrialization process which started in the 1930s. This recognition reveals a close awareness by these groups of the country's necessary re-alignment in the directions being laid down by the new techno-economic paradigm. Thus, not only along the narrow terrain of technological development, but also within the requirements of the three domains of the BNSI, it can be argued that the 1980s were not years of total loss.

Constraints in the BNSI

In the process of identifying interactions between and amongst elements of the three domains (Part II), it became clear that, despite the interactions between them, each of the three domains has an intrinsic dynamic and content of its own. The imbalances or 'mismatches' between them have not led 'automatically' to more balanced and 'smoother' configurations. These 'mismatches' should be of no surprise, though, given the economic roots of Brazil's political economy (Chapter 2); and the disequilibrating content of a change in techno-economic paradigm (Chapter 3).

The adaptability of elements of each domain to the needs of its own and/or other domains has also been shown to be bounded and limited. Illustrations of rigidities and instabilities have been provided in the analysis of all three domains. That is not just the case of the perverse effects on the BNSI as a whole of more general inflexibilities such as the country's institutional path--dependence, and of its general macroeconomic instabilities. Financial instability was shown to be a major obstacle for R&D activities; rigidities in the educational system were shown to place major constraints for the process of 'changing spectacles' towards the IT techno-economic paradigm. Major problem also identified as major obstacles emphasis has been given to the environment of institutional and financial instability that surrounds R&D activities and to the rigidities of the educational system.

The analysis shows (Chapter 6) that the existing research capabilities within universities and R&D institutes (mainly those sponsored by state-owned enterprises) have, indeed, suffered some degree of wasted opportunities as a result of constraints imposed upon them by stabilization policies. Wasted opportunities were also caused by the rigidities of the educational system which created two forms of constraint on the BNSI. Firstly, it has not been able to meet the quantitative aspects of universality of primary education. On the other hand, it has failed to respond to the qualitative requirements of systemic knowledge which is expected to prevail under the new paradigm.

Two roots were identified for these wasted opportunities in the educational and R&D systems (Chapter 4); firstly, the perverse effects of short-term macroeconomic policies which prevailed throughout most of the 1980s; and, secondly, the absence of more stable and coherent scientific and technological policies. In some ways, the latter can be seen as a consequence of the former since it creates the presumption that state-owned enterprises are a major source of the country's difficulties. In practice many SOEs have been instrumental in the strengthening of the country's industrial and technological capabilities.

The BNSI and technological capabilities under the IT techno-economic paradigm

Contrary to the more pessimistic tune of the 'lost decade' diagnosis, this work argues that Brazil is well-positioned to take advantage of some 'windows of opportunities' which have been opened by the emergence of the IT techno--economic paradigm. The analysis of the BNSI (Part II) provides evidence for the argument that the Brazilian socio-economic formation can take its associated-dependency beyond the spheres of exchange and production of goods and services. In other words, it can search for 'windows of opportunities' in the technological and production networks which are being built amongst industrialized countries.

The degree of familiarity that the BNSI has gained with the functionality of informatics and telecommunications technologies is one of its most important assets for the transformation of the country's dependence. Despite their small scale, capabilities exist today and are based on the country's manufacturing and product innovation capabilities in these two dynamic industries.

These capabilities are spread throughout the system in state-owned, local and multinational enterprises; in R&D institutes; and in universities. As a result, these agents' negotiation position in the acquisition of foreign technology in the core areas of the new paradigm has been strengthened.

Despite the possible identification of these capabilities with the seeds of 'collective entrepreneurship' under the IT techno-economic paradigm, they are not, by any means, sufficient conditions for the transformation of dependency. The rigidity of the country's institutions has been a major obstacle to the emergence of a new hegemonic project aimed at the transformation of dependency under the new paradigm. This is not to say that there is lack of awareness of the need for a 'national project' which can take the country to a new development path. What is lacking is the ability to create a new regime of accumulation with appropriate institutional forms, social relations, and balance of social forces in the power bloc and amongst the population more generally.

Under these circumstances, the neo-liberal appeal for less state intervention as such is misplaced [6]. In the past the state in Brazil has established policies which stimulated progress both along existing trajectories and in sectors which were to become 'core' areas of the new techno-economic paradigm. As shown in Chapter 2 and in Part II, the Brazilian State has played an important role in establishing some of the most positive features of the BNSI. That has been the case in (i) policies towards industrial and technological autonomy carried out by state-owned-enterprises and the externalities of these policies to the economy as a whole; (ii) the 'market reserve for informatics' which has strengthened industrial and technological capabilities amongst local enterprises in a 'core' area of the new techno-economic paradigm; and (iii) the attraction of foreign capital which has contributed to the diversification of the country's industrial production and its new role in the international division of labour.

Refocusing losses, and redirecting challenges

Contrary to neo-liberal views that failures of the 1980s reflect inadequate liberalization, it is argued here that the major loss of the 1980s has been in the opportunity of the Brazilian State to enhance the ability of internal agents to respond more adequately to the changes needed. An example of such a lost opportunity is the passive role played by the state in reshaping the country's education system.

The analysis of the BNSI shows that if it is to face the challenges that are posed by the new techno-economic paradigm, the state must provide an institutional framework more adequate for the transformation of the country's dependency. This framework must be drawn bearing two questions in mind. Firstly, industrial, technological and infrastructural conditions must be provided to the BNSI in order to enable it to increase its dynamic advantages in 'core' industries. In the second place, a coherent foreign policy must be drawn in order to enable the BNSI to minimize the negative effects of the growing politicization of world investment and trade flows [7].

The political implications and the institutional engineering required for the transformation of the BNSI along the lines suggested above are beyond the scope of this work [8]. The experience of developed countries, however, shows that there is no easy and single solution [see Jessop et al. (1991)]. Moreover, the paradoxes that characterize the Brazilian conservative modernization process do not leave much room for innovation through imitation. Recent events in Brazilian politics show that institutional innovation is even harder because, regardless of changes in the political regime, the grip of decadent politicians in power is strong.

The challenges posed to institutions by the country's socio-economic crossroads are complex and leave no room for simplifying assumptions. The invocation of complexity, however, should not stop any analysis from going further than merely saying that the answers are all contingent. On the contrary, it should go further in identifying the social and economic factors upon which they depend.

Such an identification has been attempted here. An effort has been made in order to place issues of political economy under a perspective which is usually marginalized in mainstream economics. It has extended the concept of national system of innovation in order to draw attention to the forms of internal and external dependency which take place in the Brazilian socio-economic formation. This extension has allowed for a stress upon the distinction which exists between the challenges of transforming dependency now 'vis-à-vis' those which were faced by the country in the past.

In a nutshell: the previous transformation of dependency, internal political and institutional ingenuity partially overcame the technological constraints which were thought to make the country's industrialization impossible. In the present, internal technological capabilities exist and are constrained by the lack of a 'national project' that takes advantage of the 'windows of opportunities' and which faces the challenges under the new paradigm.

Summing up

This book does not simply introduce the issue of technological capability to the debate over industrialization, economic growth and its application to the Brazilian experience. Nor does it simply suggest that the empirical experience of Brazil contradicts the view of the eighties as a lost decade.

Rather, it situates technological development within the theories of techno--economic paradigm and of national systems of innovation. The latter, as used here, is extended in two crucial ways - by situating development and dependency within a framework of global interaction at the technological level. And by situating technological relations themselves beyond the domain of the system of technologies in order to encompass the economic machine and the system of social relations and institutions as well. Further, the analysis understands these three domains and their interactions in terms which might be recognized within orthodox terminology as depending extensively upon substantial intra- and inter-domain externalities.

Within these broad theoretical propositions, it is recognized that the Brazilian economic development over the past two decades has been confronted by a techno-economic paradigm shift at the world level, one of transition from fordism to information technology. It is associated with new forms of technological relations and new forms within which each of these are embedded within the BNSI.

This has allowed the analysis to endow an empirical work and assessment with a content that is too readily overlooked by conventional economics. In analytical terms, it has cut through the issues of market versus state and of austerity 'versus' expansion to highlight the continuing role of the state, and of other agencies, in promoting a definite, if faltering, process towards restructuring within the new techno-economic paradigm. As a consequence, it has been possible to question and reassess the proposition of the 1980s as a lost decade. The purpose is less to hold to a more optimistic stance either in retrospect or in prospect, for the book has heavily emphasized both the progress that has been made as well as those opportunities that have been missed and the constraints on further progress. Rather, through the analytical framework of national systems of innovation, and the attempt to identify its specific empirical parameters in the case of Brazil, the analysis has aimed at bringing technology policy to the fore in ways which root it within the broad economic and social framework and a correspondingly appropriate assessment of material conditions.

The book does not claim that its analytical framework is the only one capable of confronting these issues. Nor that the boundaries of techno-economic paradigm, national systems of innovation and its domains are well-defined. But it would be a mistake to dismiss the paradigm used here as being without theoretical content. For its emphases, most notably the emergence of innovation (and hence dynamic comparative advantage) within sets of economic and social relations that are not reducible to a simple market/non- -market dichotomy, place it on a totally different terrain than that of conventional economic theory. The neo-Schumpeterian approach adopted and its associated objects and methods of enquiry have allowed the book both to uncover the technological dynamic within Brazil and to contradict the partially sterile debate concerning the country's economic situation and prospects.

Two areas which require further research have not been covered here. Firstly, no consideration was given to the financing of innovation. Despite the many indications from the interviews that most in-house R&D projects have been self-financed, and that the lack of continuity in the financing of R&D institutes and research projects has caused great disturbances, little is known about the role of finance in the fostering of technological capabilities in the BNSI. The attempts made to fill this gap were frustrated; firstly, because the area has been neglected in most research; and secondly, because there have been changes in the forms of funding R&D activities which require investigations that would go beyond the scope of this book.

Secondly, more specific work is needed with respect to networking in the BNSI. This is so with respect to the ways technological and production cooperation is taking place both within the system and between its elements and their counterparts in other systems of innovation in the industrialized world.

Despite these and other limitations of the present work, an attempt has been made to show that a new form of dependency can emerge from the BNSI. There is no indication, however, that this emergence can take place 'naturally'. On the contrary, the analysis has shown that a new form of interdependency will only emerge if a favourable n.s.i. project is consciously constructed by social forces with that goal in mind.

Notes

1. Emphasis on the 'lost decade' can also be found in the 'forum em busca da modernidade' [Velloso (1990a,b,c)] and in works concerned with the social dimensions of the Brazilian crisis [inter alia Draibe (1991) and Camargo and Giambiagi (1991)]. Further, the 'lost decade' debate can also be used to draw differences between the two main contenders in the 1989 Presidential election. Whilst the 'modernizer' Collor claimed that the losses were caused by too much state and incompetence/corruption of the state apparatus, the left-wing Lula emphasized the lack of the use of the state as a solution to crucial social problems. The main critique of this book is to the approach taken by the already mentioned academics and international organizations such as the World Bank and the International Monetary Fund and their way of seeing the losses of the eighties.

2. In other words, the sustainability of the convergence process became closely linked to the awareness of (and positive actions towards) the paradigmatic changes that were taking place in the technological base of world development. The awareness regarding the on-going change in techno-economic paradigm is generally absent from the 'lost decade' diagnosis because it centres its analysis mainly on the change of economic regime taking place in the industrialized countries and on the need for stabilization and structural adjustments in countries such as Brazil in order to 'fit-in' the new regime's requirements.

3. The control over technologies by a few firms could block the feasibility of a country's industrialization project. In the case of Brazil, that was certainly the case for the steel industry. The establishment of the Volta Redonda plant only came about as a result of the bargaining power that the country acquired during World War II [Fausto (1984)].

4. As emphasized by Erber (1977) whilst industrial capabilities enable a country to produce goods and services, technological capabilities allow

the country's production system to innovate in processes, and in products and services.

5   The flow of direct investment soared during the second half of the 1980s, growing 2.5 times faster than exports. But developing countries' share of this cash fell from 25% in 1980, to 17% in 1986-90. According to Ernst (1990), most of this 17% has gone to China, to the 'four tigers', and to Thailand, Malaysia and Indonesia.

6.   The misplacement of the neo-liberal 'recipe' is not only perceived by heterodox economists [see Fajnzylber (1988), for example] for whom the state has an important role to be performed in a world where much more takes place besides competition between firms. The perception that in international markets confrontations also exist between productive systems, social organizations and institutional systems is also shared by hi-tech entrepreneurs.   For John Sculley, chief executive of Apple Computer, for example, "companies don't run themselves. Countries need leadership too [in order to foster partnership between the public and the private sector in hi-tech industries]". (quoted in *The Economist*, 26/IX/1992, p. 53).

7.   The call for such a foreign policy bears in mind that international regimes are neither as flexible as the apologist for a new international order seems to imply, nor too rigid as radical dependencists suggest. Thus, despite recognizing that (i) no radical change can be expected in existing regimes such as monetary and trade relations; and (ii) there is not much room for creating a regime of technology transfer which would take into consideration the particular needs of most countries, a country with the economic and political dimensions of Brazil ought to search for a negotiation position in the international community other than that of the second largest debtor country in the world.

8.   Elsewhere [Villaschi (1992)] indications have been given of key aspects to be taken into consideration by institutional engineers if institutions in Brazil are to respond to some of the requirements of the new paradigm.

References

ABENGE/CONFEA (1990), 'Perfil do Engenheiro no Século XX', CONFEA, Brasília, mimeo;

ABIMAQ/SINDMAQ (1990), *Política Industrial para a Indústria de Máquinas e Equipamentos no Brasil*, ABIMAQ/ SINDIMAQ/FINEP, São Paulo;

Abreu, M and Fritsch, W (1988), 'Obstacles to Brazilian Export Growth and the Present Trade Negociations', *Texto para Discussão nº 187*, PUC/Dep. Economia, Rio de Janeiro, mimeo;

Adler, E (1988), 'O papel das elites políticas e intelectuais e das instituições no desenvolvimento da informática e da energia nuclear na Argentina e no Brasil', *Dados - Revista de Ciências Sociais*, 31(3): 373-403;

AFCPqD (1991), *Cadernos de Política Tecnológica*, nºs 3 and 4, AFCPqd, Campinas;

_____. (1992), *Cadernos de Política Tecnológica*, nº 6, AFCPqD, Campinas;

Albert, M (1991), *Capitalism contre Capitalism*, Editions du Seuil, Paris;

Alvstan, C (1988), 'International Trade in a Changing Environment - a Demand for a New Theory', in Tornqvist et al. (1988);

Amsdem, A (1977), 'The Division of Labour is Limited by the Type of Market: The Case of the Taiwanese Machine Tool Industry', *World Development*, 5(3): 217-34;

_____. (1989), *Asia's next giant: South Korea and late industrialization*, Oxford University Press, Oxford;

Andersen, E (1991), 'Approaching National Systems of Innovation from the Production and Linkage Structure', preliminary version of Andersen (1992);

_____. (1992), 'Approaching National Systems of Innovation, in Lundvall, B-A, ed. (1992);

Andreff, W (1984), 'The international centralization of capital and the re-ordering of world capitalism', *Capital & Class*, 22: 58-80;

ANPEI (1988), 'A associação e seu trabalho', ANPEI, São Paulo;

_____. (1990), 'A Inserção do Brasil na Economia Mundial: o desafio tecnológico', ANPEI, São Paulo, mimeo;

Araújo, J, Haguenauer, L and Machado, J (1989), 'Proteção, Competitividade e Desempenho Exportador da Economia Brasileira no Anos 80', *Revista Brasileira de Comércio Exterior*, V(26):13-25, FUNCEX, Rio de Janeiro;

Arida, P and Lara-Resende, A (1985), 'Inertial inflation and monetary reform', in Williamson, J. ed. (1985), *Inflation and indexation: Argentina, Brazil and Israel*, MIT Press, Cambridge, Mass.;

Arrow, K (1962), 'The economic implications of learning by doing', *Review of Economic Studies*, vol. XXIX, no. 80: 155-73;

_____. (1973), *Information and Economic Behaviour*, Federation of Swedish Industries, Stockholm;

_____. (1974), *The Limits of Organisation*, W.W. Norton & Company, New York;

Arthur, W (1988), 'Competing Technologies: an Overview', in Dosi et al. (1988);

_____. (1989), 'Competing technologies, increasing returns, and lock-in by historical events', *The Economic Journal*, 99: 116-31;

Baer, W (1989), *The Brazilian Economy - growth and development*, 3rd. Edition, Praeger, New York;

Baptista, M (1987), 'A Indústria Eletrônica de Consumo a Nível International e no Brasil. Padrões de Concorrência, Inovação Tecnológica e Caráter de Intervenção do Estado', M.Sc. Dissertation, IE/UNICAMP, Campinas;

Baptista, M, Caulliraux, H, Possas, M, and Tauile, J, (1990), 'A Indústria de Informática no Brasil', in Coutinho and Suzigan, coords. (1990);

Bacha, E and Klein, H, eds. (1989), *Social Change in Brazil - 1945-1985*, New Mexico University Press, Albuquerque;

Barreto, A, Gusso, D, Demo, P, coords. (1990), 'Sistema Educativo-cultural: uma visão prospectiva' in IPEA/IPLAN (1990), *Para a Década de 90*, vol. 4, IPEA, Brasília;

Bastos, M (1992), 'State policies and private interests: the struggle over information technology policy in Brazil', in Schmitz and Cassiolato, eds. (1992);

Bauman, R (1989a), 'Comportamento Recente do Capital Estrangeiro', IPLAN *Discussion Paper nº 5*, IPEA/IPLAN, Brasília;

_____. (1989b), 'BEFIEX: efeitos internos de um incentivo à exportação', *Notas para Discussão nº 7*, IPEA/IPLAN, Brasília;

Baumol, W (1985), 'Productivity Growth, Convergence and Welfare: What the Long-Run Data Show', *American Economic Review*, 76(5):1072-1085;

Berg, A and Sachs, J (1988), 'The developing country debt crisis: some structural explanations', *Journal of Development Economics*, 29(3):271-306;

Bianchi, P and Bellini, N (1991), 'Public policies for local networks of innovators', *Research Policy*, 20: 487-497;

Biato, F, Guimarães, E, Figueired, M (1971), 'Potencial de Pesquisa Tecnológica no Brasil', *Relatório de Pesquisas n° 5*, IPEA/IPLAN, Rio de Janeiro;

Bielschowsky, R and Ferraz, J (1990), 'Perspectiva do Comportamento Tecnológico de Empresas Nacionais e Transnacionais na Indústria Brasileira', IEI/UFRJ, Rio de Janeiro, mimeo;

BNDE (1974), 'FUNTEC - 10 anos de apoio a pesquisa', BNDE, Rio de Janeiro;

Bonelli, R and Sedlaceck, G (1991), 'A evolução da distrituição de renda entre 1983 e 1988', in Camargo, J and Giambiagi, F, eds. (1991);

Botelho, A, Ferro, J, McKnight, L and Manfredini, J (1992), 'Telecommunications in Brazil: Reform or Revolution?', paper prepared for *The Telecommunications in Latin America Project*, Center for Telecommunications and Information Studies, Columbia University, New York;

Boyer, R (1988a), 'Technical change and the theory of 'regulation'', in Dosi et al. (1988);

_____. (1988b), *The Search for Labour Market Flexibility*, Claredon, Oxford;

_____. (1989), 'New Directions in Management Practices and Work Organization: general principles and national trajectories', paper prepared for the OECD Conference *Technological Change as a Social Process - Society, Enterprises and the Individual*, Helsinki, December 11-13;

_____. (1990), 'The Capital Labor Relations in OECD Countries: From the Fordist 'Golden Age' to Contrasted National Trajectories', *CEPREMAP Working Paper n° 9020*, CEPREMAP, Paris;

Braga, H and Matesco, V (1986), 'Progresso Técnico na Indústria Brasileira: Indicadores e Análise de seus Fatores Determinantes, *Textos para Discussão n° 99*, IPEA/INPES, Rio de Janeiro;

_____. (1989), 'Desempenho Tecnológico da Indústria Brasileira: Indicadores e Análise de seus Fatores Determinantes', *Textos para Discussão Interna n° 162*, Rio de Janeiro: IPEA/INPES;

Braga, H and Willmore, L (1990), 'As importações e o esforço tecnológico: uma análise de seus determinantes em empresas brasileiras', *Revista Brasileira de Economia*, 44(2):131-55, FGV, Rio de Janeiro;

Bresser Pereira, L (1978), *O colapso de uma aliança de classe*, Brasiliense, São Paulo;

_____. (1983), *Introdução à Economia Brasileira*, São Paulo: Brasiliense;

_____. (1989), 'De volta ao capital mercantil: Caio Prado Jr. e a crise da Nova República', *Revista Brasileira de Ciência Política*, 1(1):45-69;

_____. (1990), 'Da crise fiscal à redução da dívida', in Velloso, ed. (1990c);

Brisolla, S (1989), 'A Relação da Universidade com o Setor Produtivo - o caso da UNICAMP', UNICAMP/DPCT, Campinas, mimeo;

Bullock, A, Stallybrass, O and Trombley, S, eds. (1988), *The Fontana Dictionary of Modern Thought*, 2nd. Edition, Fontana Press, London;

Cabral, A (1992), 'Science and technology policy: the Brazilian experience in the aeronautical industry', *Science and Public Policy*, 19(1): 35-41;

Camargo, A (1990), 'As duas faces de Janus: os paradoxos da modernidade incompleta', in Velloso, J. coord. (1990b);

Camargo, J and Giambiagi, F, eds.(1991), *Distribuição de Renda no Brasil*, Paz e Terra, Rio de Janeiro;

Cano, W (1977), *Raízes da Concentração Industrial em São Paulo*, DIFEL, São Paulo;

Caporaso, J, ed. (1987), *A Changing International Division of Labor*, Frances Pinter, London;

Cardoso, E and Fishlow, A (1990), 'The Macroeconomics of the Brazilian External Debt', in Sachs, J ed. (1990), *Developing Country Debt and Economic Performance*, Vol. 2, The University of Chicago Press, Chicago;

Cardoso, F (1980), *As Idéias e seu Lugar*, Vozes, Petrópolis;

_____. (1980), 'Dilemas do autoritarismo', in Cardoso, F and Martins, C, eds. (1980), *Política e Sociedade*, CEBRAP, São Paulo;

Cardoso, F and Faletto, E (1979), *Dependency and Development in Latin America*, University of California Press, Berkeley, Cal.;

Cassiolato, J, Brunetti, J and Paula, M (1981), 'Evolução da Política Científica e Tecnológica e o Desenvolvimento Economico Brasileiro na Última Década: Algumas Reflexões', in OEA (1982), *V Seminário Metodológico sobre Política y Planificacion Cientifica y Tecnologica*, OEA, Washington, D.C.;

Cassiolato, J, Hewitt, T and Schmitz, H (1992), 'Learning in industry and government', in Schmitz and Cassiolato, eds. (1992);

Castilhos, C (1992), *Les conditions de la production e de l'assimilation de technologies nouvellles dans l'industrie manufacturiere bresilienne*, Ph.D. Dissertation, Universite de Paris- X - Nanterre, Paris;

Castro, A (1971), *Sete ensaios sobre a economia brasileira*, 2 vols., Forense, Rio de Janeiro;

_____. (1985), 'Ajustamento x Transformação. A Economia Brasileira de 1974 a 1984', in Castro, A and Souza, F (1985), *A Economia Brasileira em Marcha Forçada*, Paz e Terra, Rio de Janeiro;

Castro, M (1990), 'Uneven Development and Peripheral Capitalism: The case of Brazilian informatics', LSE, London, mimeo;

Castro, P. and Ronci, M. (1991), 'Brazilian Hyper-inflation: an Institutional Approach', *Conference Out of Debt and into Development: Prospects for Emerging Economies*, Steyning, West Sussex, 25-28 February;

CEC (1987), 'Towards a Dynamic European Economy', *Green Paper on the Development of the Common Market for Telecommunications Services and Equipment*, CEC, Brussels;

Chesnais, F. (1988), 'Multinational entreprises and the international diffusion of technology', in Dosi et al. (1988);

Clements, B and McClain, J (1990), 'The Political Economy of Export Promotion in Brazil', in Graham and Wilson, eds. (1990);

CNI (1990), 'Competitividade e estratégia industrial: a visão de líderes industriais brasileiros', CNI, Rio de Janeiro;

CNPq (1988), *Evolução dos Recursos da União para C&T - 1980 a 1987*, CNPq, Brasília;

CNPq (1990), 'Quadro Sinóptico - Indicadores de C&T no Brasil', CNPq, Brasília, mimeo;

Cohen, D (1991), *Private lending to sovereign states: a theoretical autopsy*, MIT Press, Cambridge, Mass.;

Cohen, S (1987), 'A Labour Process to Nowhere?', *New Left Review*, 165;

Colombo, U (1988), 'The Technology Revolution and the Restructuring of the Global Economy', in Muroyama, J and Stever, G, eds. (1988), *Globalization of Technology*, National Academy Press, Washington, D.C.;

Conjuntura Econômica (1990), 44(6), FGV, Rio de Janeiro;

Cooper, C (1973), 'Science, Technology and Production in the Underdeveloped World', in Cooper, C, ed. (1973), *Science, Technology and Development*, Frank Cass, London;

_____. (1974), 'Science Policy and Technological Change in Underdeveloped Economies', *World Development*, 2(3);

Correa do Lago, L. (1987), 'Investimentos diretos no Brasil e a conversão de empréstimos em capital de risco', *Texto para Discussão n° 161*, PUC/Dep. Economia, Rio de Janeiro, mimeo;

Coutinho, L and Suzigan, W, coords. (1990), *Desenvolvimento Tecnológico da Indústria e a Constituição de um Sistema Nacional de Inovação no Brasil*, UNICAMP/IE, Campinas, SP;

Coutinho, L and Ferraz. J. coords. (1994), *Estudo da Competitividade da Indústria Brasileira*, IEI/UNICAMP, Rio de Janeiro;

Cruz, H (1983), 'Recessão, Mudança Tecnológica e o Setor de Bens de Capital', IPE/USP, São Paulo, mimeo;

Cruz, H and da Silva, M (1990), 'A Situação do Setor de Bens de Capital e suas Perspectivas', in Coutinho and Suzigan, coords. (1990);

CUT (1987), 'A Tecnologia e os Trabalhadores', *Cadernos da CUT*, setembro, CUT, São Paulo;

Dahlman, C and Fonseca, F (1978), 'From Technological Dependence to Technological Development: the Case of Usiminas Steel Plant in Brazil', *Working Paper 21*, IDB / ECLA / UNDP/IDRC, Bueno Aires, mimeo;

Dahlman, C and Frischtak, C (1989), 'National Systems Supporting Technical Advance in Industry: The Brazilian Experience', in Nelson, R, ed. (forthcoming), *National Systems of Innovation: A Comparative Study*, Oxford University Press, Oxford;

Dahmen, E (1988), ' 'Development Blocks' in Industrial Economics', *Scandinavian Economic History Review & Economy and History*, XXXVI(1): 3-14;

da Matta, R (1989), *O que faz o Brasil, Brasil*, Rocco, Rio de Janeiro;

da Silva, M (1982), 'Inovação Tecnológica no Setor de Máquinas-Ferramenta no Brasil', *Monografia de Trabalho 46*, BID/CEPAL/PNUD, Argentina, mimeo;

David, P (1985), 'Clio and the economics of QUERTY', *American Economic Review*, 72(2): 332-337;

Delbeke, J (1981), 'Recent Long Wave Theories. A critical survey', *Futures*, 13(4);

de Mello, G, coord. (1990), *Microeletrônica e Informática: uma abordagem sob o enfoque do Complexo Eletrônico*, BNDES, Rio de Janeiro;

Dertouzos, M, Lester, R and Solow, R, eds. (1989), *Made in America*, MIT Press, Cambridge, Mass.;

Devine, W (1983), 'From Shaft to Wires: Historical Perspective', *Journal of Economic History*, 43: 347-373;

de Vroey, M (1984), 'A Regulation Approach Interpretation of the Contemporary Crisis', *Capital and Class*, 23: 45-66;

DIEESE (1988), 'A visão das entidades sindicais de trabalhadores sobre a política científica e tecnológica', in *Setores Sociais e a C&T*, CNPq, Brasília;

Diebold, J (1952), *Automation: The Advent of the Automatic Factory*, Van Nostrand, New York;

Diniz, E (1981), 'O Estado Novo: estrutura de poder e relações de classes', in Fausto, org. (1981);

Dornbusch, R (1991), 'Latin America after Collor and Castro: stabilization, reform and after', Lecture at the Institute of Latin American Studies / University of London, November 1991;

Dornbusch, R and Cardoso, E (1989), 'Brazilian debt: a requiem for muddling through', in Edwards, S and Larrain, F, eds. (1989), *Debt, Adjustment and Recovery: Latin America's prospects for growth and development*, Basil Blackwell, Oxford;

Dosi, G (1983), 'Technological paradigms and technological trajectories. The determinants and directions of technical change and the transformation of the economy', in Freeman, C, ed. (1983);

_____. (1984), 'Technology and Conditions of Macroeconomic Development', in Freeman, C, ed. (1984);

_____. (1988), 'Sources, Procedures, and Microeconomic Effects of Innovation', *Journal of Economic Literature*, XXVI: 1120-1171;

Dosi, G, Freeman, C, Nelson, R, Silverberg, G and Soete, L, eds. (1988), *Technical Change and Economic Theory*, Pinter Publishers, London;

Dosi, G, Pavitt, K and Soete, L (1990), *The Economics of Technical Change and International Trade*, Harvester Wheatsheaf, London;

dos Santos, W (1985), 'A Pós-"Revolução" Brasileira', in dos Santos, W, ed. (1985), *Brasil, Sociedade Democrática*, José Olympio, Rio de Janeiro;

_____. (1990), 'Modernização política: algumas questões pós-Constituinte', in Velloso, ed. (1990b);

Draibe, S (1985), *Rumos e metamorfoses*, Paz & Terra, Rio de Janeiro;

Draibe, S, de Castro, M and Azeredo, B (1991), 'O Sistema de Proteção Social no Brasil', in NEPP (1991), *Social Policies for the Urban Poor in Southern Latin America*, UNICAMP, Campinas;

Dunning, J (1981), *International Production and the Multinational Enterprise*, George Allen & Unwin, London;

Dunleavy, P and O'Leary (1987), *Theories of the State - politics of liberal democracy*, MacMillan, London;

E.C.L.A. (1951), *Economic Survey of Latin America - 1949*, United Nations, New York;

Elam, M (1990), 'Puzzling Out the Post-Fordist Debate: Technology, Markets, and Institutions', *Economic and Industrial Democracy*, 11(1): 9-38;

Elliot, J (1980), 'Marx and Schumpeter on Capitalism's Creative Destruction: a Comparative Restatement', *Quaterly Journal of Economics*, XCV(1): 45-68;

Elster, J (1983), *Explaining Technical Change*, Cambridge University Press, Cambridge;

Erber, F (1977), *Technological Development and State Intervention: a Study of the Brazilian Capital Goods Industry*, Ph.D. Thesis, University of Sussex, Falmer;

_____. (1981), 'Science and Technology Policy in Brazil', *Latin American Research Review*, XVI(1): 3-56;

_____. (1982), 'Technology Issues in the capital goods sector', UNCTAD, Geneve, mimeo;

_____. (1983), 'Technological Dependence and Learning Revisited', UFRJ/IEI, Rio de Janeiro, mimeo;

_____. (1985), 'The Development of the 'Electronics Complex' and government Policies in Brazil', *World Development*, 13(3): 293-309;

Erber, F, Tigre, P and Wasserman (1974), 'Absorção e Criação de Tecnologia na Indústria de Bens de Capital', *Relatório de Pesquisa*, FINEP, Rio de Janeiro, mimeo;

Erber, F, coord. (1974), 'Reflexões sobre a Demanda pelos Serviços dos Institutos de Pesquisa', *Relatório de Pesquisa*, FINEP, Rio de Janeiro;

Erber, F, Araujo, J and Guimarães, E (1985a), *A Política Científica e Tecnológica no Brasil*, Zahar, Rio de Janeiro;

Erber, F, Araujo, J and Tauile, J (1985b), 'Restrições Externas, Tecnologia e emprego: uma análise do caso brasileiro', OIT/UNDP, Rio de Janeiro, mimeo;

Ernst, D (1990), 'Global Competition and New Information Technologies', paper presented at the *Conference Technology and Competitiveness*, 24-27 June 1990, OECD/French Government, Paris;

Ernst, D and O'Connor, D (1989), *Technology and Global Competition*, OECD, Paris;

Evans, P (1979), *Dependent Development: the Alliance of Multinational, State, and Local Capital in Brazil*, Princenton University Press, Princenton;

_____. (1986), 'State, Capital, and the Transformation of Dependence: The Brazilian Computer Case', *World Development*, 14 (7): 791-808;

Evans, P and Tigre, P (1989a), 'Brasil e Coréia: para além dos Clones', *Novos Estudos CEBRAP*, 24:110-130, CEBRAP, São Paulo;

_____. (1989b), 'Estratégias de desenvolvimento de indústrias de alta tecnologia: análise comparativa da informática no Brasil e na Coréia do Sul', *Revista Brasileira de Economia*, 43(4):549-73, FGV, Rio de Janeiro;

Exame (1980), 'Melhores e Maiores 1980', agosto, Editora Abril, São Paulo;

_____. (1985), 'Melhores e Maiores 1985', agosto, Editora Abril, São Paulo;

_____. (1990), 'Melhores e Maiores 1990', agosto, Editora Abril, São Paulo;

Fagerberg, J (1987), 'A technology gap approach to why growth rates differ', *Research Policy*, 16: 87-99;

Fajnzylber, F (1983), *La industrializacion trunca de America Latina*, Editorial Nueva Imagen, México;

_____. (1988) 'International Competitiveness: Agreed Goal, Hard Task', *Cepal Review*, n° 36;

Fausto, B (1970), *A Revolução de 1930 - história e historiografia*, Brasiliense, São Paulo;

Fausto, B, org. (1981), *História Geral da Civilização Brasileira - O Brasil Republicano: sociedade e política*, DIFEL, São Paulo;

_____. (1984), *História Geral da Civilização Brasileira - O Brasil Republicano: economia e cultura*, DIFEL, São Paulo;

Fernandes, F (1985), *Nova República?*, Zahar, Rio de Janeiro;

Ferraz, F (1990), 'A construção da modernidade', in Velloso, ed. (1990b)

Ferraz, J (1984), *Technological development and conditioning factors: the case of the Brazilian ship-building industry*, Ph.D. Thesis, University of Sussex / SPRU, Falmer;

_____. (1989), 'A heterogeneidade tecnológica da indústria brasileira: perspectivas e implicações para política', _Revista Brasileira de Economia_, 43(3): 372-92, FGV, Rio de Janeiro;

Ferri, M and Motoyama, S, coords. (1979), _História das Ciências no Brasil_, EPU/EDUSP, São Paulo;

Figueiredo, N (1974), 'Condições e Fatores Determinantes para uma Política Nacional de Desenvolvimento Tecnológico', _Revista de Administração de Empresas_, 14(3), FGV, Rio de Janeiro;

Fine, B and Harris, L (1979), _Rereading Capital_, MacMillan, London;

Fiori, J (1990), 'Sonhos prussianos, crises brasileiras - leitura política de uma industrialização tardia', _Ensaios FEE_, 11(1):41-61, FEE, Porto Alegre;

Fleischer, D (1990), 'The Constituent Assembly and the Transition', in Graham and Wilson, eds. (1990);

Fleury, A (1988), _Análise a nível da empresa, dos impactos da microeletrônica sobre a organização da produção e do trabalho_, Tese de Professor Titular, Escola Politécnica/USP, São Paulo;

Forrester, H, Graham, A, Senge, P and Sterman, J (1983), 'Implications for National and Regional Economic Policy', in _Background Material of the IIASA.IRPET Conference on Long Waves, Depression, and Innovation_, held at Siena/Florence, October 1983;

Frank, G (1964), 'A Agricultura Brasileira: Capitalismo e o Mito do Feudalismo', _Revista Brasiliense_, jan./fev., Brasiliense, São Paulo;

Fransman, M (1985a), 'Conceptualising Technical Change in the Third World in the 1980s: An Interpretive Survey', _The Journal of Development Studies_, 1985: 572-652;

Fransman, M, ed. (1985b), _Capital Goods in Economic Development_, Mac Millan, London;

Freeman, C (1982), _The Economics of Industrial Innovation_, Pinter Publishers, London;

_____. (1984), 'Prometheus Unbound', _Futures_, October: 494-507;

_____. (1987), _Technology and Economic Performance - lessons from Japan_, Pinter Publishers, London;

_____. (1988), 'Formal Scientific and Technical Institutions in the National Systems of Innovation', draft for the IKE-book, SPRU, Sussex, mimeo;

_____. (1988), 'Diffusion: the spread of new technology to firms, sectors, and nations', in Heertje, A, ed. (1988), _Innovation, Technology, and Finance_, Basil Blackwell for the European Investment Bank, London;

_____. (1989), 'The Diffusion of Biotechnology Through the Economy: The Time Scale', in O.E.C.D. (1989);

_____. (1991), 'Networks of innovators: a synthesis of research issues', _Research Policy_, 20: 499-514;

_____. (1992), 'Formal Scientific and Technical Institutions in the National Systems of Innvation', in Lundvall, ed. (1992).

Freeman, C, Clark, J and Soete, L (1982), *Unemployment and Technical Innovation - a study of long waves and economic development*, Frances Pinter, London;

Freeman, C, ed. (1983), *Long Waves in the World Economy*, Butterworths, London;

_____. (1984), *Design, Innovation and Long Cycles in Economic Development*, Frances Pinter (1986 re-set edition), London;

Freeman, C and Perez (1984), 'Long waves and new technologies', *Tidssdrift for Polistist Ekonomi*, 17: 5-14;

Freeman, C and Lundval, B-A, eds. (1988), *Small Countries Facing the Technological Revolution*, Pinter Publishers, London;

Freeman, C and Perez, C (1988), 'Structural crises of adjustment: business cycles and investment behaviour', in Dosi et al., eds. (1988);

Freeman, C and Soete, L, eds. (1990), *New Explorations in the Economics of Technical Change*, Pinter Publishers, London;

Frenkel, J, coord. (1978), 'Tecnologia e Competição na Indústria Farmacêutica Brasileira', FINEP, Rio de Janeiro, mimeo;

Fritsch, W and Franco, G (1988), 'Investimento Direto: Tendencias Globais e Perspectivas para o Brasil', *Texto para Discussão nº 195*, PUC/Dep. Economia, Rio de Janeiro, mimeo;

Frischtak, C (1990), *Specialisation, Technical Change and Competitiveness of the Brazilian Electronics Industry*, World Bank, Washington, D.C.;

Furtado, C (1971), *Formação Econômica do Brasil*, 11ª ed., Cia. Editora Nacional, São Paulo;

Gaio, F (1992), 'Software strategies for developing countries: lessons from the international and Brazilian experiences', in Schmitz and Cassiolato, eds. (1992);

Gazeta Mercantil, 'Edição Especial', 14/9/90, GM, São Paulo;

Gerschenkron, A (1966), *Economic Backwardness in Historical Perspective*, The Belknap Press, Cambridge, Mass.;

Goes, W (1990), Um novo modelo de participação', in Velloso, ed. (1990b);

Gomes, S and Cerqueira Leite, R eds. (1977), *Ciência, Tecnologia e Independência*, Duas Cidades, São Paulo;

Gondim, A (1992), 'Nem modernidade nem 1º mundo', *InforANDES*, agosto, ANDES, Brasília;

Gonçalves, R (1987), 'Competitividade Internacional, Vantagem Comparativa e Empresas Multinacionais: o caso das exportações brasileiras de manufaturados', *Pesquisa e Planejamento*, 17(2), INPES/IPEA, Rio de Janeiro;

Graciosa, H (1989), 'Telecommunications Research and Development in Brazil', *IEEE Comunications Magazine*, September: 33-41;

Graham, L (1990), 'Dilemmas for democracy in Brazil', in Graham and Wilson, eds. (1990);

Graham, L and Wilson, R, eds. (1990), *The political economy of Brazil: Public Policies in a Era of Transition*, University of Texas Press, Austin;

Gramsci, A (1971), *Selections from the prison notebooks*, Lawrence and Wishard, London;

Grupp, H and Schnoring, T (1992), 'Research and development in telecommunications', *Telecommunications Policy*, Jan./Feb.: 46-66;

Guimarães, E and Ford, E (1975), 'Ciência e Tecnologia nos Planos de Desenvolvimento', *Pesquisa e Planejamento*, 5(2):385-432;

Guimarães, T, coord. (1988), 'Questões Relativas `a Competitividade da Indústria de Bens de Capital', *Estudos BNDES n° 8*, BNDES, Rio de Janeiro;

Haustein, H-D (1987), 'The Pathway of Dynamic Efficiency: Economic Trajectory of a Technical Revolution', in Vasko et al. (1987);

Hagedoorn, J and Schakenraad, J (1990), 'Inter-firm partnerships and co-operation strategies in core technologies', in Freeman et al. (1990);

Hewitt, T (1988), *Employment and skills in the electronics industry: the case of Brazil*, D. Phil. Thesis, University of Sussex;

_____. (1992), 'Employmenty and skill in the Brazilian electronics industry', in Schmitz and Cassiolato, eds. (1992);

Hirschman, A (1958), *A Strategy of Economic Development*, Yale University Press, New Haven, Conn.;

_____. (1981), *Essays in Trespassing - economics to politics and beyond*, Cambridge University Press, Cambridge;

Hobday, M (1985), 'The Brazilian Telecommunications Industry: Accumulation of microelectronic technology in the manufacturing and service sectors', UNIDO, Geneve, mimeo;

_____. (1990), *Telecommunications in Developing Countries - The Challenge from Brazil*, Routledge, London;

Hohn, H-W and Schneider, V (1991), 'Path-dependency and critical mass in the development of research and technology: a focused comparison', *Science and Public Policy*, 18(2): 111-122;

Husain, S, (1991), 'Latin America Economic Reform and the World Bank', paper presented at ILAS/U.L., February;

IBICT (1984), *Guia das Sociedades e Associações Científicas e Tecnológicas do Brasil*, SEPLAN, Brasília;

IEDI (1990), 'Carta de Principios', IEDI, São Paulo;

IPT (1987), *Comportamento dos Institutos de Pesquisa Tecnologica Industrial no Brasil*, IPT, São Paulo;

Jaguaribe, A. (1987), 'A Política Tecnológica e sua Articulação com a Política Econômica. Elementos para uma Análise da Ação do Estado', *Texto para Discussão n° 115*, IEI/UFRJ, Rio de Janeiro;

Jenkins, R. (1984), 'Divisions over the International Division of Labour', *Capital and Class*, 22: 28-57;

Jessop, B (1990), 'Fordism and post-Fordism. A Critical Reformulation', *COS Research Report*, 16/1990, Copenhagen Business School, Copenhagen;

Jessop, B, Kastendiek, H, Nielsen, K and Pedersen, O, eds. (1991), *The Politics of Flexibility - restructuring State and Industry in Britain, Germany and Scandinavia*, Edward Elgar. London;

Johannisson, B. (1988), 'Local Entrepreneurship - Relict or Potential in Regional Development', in Tornqvist et al. (1988);

Johnson, B (1991), 'Institutional learning', draft (2.5.91) of Johnson (1992);

_____. (1992), 'Institutional learning', in Lundvall, ed. (1992);

Johnson, B and Lundvall, B-A (1991), 'Flexibility and Institutional Learning', in Jessop et al., eds. (1991);

Jorge, M (1978), 'Seleção, Absorção, e Criação de Tecnologia na Petroquímica Brasileira', FINEP, Rio de Janeiro, mimeo;

Kaplinsky, R (1985), 'Electronics-based Automation Technologies and the Onset of Systemofacture: Implications for Third World Industrialization', *World Development*, 13(3):423-439;

_____. (1988), 'Reestructuring the capitalist labour process: some lessons from the car industry', *Cambridge Journal of Economics*, 12: 451-470;

Katz, J (1984), 'Domestic Technological Innovations and Dynamic Comparative Advantages', *The Journal of Development Studies*, 16(1/2): 13-37;

Katz, J and Bercovich, N (1989), 'Science, technology and social economic re-structuring: The case of Argentina', paper presented at the *Workshop National Systems Supporting Technical Advance in Industry*, Maastricht: November 3-4, 1989;

Katzman, M (1989), 'Urbanization since 1945', in Bacha and Klein, eds. (1989);

Kennedy, P (1988), *The Rise and Fall of the Great Powers*, Fontana Press, London;

Kleinknecht, A (1987), *Innovation Patterns in Crisis and Prosperity*, MacMillan, London;

Kuhn, T (1970), *The Structure of Scientific Revolutions*, second edition, The University of Chicago Press, Chicago;

Kuznets, S (1989), *Economic Development, the family and income distribution - selected essays*, Cambridge University Press, Cambridge;

Lamounier, B and Souza, A (1990), 'As Elites Brasileiras e a Modernização do Setor Público', *Relatório da Pesquisa*, IDESP, São Paulo;

Landes, D (1969), *The Unbound Prometheus*, Cambridge University Press, Cambridge;

Langer, E (1989), 'Generations of Scientists and Engineers - origins of the computer industry in Brazil', *Latin American Research Review*, XXIV(2): 95-111;

Lara-Resende, A (1990), 'Da inflação crônica à hiperinflação: observações sobre o quadro atual', in Velloso, J ed. (1990a).

Lee, C-O (1991), 'Stages of economic development and technology policy: the experience of Korea', *Science and Public Policy*, August, 1991: 219-224;

Lessa, C (1978), *A estratégia de desenvolvimento 1974-76: sonho e fracasso*, Tese para concurso de Professor Titular, UFRJ/ FEA, Rio de Janeiro;

Levinsen J and Kristinsen, P (1983), *The Small Country Squeeze*, Forlaget for Samfundsekonomi og Planlaegning, Stockolm;

Lipietz, A (1985), 'Le national et le regional: quelle autonomie face la crise capitaliste mondiale?', *CEPREMAP Working Paper n° 8521*, CEPREMAP, Paris;

_____. (1987), *Mirages and Miracles*, Verso, London;

List, F (1856), *National System of Political Economy*, J.B. Lippincott & Co., Philadelphia;

Locatelli, R (1985), *Industrialização, crescimento e emprego: uma avaliação da experiência brasileira*, IPEA/INPES, Rio de Janeiro;

Lundvall, B-A (1985), *Product Innovation and User-Producer Interaction*, Aalborg University Press, Aalborg, Denmark;

_____. (1988), 'Innovation as an interactive process: from user-producer interaction to the national system of innovation', in Dosi et al. (1988);

_____. (1989), 'Innovation, the Organized Market and the Productivity Slow--down', paper presented at *OECD's International Seminar on Science, Technology and Economic Growth*, Paris, 6-9 June, 1989;

_____. (1990), 'Explaining Inter-firm Cooperation and Inovation - Limits of the Transaction Cost Approach', paper presented at the workshop on *The Socio-Economics of Inter-firm Cooperation*, Berlin: Wissenschafts--Zentrum, June 11-13, 1990;

_____. (1992a), 'Introduction', in Lundvall, ed. (1992);

_____. (1992b), 'User-Producer Relationships, National Systems of Innovation and Internationalisation', in Lundvall, ed. (1992);

_____. ed. (1992), *National Systems of Innovation - Towards a Theory of Innovation and Interactive Learning*, Pinter Publishers, London;

Luz, N (1973), *A Luta pela Industrialização do Brasil (1880-1945)*, Difel, São Paulo;

Maddison, A (1989), *The World Economy in the 20th Century*, OECD, Paris;

Malan, P (1979), 'Economia brasileira no futuro próximo', in Centro Brasil Democrático (1979), *Painéis da Crise Brasileira - tomo II*, Avenir / Civilização Brasileira / Paz e Terra, Rio de Janeiro;

_____. (1982), 'O 'problema' da divida brasileira', in Tavares, M and David, M (1982), *A economia política da crise*, Vozes/Achiamé, Rio de Janeiro;

Maizels, A (1963), *Industrial Growth and World Trade*, Cambridge University Press, London;

Mammana, C (1989), 'Exposição', *Seminário de Avaliação da Política Nacional de Informática*, UNICAP/IE - SEI - CNPq, Campinas;

Mandel, E (1980), *Long Waves of Capitalist Development*, Cambridge University Press, Cambridge;

Mansel, R (1990), 'Rethinking the telecommunications infrastructure: the new 'black box", *Research Policy*, 19:501-515;

Mantega, G (1984), *A Economia Política Brasileira*, Polis/Vozes, São Paulo;

Marcovitch, J (1978), *Interação da instituição de pesquisa industrial com seu meio ambiente e suas implicações na eficácia industrial*, Ph.D. Thesis, USP, São Paulo;

Marini, R (1969), *Subdesarrollo y Revolucion*, Siglo XXI, México;

Marx, K (1954), *Capital*, vol. I, Lawrence & Wishart, London;

Masterman, M (1970), 'The Nature of a Paradigm', in Lakatos, I and Musgrave, A, eds. (1970), *Criticism and the Growth of Knowledge*, Cambridge University Press, Cambridge;

Meade, J (1952), 'External Economics and Diseconomies in a Competitive Situation', *Economic Journal*, 62: 54-67;

Medeiros, A (1986), *The Politics of Intergovernmental Relations in Brazil - 1964-1982*, Garland Publishing, New York;

_____. (1991), 'The Politics of Decentralization in Brazil', paper presented at the Workshop *Institutional Building in Brazil*, 5-6 June, 1991, ILAS, London;

Medeiros, J, Torkomian, A and Perilo, S (1989), 'Os Polos Tecnológicos de Campinas, S. José dos Campos e São Carlos e a Vinculação Universidade--Setor Produtivo', CNPq/ASP, São Paulo, mimeo;

Medeiros, J and Perilo, S (1990), 'Implantação e Consolidação de um Polo Tecnológico: o caso de São José dos Campos', *Revista de Administração de Empresas*, 30(2): 35-45, FGV, São Paulo;

Medeiros, J, Stal, E, Mattedi, A and March, M (1990), 'Perfil dos Polos Tecnológicos Brasileiros', CNPq/ASP - ANPROTEC, São Paulo, mimeo;

Melo, L (1989), 'O programa de apoio ao desenvolvimento tecnológico da empresa nacional - PADTEN - (1973-1988)', *Texto para Discussão nº 203*, UFRJ/IEI, Rio de Janeiro;

Mendes, I. (1988), 'Tecnologia, Capital e Nacionalismo na Constituinte', Brasília, mimeo;

Meyer-Stamer, J (1992), 'The end of Brazil's informatics policy' *Science and Public Policy*, 19(2): 99-110;

Ministério de Ciência e Tecnologia (1986), 'Relatório final dos grupos de trabalho de recursos humanos em informática', Ministério de Ciência e Tecnologia, Brasília mimeo;

Ministério da Educação (1989), *Censo Escolar 1988*, ME, Brasília;

Ministério do Planejamento e Coordenação Geral (1967), *Plano Estratégico de Desenvolvimento*, MINIPLAN, Rio de Janeiro;

_____. (1969), *I Plano Nacional de Desenvolvimento*, MINIPLAN, Brasília;

Modiano, E. (1990), 'Terceiro choque versus primeiro pacto', in Velloso, ed. (1990b);

Moreira, M. (1989), *Progresso Técnico e Estrutura de Mercado: O Caso da Indústria de Telequipamentos*, BNDES, Rio de Janeiro;

Moura Castro, C (1985), 'É Possível uma Tecnologia 'Made in Brazil'?', CNPq, Brasília, mimeo;

Moura Castro, C (1989), 'What's Happening in Brazilian Education?', in Bacha and Klein, eds. (1989);

Neder, R (1989), 'Novas Tecnologias e Ação Sindical em São Paulo', *Revista de Administração de Empresas*, 29(1):23-33, FGV/SP, São Paulo;

Nelson, R (1982), 'The Role of Knowledge in R&D Efficiency', *Quartely Journal of Economics*, 97(3): 453-70;

Nelson, R (1988), 'National systems of innovation - preface', in Dosi et al., eds. (1988);

Nelson, R and Winter (1977), 'In Search of a Useful Theory of Innovations', *Research Policy*, 6(1);

Nielsen, K (1991), 'Towards a Flexible Future - Theories and Politics', in Jessop et al., eds. (1991);

Nilsson, J-E (1988), 'An Old Theory for a New Reality', in Torqvist et al. (1988);

Nogueira, M and Nogueira, JM (1990), 'Perspectiva do Setor de Informática no Contexto da Nova Política Industrial', proceedings of the *XVIII Encontro Anual da ANPEC*, ANPEC, Brasília;

North, D (1991), 'Institutions', *Journal of Economic Perspectives*, 5(1): 97-112;

O'Connor, D (1985), 'The Computer Industry in the Third World: Policy Options and Constraints', *World Development*, 13(3): ;

O'Connor, J (1987), *The Meaning of Crisis*, Basil Blackwell, Oxford;

O'Donnel, G, Schmitter, P and Whitehead, L, eds. (1986), *Transitions from Authoritarian Rule: comparative perspectives*, John Hopkins University Press, Baltimore;

O.E.C.D. (1987), *International Investment and Multinational Enterprises*, OECD, Paris;

_____. (1989), *Biotechnology - economic and wider impacts*, Paris: OECD;

_____. (1990), 'Human Resources in the Production System and New Technologies', OECD/Technology Economy Programme, Paris, mimeo;

O.E.C.D. (1991), *Strategic Industries in a Global Economy*, OECD, Paris;

Oliveira, F (1981), *A economia brasileira: crítica à razão dualista*, CEBRAP/Vozes, São Paulo;

Oliveira, F (1984), in Fausto, org. (1984);

Orsenico, L (1989), *The emergence of biotechnology*, Pinter Publishers, London;

Palma, G (1981), 'Dependency and development: a critical overview', in Seers, D, ed. (1981), *Dependency theory - a critical reassessment*, Frances Pinter, London;

Paloni, A (1992), 'External balance and domestic policy in Argentina, Brazil and Mexico', forthcoming in *Scottish Journal of Political Economy;*

Perez, C. (1983), 'Structural change and the assimilation of new technologies in the economic and social system', *Futures*, 15(4):357-75;

_____. (1985), 'Microelectronics, Long Waves, and World Structural Change: New Perspectives for Developing Countries', *World Development*, 13(3): 441-63;

Perez, C (1989), 'Technical Change, Competitive Restructuring and Institutional Reform in Developing Countries', *Discussion Paper n° 4*, World Bank/SPR Publications, Washington, D.C.;

Perroux, F (1955), 'Note sur la Notion de Pole de Croissance', reprinted in Perroux, F (1969), *L'Economie du XX Siecle*, Presses Universitaires de France, Paris;

Pessanha, C (1981), 'O Estado e a Economia no Brasil: a campanha contra a estatização 1974-76', M.Sc. Dissertation, IUPERJ, Rio de Janeiro;

Pessini, J. (1986), 'A Indústria Brasileira de Telecomunicações: uma tentativa de reinterpretação dos mercados recentes', M. Sc. Dissertation, IE/ UNICAMP, Campinas;

Piragibe, C (1988), 'Electronics industry in Brazil and the role of the State: some aspects', in Piragibe, C, ed. (1988), *Electronics industry in Brazil*, MCT/ CNPq, Brasília;

Porteous, M (1992), 'Revolution in recession? advanced technologies and Brazil's machine tool sector in the crisis', in Schmitz and Cassiolato, eds. (1992);

Porto, J, da Silva, A and Laplane, M (1990), 'Avaliação da Política Nacional de Informática', UNICAMP/IE, Campinas, mimeo;

Prado Jr., C (1945), *História Econômica do Brasil*, São Paulo: Brasiliense;

Quadros Carvalho, R (1992), 'Why the market reserve is not enough: lessons from the diffusion of industrial automation technology in Brazilian process industries', in Schmitz and Cassiolato (1992);

Quadro da Silva, S (1991), 'Sistema financeiro: participação na renda, funções e disfunções', in Camargo and Giambiagi, eds. (1991);

Rattner, H (1974), 'O Controle da Transferência de Tecnologia para Países em Desenvolvimento', *Revista de Administração de Empresas*, 13(1), FGV, Rio de Janeiro;

Rebouças, O (1990), 'Avaliação dos choques antiinflacionários', in Velloso, ed. (1990a).

Reichstul, H and Coutinho, L (1983), 'Investimento Estatal 1974-1980: Ciclo e Crise', in Belluzzo, L and Coutinho, R, orgs. (1983), *Desenvolvimento Capitalista no Brasil* - Vol. 2, Brasiliense, São Paulo;

República Federativa do Brasil (1988), *Constituição do Brasil*, JB, Rio de Janeiro;

Resende, F (1990), 'Descentralização e Eficiência na Tomada de Decisões para o Desenvolvimento sob a Constituição de 1988', in PNUD (1990), *Políticas de Desenvolvimento para a Década de 90*, PNUD, Brasília;

Rezende Neto, L (1991), 'Exposição', in *CPI Atraso Tecnológico*, Brasília: Congresso Nacional, Notas Taquigráficas, 26/08/91;

Rocha Neto, I (1990), 'The Brazilian Technical and Scientific Basis on Engineering', Brasília, mimeo;

Romanini, J (1977), 'Apoio Institucional à Ciência e Tecnologia no Brasil', Conselho Nacional de Pesquisa/CET-SUP, São Paulo, mimeo;

Romão, M (1991), 'Distribuição de renda, pobreza e desigualdades regionais no Brasil', in Camargo and Giambiagi, eds. (1991).

Romer, P (1986), 'Increasing Returns and Long-run Growth', *Journal of Political Economy*, 94: 1002-1038;

Rosenberg, N (1976), *Perspectives on Technology*, Cambridge University Press, Cambridge;

_____. (1982), *Inside the Black Box: Technology and Economics*, Cambridge University Press, Cambridge;

Rosenthal, D (1987), *Microelectronics and industrial policies in developing countries: the case of the semiconductor industry in Brazil*, Ph.D. Thesis, University of London, London;

Rosenthal, D and Moreira, I (1991), 'A Finada Política Nacional de Informática: Supostos, Objetivos e Instrumentos', *Texto Para Discussão nº 251*, UFP/Dept. Economia, Recife, mimeo;

Rossi, J (1986), 'Distribuição da Renda', IPEA/INPES, Rio de Janeiro, mimeo;

Rostow, W (1978), *The World Economy. History and Prospect*, Macmillan, London;

Rouquier, A, Lamounier, B and Schwarzer, J, eds. (1985), *Como nascem as democracias*, Brasiliense, São Paulo;

Ruggie, J (1983), 'International Interdependence and National Welfare', in Ruggie, J, ed. (1983), *The Antinomies of Interdependence*, Columbia University Press, New York;

Sá, E, coord. (1989), *Automação Industrial: um suporte à competitividade*, BNDES, Rio de Janeiro;

Sachs, J (1987), 'Trade and Exchange Rate in Growth-Oriented Adjustment Programs', in Corbo et al., eds. (1987), *Growth Oriented Adjustment Programs*, World Bank and IMF, Washington, D.C.;

Sachs, J, ed. (1990), *Developing country debt and economic performance*, vol. 1, The University of Chicago Press, Chicago;

Salm, C, coord. (1990), 'Cenários da Indústria Brasileira e da Formação Profissional', IEI/UFRJ, Rio de Janeiro, mimeo;

Schmitz, H and Cassiolato, J, eds. (1992), *Hi-tech for industrial development - Lessons from the Brazilian experience in electronics and automation*, Routledge, London;

Schmitz, H and Hewitt, T (1992), 'An assessment of the market reserve for the Brazilian computer industry', in Schmitz and Cassiolato, eds.(1992);

Schumpeter, J (1934), *The theory of economic development*, Harvard University Press, Cambridge, Mass.;

_____. (1938), *Business Cycles: A Theoretical, Historical, and Statistical Analysis of the Capitalist Process*, 2 vols., McGraw-Hill, New York;

_____. (1942), *Capitalism, socialism and democracy*, McGraw-Hill, New York;

Schwartzman, S, coord. (1979), *Formação da Comunidade Científica no Brasil*, Companhia Editora Nacional/FINEP, Rio de Janeiro;

Schwartzman, S (1988), 'Brazil: opportunity and crisis in higher education', *Higher Education*, 17: 99-119;

Scitovsky, T (1954), 'Two Concepts of External Economies', *Journal of Political Economy*, LXII(2): 143-151;

SEI (1989), *Panorama do Setor de Informática - séries estatisticas v.2*, SEI, Brasília;

Secretaria de Planejamento da Presidência da Republica (1974), *II Plano Nacional de Desenvolvimento*, SEPLAN, Brasília;

Serra, J (1982), 'Ciclos e Mudanças Estruturais na Economia Brasileira do Pós-Guerra', in Belluzzo, L and Coutinho, R (1982), *Desenvolvimento Capitalista no Brasil - vol. 1*, Brasiliense, São Paulo;

Silva, L and Buarque, C (1990), 'Educação Urgente', PT/Governo Paralelo, São Paulo, mimeo;

Silverberg, G, Dosi, G and Orsenigo, L (1988), 'Innovation, Diversity and Diffusion: A Self-Organisation Model', *The Economic Journal*, 98: 1032-1054;

Simonsen, M (1990), 'A inflação e o pensamento econômico brasileiro', in Velloso, ed. (1990a);

Simonsen, R (1977), 'O planejamento da economia brasileira', in IPEA/INPES (1977), *A controvérsia do planejamento na economia brasileira*, Série Pensamento Econômico Brasileiro, IPEA/INPES, Rio de Janeiro;

Smith, A (1776), *An Inquiry into the Nature and Causes of the Wealth of Nations*, reprinted in Penguin Books, Penguin, London;

Singer, P (1984), 'Interpretação do Brasil: Uma Experiência Histórica de Desenvolvimento' in Fausto, org. (1984);

Stavrous, M (1990), *Regulation approach: a critical appraisal*, Ph.D. Thesis, Birkbeck College/University of London, London;

Stewart, F and Ghani, E (1989), 'Externalities, Development and Trade', *Development Studies Working Papers*, Queen Elizabeth House, Oxford, mimeo;

Suzigan, W (1975), 'Industrialização e política econômica: uma interpretação em perspectiva histórica', *Pequisa e Planejamento Econômico*, 5(2): 433-474;

Suzigan, W, coord. (1989), 'Estratégia e Desenvolvimento de C&T nas Empresas Privadas Nacionais', FECAMP/UNICAMP, Campinas, mimeo;

Swavely, (1990), 'Labour power and politics in Brazil', in Grahman and Wilson, eds. (1990);

Tavares, M (1972), *Da Substituição de Importação ao Capitalismo Financeiro*, Zahar, Rio de Janeiro;

Tavares, M. (1975), *Acumulação de Capital e Industrialização no Brasil*, Tese de Livre Docência, UFRJ, Rio de Janeiro;

Taylor, F (1903), *Shop Management*, reprinted in Taylor, F (1947), *Scientific Management*, Harper and Brothers, New York;

TELEBRASIL (1992), *Revista Brasileira de Telecomunicações e Informática*, Assoc. Brasil. de Telecomunicações, Rio de Janeiro;

Teitel, S and Toumi, F (1986), 'From Import Substitution to Exports: the manufacturing exports experience of Argentina and Brazil', *Economic Development and Cultural Change*, April;

Tigre, P (1983), *Technology and Competition in Brazilian Computer Industry*, Frances Pinter, London;

Tigre, P and Ferraz, J, coords. (1989), 'Avaliação e Perspectivas Tecnológicas das Empresas Estatais', CNPq, Brasília, mimeo;

Tornqvist, G, Gyllstrom, B, Nilsson, J-A, Stevensson, L, eds. (1988), *Division of Labour, Specialization, and Technical Change*, Liber, London;

Vasko, T, ed. (1987), *The Long-Wave Debate*, Springer-Verlag, London;

Veblen, T (1919), *The Place of Science in Modern Civilization*, reprint, Augustus M. Kelley, New York, 1965;

Velloso, J (1977), *Brasil: A Solução Positiva*, Abril, São Paulo;

_____. (1990), 'Bases para o reordenamento financeiro do setor público: primeiras idéias', in Velloso, ed. (1990a).

Velloso, J ed. (1990a), *Brasil: agenda para sair da crise - inflação e deficit público*, José Olympio, Rio de Janeiro;

_____. (1990b), *Modernização Política e Desenvolvimento*, José Olympio, Rio de Janeiro;

_____. (1990c), *Dívida externa e desenvolvimento*, José Olympio, Rio de Janeiro;

Villaschi, A (1990), 'The Brazilian National System of Innovation in the 1980s: a decade of wasted opportunities?', paper prepared for FECAMP/ UNDP Project on *Technological development of industry and the constituion of a national system of innovation in Brazilin*, UNICAMP/Instituto de Economia, Campinas, SP;

202

_____. (1991), 'Convergence of economic growth: should NICs feel confortable about past achievements?', *CQD Working Papers*, CQD, Vitória, ES;

_____. (1992), 'O Brasil e o novo paradigma tecnológico de desenvolvimento economico mundial', *Ensaios FEE*, 13(1): 43-87;

Villela, A. (1984), *Empresas de Governo como Instrumento de Política Econômica*, IPEA, Rio de Janeiro;

Viner, J (1931), 'Cost Curves and Supply Curves', reprinted in American Economic Association (1953), *Reading in Price Theory*, Allen and Unwin, London;

Weffort, F (1984), *Por que democracia?*, Brasiliense, São Paulo;

Williamson, O (1975), *Markets and Hierarchies: Analysis and Anti-trust Implications*, The Free Press, New York;

_____. (1985), *The Economic Institutions of Capitalism*, The Free Press, New York;

Willmore, L (1987), 'Controle estrangeiro e concentração na indústria brasileira', *Pesquisa e Planejamento*, 17(1):161-89, INPES/ IPEA, Rio de Janeiro;

World Bank (1981), *World Economic Report 1980*, Oxford University Press, New York.